STAR WARS AFTER LUCAS

STAR WARS
AFTER LUCAS

A CRITICAL GUIDE TO THE
FUTURE OF THE GALAXY

Dan Golding

University of Minnesota Press
Minneapolis
London

Published by the University of Minnesota Press
111 Third Avenue South, Suite 290
Minneapolis, MN 55401-2520
http://www.upress.umn.edu

Printed in the United States of America on acid-free paper

The University of Minnesota is an equal-opportunity educator and employer.

30 29 28 27 26 25 24 23   10 9 8 7 6 5 4 3 2 1

Library of Congress Cataloging-in-Publication Data
Golding, Dan, author.
Star wars after Lucas : a critical guide to the future of the galaxy / Dan Golding.
Minneapolis : University of Minnesota Press, 2019. | Includes bibliographical references and index.
Identifiers: LCCN 2018039743 (print) | ISBN 978-1-5179-0542-2 (hc/j) | ISBN 978-1-5179-0541-5 (pb)
Subjects: LCSH: Star Wars films—History and criticism.
Classification: LCC PN1995.9.S695 G65 2019 (print) | DDC 791.43/75—dc23
LC record available at https://lccn.loc.gov/2018039743

CONTENTS

STAR WARS AND THE HISTORY OF NOSTALGIA

t was December 2015, and *Star Wars* ruled the box office again. It had been unthinkable: George Lucas, the creator and overseer general of all things *Star Wars* and Lucasfilm, had promised us, repeatedly and over several years, that this would never happen. After six films, he was done. Following the bitter taste of the prequel trilogy, the last of which was released in 2005, there was to be no more *Star Wars* stories on the big screen. No more galaxy far, far away. No more Jedi Knights, no more Wookiees, no more Darth Vader. This was the end of the Skywalkers.

Except that wasn't to be. That, somehow, couldn't be. And so here was *The Force Awakens* in December 2015, with a new director, J. J. Abrams, introducing us to Rey, Finn, and Poe, and reintroducing us to Han Solo, Leia Organa, and Luke Skywalker—aged, but still familiar. It worked. Despite the lingering ire over the three prequel films, despite the general skepticism surrounding the idea of new *Star Wars* movies, people weren't just happy to see *Star Wars* return; they were overwhelmed. There were breathless reviews, teary YouTube reaction videos, and screaming fans at red carpet events. "What a beautiful, thrilling, joyous, surprising and heart-thumping adventure this is," wrote Richard Roeper for the *Chicago Sun-Times*. "It's a return to greatness."[1] Patton Oswalt, the actor and comedian, was even more succinct in his praise. "JJ did it," was all he tweeted.[2] The film was a creative and financial success, the second *Star Wars* film, *Rogue One*, was on its way and looking good, and the animated series *Star Wars: Rebels* was steadily puttering along on Disney's cable channels. A new era of *Star Wars* was here.

Everyone was happy. Except, as it happened, George Lucas. "They wanted to do a retro movie," Lucas told Charlie Rose on his talk show. "I don't like that." This was the other major point in time that *The Force Awakens* marked: it wasn't just the first new *Star Wars* film in a decade; it was the first one made with no input from the creator himself. After four decades, Lucas had in 2012 sold Lucasfilm and *Star Wars* to the Disney Corporation for $4 billion. Lucas would see *The Force Awakens* for the first time in a darkened theater just like the rest of us.

This hadn't necessarily been Lucas's original idea. To sweeten the Disney deal, he had written story treatments for three more *Star Wars* films—the very idea of which had been chimeric for so long. Lucas was so sure that Disney would be keen to make more *Star Wars* in his mold that he didn't even let Disney executives look at his treatments until the deal was done. "Buying my stories is part of what the deal is," Lucas later told *Bloomberg*.[3]

On reception of the goods, though, it seems that Disney was not impressed. "They looked at the stories," Lucas told Rose, "and they said, 'We want to make something for the fans.'" Lucas's 2015 interview with Rose is thick with displeasure and insinuation, but it boils down to one clear point: Disney had not taken *Star Wars* in the direction that Lucas would have preferred. *The Force Awakens* was not the new Disney-era *Star Wars* film that he had wanted to see. It was "retro," and it was "for the fans."

Perhaps we could write Lucas's reaction off to simple discomfort at a creative separation (Lucas used the metaphor of a divorce or a breakup at multiple points). Nonetheless, he had more positive things to say about the second Disney-era *Star Wars* film, *Rogue One*, in 2016. Though this time, Lucas's reaction didn't quite cause the same headlines, a year later, and perhaps with some more controlled public relations mechanisms in place, the story was different. Lucas, who after the Rose interview had offered a chastened press release "clarifying" his comments ("Disney is doing an incredible job of taking care of and expanding the franchise," he wrote[4]), had otherwise kept a low profile. But, when it came to drumming up marketing for *Rogue One*, Lucas reappeared by proxy. Though we didn't hear it directly, Lucas was said to have loved *Rogue One*. "I don't want to put words into his mouth, but I can honestly say that I can die happy now," the director Gareth Edwards said at a press conference promoting the film. "He really liked the movie. It meant a lot. To be honest, and no offense to [any of the critics at the press conference], it was the most important review to me."[5]

There's an irony to all of this. In among some of the most financially successful films of our times, in the middle of an unparalleled marketing storm mounted by one of the world's biggest entertainment corporations, and a nostalgic, emotional audience reaction en masse, one man still has the power to turn heads and derail publicity with a single thumbs-up or thumbs-down. Lucas was done making *Star Wars*, but, it seemed, he could still break *Star Wars*.

But what does all of this actually mean? Disney's strategy was otherwise a success on the largest imaginable scale. Both *The Force Awakens* and *Rogue One* were critically lauded and financially massively profitable, to the point where Disney's $4 billion was almost returned on the first two films alone. This is also to say nothing of the presumably handsome licensing and merchandise profits. *The Force Awakens* is now the highest-grossing film in North America ever, and third-highest globally after *Titanic* (dir. James Cameron, 1997) and *Avatar* (dir. James Cameron, 2009). In the process, *Star Wars* itself was restored as a defining force in contemporary popular culture. For many of the fans of the franchise, something inexpressible was redeemed. So why the focus on the reactions of one man, we might wonder?

Here's what Lucas's reactions tell us about this new era of *Star Wars*: far from a simple continuation of the *Star Wars* legacy, something had in fact changed here. For all that has been made about these new films' ability to deliver something quintessentially "*Star Wars*-y," their atonement for past sins, and their renewal of the franchise, there are discontinuities here, too. Lucas can recognize the changes, but can we? This is, after all, an important task for understanding popular culture today. Disney's strategy in reviving *Star Wars* can tell us much about not just how American, globalized media functions today but also the power of the contemporary audience's thirst for revisiting the past, and culture that deals with questions of legacy and myth. It can tell us about how seriality works in today's franchises, as reflected in the judgment of the man who pioneered the mainstream form in its heyday. It gives us a clue about what one of the largest entertainment corporations on the planet is doing with one of the largest media franchises in history. And of course, Lucas's reactions can go a long way in telling us what *Star Wars* looks like, after he has ceased to be involved and handed over control to a major entertainment corporation. Lucas, after all, was "God" for the franchise, as Edwards put it in that same press conference. So why would God forsake the universe he built?

GOD'S GIFT TO DISNEY

The sale of Lucasfilm to Disney had caught most, including Hollywood and Wall Street, off guard.[6] Even *Star Wars* icons were surprised: "Oh my gosh, what a shock that was," Mark Hamill told *Entertainment Weekly*. "I had no idea that George was going to sell to Disney until I read it online like everybody else."[7] Lucasfilm Ltd. was Lucas's company: he had founded it all the way back in 1971, when he was just an up-and-coming film brat under the wing of Francis Ford Coppola. In 1978 he'd built Skywalker Ranch, in Marin County, California, intending it to be an artists' paradise of sorts, a place where he and others could escape the trappings of corporate Hollywood. Despite creating some of Hollywood's most enduring brands, Lucas was never comfortable being part of the machine and spent much of his time trying to escape its reach. Even in 2012, Lucasfilm was hardly creatively dormant. Before the sale to Disney, Lucasfilm was still busily working on material: though a planned live-action *Star Wars* television series had never panned out, Lucasfilm had recently released a 3-D conversion of *The Phantom Menace*, and had plans for 3-D conversions of all six *Star Wars* films; the fourth season of the animated *Clone Wars* television series was being broadcast on Cartoon Network (there would be a further two); a new *Star Wars* game, *Star Wars 1313,* was being made by the company's games division, LucasArts; and a relaunch of the *Star Wars* ride at Disneyland, *Star Tours,* was underway. The world that Lucas had built was continuing to simmer along.

Still, cracks were appearing in Lucas's empire, and in retrospect, the signs that things might be coming to an end were there. *Red Tails,* the first nonfranchise Lucasfilm project since 1994's *Radioland Murders,* had been released in January 2012 and had not done well. Lucas vented his frustrations with the project in an interview with Jon Stewart, saying that the film (a project about the African American World War II Tuskegee airmen that Lucas had been pursuing since the 1980s) struggled to get a release because "there's no major white roles in it at all."[8] The latest Indiana Jones film, *The Kingdom of the Crystal Skull,* had done well at the box office but had struggled critically (winning the Razzie Award in 2009 for "Worst Prequel, Remake, Rip-off, or Sequel," something even the maligned *Star Wars* prequels never achieved[9]). *Crystal Skull* seemed to derail plans for future Jones films despite an ending that suggested future sequels. Even Lucas's old friend, Steven Spielberg, demurred on the film's legacy, telling *Empire Magazine,* "When [George] writes a story he believes in—even if I don't believe in it—I'm going to shoot the movie the way George envisaged it."[10] *Crystal Skull* star Shia LeBeouf was less diplomatic: "I feel like I dropped the ball on the legacy that people loved and cherished."[11]

Franchise fatigue was nothing new to Lucas. It had often felt like he had tried to get away from *Star Wars* from the beginning. As early as 1976, before the release of the first film, Lucas claimed that after *Star Wars,* "I'm going to retire and make small experimental films," a declaration he continued to repeat for many decades afterward.[12] He often seemed to deliberately give the impression of someone who had been just as caught off guard by the success of *Star Wars* as any film commentator or moviegoer. "*Star Wars* obviously snuck up and grabbed me and threw me across the room and beat me against the wall," he joked in 2010.[13] Chris Taylor suggests in his book *How Star Wars Conquered the Galaxy* that Lucas persevered with the *Star Wars* machine because it allowed him to fund Lucasfilm, the company that he loved, and the emblem of making films outside the Hollywood corporate machine.[14] To an extent, it's convincing: Lucas always seems like a reluctant convert to the *Star Wars* cause in interviews (beyond his usual introversion) and describes himself in interviews as a Darth Vader–like character more than once.[15] "Don't suddenly find yourself making the same film you made thirty years ago," Lucas warned Simon Pegg on the red carpet for *Revenge of the Sith* in 2005.[16]

Still, Lucas also keenly guarded the legacy of his space saga and always resisted the strong criticism his films frequently faced. In fact, he seemed to take some of the criticism personally and often spoke of the detrimental impact of online and fan culture on his psyche and his films. *Star Wars* always seemed personal to Lucas: he could have stepped away from *Star Wars* as early as 1978 and let someone else write, produce, and oversee the sequels, just as he directed only the first of the original three. He could have chosen instead to make *Apocalypse Now* (which was his project for many years before it became Coppola's), or any other number of films that he frequently claimed to have on the backburner. He could have left the original trilogy alone and not attempted to digitally update them in the 1990s with the Special Editions; he could have not made the prequels at all, or farmed them out to another director, or producer, or studio.

But Lucas never took an opportunity to step back from *Star Wars*. For better or worse, he spent most of his creative life making *Star Wars* films. "'George Lucas, creator of Star Wars,' is what my obituary will read," he once told Disney CEO Bob Iger.[17] A 1977 interview with Lucas, conducted by Stephen Zito for *American Film*, seems somehow to capture his relationship with the franchise, even before the first film was released. Zito paints Lucas as at once staunchly defensive of his new space opera and its "low culture" roots, and also nervy, exhausted, and as Zito wryly notes, "with the manner of someone on whom fate has played a dirty trick."[18] This was Lucas and *Star Wars*, distilled.

Yet by 2012, the sixty-eight-year-old Lucas had finally done it: he'd called off the prospect of future *Star Wars* films. "There will definitely be no Episodes VII–IX," he told *Total Film* in 2008, even going as far as to suggest that he'd left instructions barring future films after his retirement or death. "That's because there isn't any story. I mean, I never thought of anything!"[19] In January 2012 he announced that he was retiring from the day-to-day running of Lucasfilm, and yet again claimed to be pursuing small and personal films. There was also change on the horizon in Lucas's personal life: by 2013 he was married for the second time (his first marriage to the well-regarded editor Marcia Lucas ended in 1983). His new partner was Mellody Hobson, chair of DreamWorks Animation and a personal friend of the Obamas. Hobson and Lucas's first child, Everest, was born in August 2013. This is what the future looked like for George Lucas: private, focused on his family—and most definitely retired.

The sale of Lucasfilm itself had apparently been in the cards since 2011, when Lucas had had breakfast with Iger at Walt Disney World Resort in Florida. Lucas was there for the opening of the new Star Tours ride, which he had been heavily involved with. As the two breakfasted in the Hollywood Brown Derby restaurant, which had been closed for their privacy, Iger asked Lucas if he'd ever consider selling Lucasfilm. I'm not ready yet, Lucas replied. "But when I am, I'd love to talk."[20]

Just a year later, Lucas was having another important meal: this time, with Kathleen Kennedy, the producer, cofounder of Amblin Entertainment, and longtime collaborator of Spielberg's. Over lunch, Lucas asked Kennedy to take over Lucasfilm, an offer that she quickly accepted ("I kind of surprised myself," she recalls, almost paraphrasing Han Solo[21]). After taking stock of where Lucasfilm sat, Kennedy and Lucas's next move was a bold one: to start laying the groundwork for a new trilogy of *Star Wars* films. Michael Arndt, the Oscar-winning screenwriter of *Little Miss Sunshine*, was brought in to write a script based on Lucas's ideas, with *The Empire Strikes Back* screenwriter Lawrence Kasdan on hand as a consultant. In June 2012 Lucas called Iger, and a few months later the sale was announced. Iger says that the day after the deal was signed—it was Halloween—he went trick or treating, dressed as Darth Vader.[22]

After the shock of the sale, it quickly became clear to the world that Disney was not interested in performing any caretaker function with Lucasfilm or simply mining the existing *Star Wars* films for profit. A new *Star Wars* trilogy, set after the original trilogy—the long-touted Episodes VII, VIII, and IX—would be made, with the first released in 2015. Later came an even more ambitious calendar of releases: beyond this new sequel trilogy, Disney would release a "*Star Wars* Story" film that would sit adjacent to the main plotline every other year, starting with *Rogue One* in 2016 and *Solo* in 2018. This meant that after nearly four decades with only six *Star Wars* films between them, Disney would add five more in just five years.

To find room for these new stories in a fictional universe weighed down not just by the films but by an expanded universe of books, comics, and video games, Disney convened a story group at Lucasfilm to decide what was to be in the "canon" universe, and what was out. This ecumenical council for the galaxy far, far away eventually settled on the simplest solution: clear the decks. Everything that wasn't in the six films, or *The Clone Wars* television series, was out. All those stories—charting everything from Han and Leia's kids to Luke's lovers, the Emperor's unbalanced clone, the origins of the Republic, the Sith, and the Jedi, and even Chewbacca's controversial death—would be demoted to something just above fan wish-fulfillment. These stories would be known as the "*Star Wars* Legends" from now on, implying both mythical status and obsolescence simultaneously. Disney would forge its own path.

The new era of *Star Wars* would have its work cut out for it. The prequel trilogy still cast a long shadow, and there was an expectation that any new *Star Wars* film would have to perform some significant and difficult work in order to allow fans to move on. Such was the vehemence of the animosity toward the prequels that it had apparently gone some way to urging Lucas into retirement. "It was fine before the Internet," Lucas said. "But now with the Internet, it's gotten very vicious and very personal. You just say, 'Why do I need to do this?'"[23] That Disney's new films would be very much products of the internet era, though, was already a foregone conclusion: on the day of the sale announcement, mocking Darth Vader–Mickey Mouse memes were everywhere. Many fans were ready to be upset, and barbs were brought out preemptively. This first new Disney-era *Star Wars* film would have ten years of anticipation and half a franchise's worth of disappointment and frustration to live up to.

Despite Disney's success with its Marvel and Pixar films, there was also some suspicion as to whether Disney could be trusted not to meddle or water down the world of *Star Wars*. Only 37 percent of fans spoken to by the researcher William Proctor shortly after the deal was announced were optimistic about the sale to Disney. One respondent, a forty-four-year-old college professor, confessed that the sale "left a bad taste in my brain, much like when I learned Michael Jackson had acquired the publishing rights to all those Lennon/McCartney songs. . . . I just don't want to see Star Wars 'Disney-fied.'"[24] Some extreme fan reactions seemed to forget that Disney was a corporation with numerous subsidiaries (Pixar and Marvel have both continued to operate with relative autonomy), and instead imagined a future for *Star Wars* that contained animated princesses, Mickey Mouse, and musical numbers.

All this added up to one thing: if the first new *Star Wars* film was anything less than high quality, it was going to be relentlessly pilloried. A negative reception for the new film would have the capacity to derail Disney's hopes for expanding the franchise into a multi-pronged, multimovie property like its Marvel Cinematic Universe films, and the potential to further alter the cultural legacy of a film series that had already suffered dreadfully in the 2000s. "*The Force Awakens* has to do more than not disappoint," wrote *Wired* in its review of the film. "It has to *redeem*."[25]

There was also uncertainty: the last time a new *Star Wars* trilogy was announced, it was at least clear in broad strokes what it would cover. The prequels were always going to chart the fall of Anakin Skywalker and the Clone Wars, but what would these new films be about? Would Luke, Leia, and Han return? Would Chewbacca have gray hair? What would *Star Wars* look like, after Lucas?

THE NOSTALGIA DISEASE

Then there was Lucas himself, an industry-changing creator now bereft of his creations. What would he do, in this post-Lucas era of *Star Wars*? If he could find time while making his long-promised "little films," would he be invited to the *Star Wars* set? Would he be on call to mentor these new custodians of *Star Wars*? And would he even like these new films? "One thing I regret about *Star Wars* is that I never got to see it, you know?" Lucas said in an interview in early 2015. "I never got to be blown away by the big ship coming over the thing, or anything. But this time I'm going to be, because I have no idea what they're doing."[26] He would sit back, so it seemed, and watch.

Lucas didn't wait long before making his feelings known about how he thought the whole approach was going. As well as his "retro" comments, Lucas also infamously told Rose in the same interview in December 2015 that he'd "sold [his films] to the white slavers" and was immediately and rightly censured for it. In context, Lucas made the remark in response to Rose suggesting that the *Star Wars* films were his "kids" and that he might have a responsibility for their ongoing well-being. Lucas trails off after making the comment, and his uncomfortable smile suggests he knows he's gone too far (in a subsequent apology, he said that "I misspoke and used a very inappropriate analogy"[27]).

But then there are still the other remarks: the ones about *The Force Awakens* being "retro" and "for the fans," as well as the later alleged embrace of *Rogue One*. So what, exactly, do the labels that Lucas used to describe *The Force Awakens*—so clearly intended to stand in for less diplomatic comments—actually mean? How could *The Force Awakens*, a film made in 2015 with the full financial and technological acumen of Disney, be "retro"? And how could a new entry in one of the most popular film franchises of all time be criticized as being "for the fans"? On the other hand, why might Lucas prefer *Rogue One*? Would it not also be considered "retro," with its carefully re-created 1970s sets, costumes, and moustaches, or "for the fans," with its myriad of original trilogy references?

Perhaps we might understand Lucas's comments to be about the broad similarities between *The Force Awakens* and his earlier *Star Wars* films. For all that is made about the points of similarity between the original trilogy and the prequels ("It's like poetry," says Lucas in an oft-mocked line in a making-of documentary for *The Phantom Menace*, "it rhymes."), Lucas steadfastly avoided allowing *The Phantom Menace* to tell a standard hero's journey tale.[28] For all their flaws, the prequels do tell a genuinely different story than the original films. Where the originals are about the rise of a hero and the defeat of an evil Empire, the prequels chart the collapse of a bu-reaucratic republic at the hands of a Machiavellian politician. Even *The Phantom Menace* is structurally quite different from all that came before it, as it follows a wide spread of protagonists, none of whom are clearly the film's lead (Qui-Gon Jinn and Obi-Wan Kenobi are in the film from the beginning but drift in and out of focus; Anakin Skywalker leads two major action sequences yet is introduced only halfway through; and Padmé Amidala and even Jar Jar Binks take the lead at various points and can also make claim to being protago-nists of sorts).

In contrast, *The Force Awakens* is certainly closer in plot to the first *Star Wars* film than anything Lucas was involved with. As is often pointed out in comment threads and by some critics, if we squint, we can see *The Force Awakens* as a broad-strokes remake of *A New Hope*. "*The Force Awakens* worships at the feet of the original *Star Wars* trilogy on a beat-for-beat, moment-for-moment, even prop-for-prop basis," wrote Tasha Robinson for *The Verge*.[29]

Certainly, this is the most common criticism of *The Force Awak-ens* (one that I address in detail in chapter 3), and if this is what Lucas meant by his "retro" remark, then he is not alone in his res-ervations. Despite the other successes of *The Force Awakens,* the film seems certain to be remembered by a strand of critic and fan com-munity as entirely derivative of earlier *Star Wars* films. "I usually have no problem with sequels following certain formulas from its predecessors but *The Force Awakens* is more like a remake of *A New Hope* and in many instances it feels we are basically watching the same movie," wrote the film critic Gerardo Valero, in a reproof typical of a larger genre of similar work.[30] Where the prequels had apparently strayed too far from the central appeal of *Star Wars, The Force Awakens* hewed too close to the line. For these critics, *The Force Awakens* was too nostalgic, too simple, and too shallow to truly lay claim to be a genuine revival of the *Star Wars* franchise. With a new *Star Wars* film about to arrive annually, for these critics every fear about the Disney era was proving all too founded.

The most interesting thing about all this, of course, is that these objections are themselves quite familiar for *Star Wars*. In fact, in many respects these complaints feel startlingly similar to the same broad criticisms that *Star Wars* has faced ever since the first film was released. These are the recurrent objections to *Star Wars*: it is nostalgic for a comforting past, it prioritizes spectacle over meaning, and it contains shallow political relevance or, worse, might even serve as a distraction from more important topics.

Indeed, nostalgia and politics seem to be the two reliable constants in the way that *Star Wars* films are talked about across decades. Fredric Jameson, the famed theorist of postmodernism, claimed *Star Wars* as a key illustration of what he described as the "nostalgia film": not a film that directly evokes nostalgia by depicting another era (unlike Lucas's other megahit, *American Graffiti,* and its 1950s rock and roll tunes and muscle car races), but by reworking the cultural experiences of that era. In other words, the first *Star Wars* is a nostalgia film because it reclaims the Saturday afternoon adventure short-film serial that was popular in the 1930s, 1940s, and 1950s, but that was extinct by the time of its release in 1977. For Jameson:

> *Star Wars,* far from being a pointless satire of such now
> dead forms, satisfies a deep (might I even say repressed?)
> longing to experience them again: it is a complex object in
> which on some first level children and adolescents can take
> the adventures straight, while the adult public is able to
> gratify a deeper and more properly nostalgic desire to return
> to that older period and to live its strange old aesthetic arte-
> facts through once again.[31]

The many and varied influences of *Star Wars* have long since been noted by critics, from the kinds of B-movie serials that Jameson is referring to here (such as *Flash Gordon* and *Buck Rogers*), to Akira Kurosawa (particularly *The Hidden Fortress* from 1958), *The Searchers* (dir. John Ford, 1956), *Metropolis* (dir. Fritz Lang, 1927), and World War II fighter pilot films *The Dam Busters* (dir. Michael Anderson, 1955) and *633 Squadron* (dir. Walter Grauman, 1964). "Lucas looked *everywhere* for ideas for *Star Wars,* which is at the same time derivative and original," writes Dale Pollock in his biography of the director.[32] Indeed, Lucas went as far as to edit together reels of World War II dogfight footage as a style guide of sorts for his visual effects team to model the Death Star battle on during the making of the original film.[33] He was, quite literally, making new images out of old.

This is not simple plagiarism or borrowing, however. As Jameson argues, "By reinventing the feel and shape of character-istic art objects of an older period (the serials), [*Star Wars*] seeks to reawaken a sense of the past associated with those objects."[34] There is a strategy at work, then, in *Star Wars'* evocation of older cultural objects. When Lucas's film recalls a sense of the B-movie serial to audiences, they might also remember who they were at the time, what they were feeling, and what they most love about these memo-ries. While Lucas's film school contemporaries like Martin Scorsese made literate allusions to highbrow directors like Federico Fellini and Jean-Luc Godard,[35] Lucas instead spoke to a mass audience by citing older popular media set in a nostalgic mode. "He showed people it was all right to become totally involved in a movie again," said Alan Ladd Jr., president of Twentieth Century Fox and an early champion of *Star Wars,* "to yell and scream and applaud and really roll with it."[36]

So, just as *The Force Awakens* was criticized for being too unorigi-nal and for borrowing too much from other sources, so too was the first *Star Wars* film, right from the beginning. Yet there is a key dif-ference. Lucas was almost obsessive in his borrowings from different media forms, each with their own results; *The Force Awakens,* on the other hand, took the same model and looks to the *Star Wars* fran-chise as a whole rather than the wider gamut of cinema that Lucas drew on. Nonetheless, though the nostalgic objects referenced have changed, the logic and the accompanying criticism remains similar. Perhaps, in an odd way, this is part of Lucas's objection to *The Force Awakens*: finally, he knows what it is like to be the Akira Kurosawa, the John Ford, or the Walter Grauman to his *Star Wars* world.

For many, however, labeling a film like *The Force Awakens* as "too nostalgic" is seemingly enough to substantiate criticism by it-self. This is not just because it implies a level of unoriginality or simplicity. Indeed, nostalgia is, for many, always a suspect emotion, especially for critics who might see appeals to a happier past as re-gressive.[37] For those advocating social change, nostalgia is usually a negative sentiment, and even possibly a strategy of repression.

Nostalgia looks backward. It seeks to empower the present with what has been lost to the past, and for some, it represents an uncritical return to history. "Nostalgia, with its wistful memories, is essentially without guilt," contends Michael Kammen.[38] In recent years, too, nostalgia as an aspect of popular entertainment media has been seemingly pervasive, from television (nostalgic fictions like *Mad Men, The Hour,* and *Babylon Berlin* and remakes like *Knight Rider* and *Hawaii Five-0*) to music (Bruno Mars's use of "retro" musical styles and synth instrumentation) to video games (the revival of pixel art and chip tunes among independent game makers as an aesthetic). *Star Wars* is hardly alone in the battle over nostalgia: for critics, it is just simply one of the biggest targets.

There is a political significance to such charges of nostalgia, however. Writing about feminism in the 1980s, Janice Doane and Devon Hodges describe nostalgia as a way to "authenticate woman's traditional place and to challenge outspoken feminist criticisms of it."[39] Such a "traditional" past may well be an illusory symbol, too: writing in *Jacobin* magazine, Samuel Earle points out that the racist mentality that demands migrants "go back to where you came from" presumes a pure point of origin that surely never actually existed: "The racist, like all great nostalgists, is homesick for a home they never had."[40]

For a Marxist view of history, on the other hand, nostalgia suggests a retrograde embrace of the past that implicitly goes against an understanding of history as progressing toward a more just future. "Let the dead bury their dead," wrote Karl Marx in 1852,[41] a proclamation that Marcos Piason Natali argues "transformed nostalgia into a sort of political crime, causing well-intentioned leftists of several varieties to flee even the appearance of any connection to nostalgia."[42] Even the words used to describe left and right politics imply some sort of relationship to the past: "progressive" politics implies a future of change and improvement; "conservative," "traditionalist," or "reactionary" politics implies stasis or even a restoration. Nostalgia's fond reminisces for the past therefore seems to fundamentally align it with conservatism. You can, in a way, even imagine the villains of *The Force Awakens* being similarly chided for their nostalgia for the bygone days of Empire. "I will finish what you started," Kylo Ren promises Darth Vader's disfigured helmet, consciously connecting his actions to an antiquated era. Ren, with his own wholly unnecessary mask, is sometimes little more than a glorified Vader cosplayer in *The Force Awakens*, such is his nostalgic devotion to his grandfather's legacy.

If the political or historical associations weren't enough for us to distrust nostalgia, we need only take a look at the word's origins. Nostalgia began as a disease. The word itself was coined in 1688 by a Swiss physician named Johannes Hofer, who used it to diagnose acute psychological yearning—from the Greek *nostos* (homecoming) and *algos* (pain). In its earliest implementation, nostalgia was particularly used to describe acute homesickness felt by Swiss soldiers on a foreign campaign—many of whom were so susceptible to this nostalgia that a homely Swiss milking song, "Khue-Reyen," was apparently banned from being played, an offense punishable by death.[43] Yet nostalgia's status as a medical condition was short-lived—though doctors searched high and low to no avail for a bone that produced nostalgia and similar maladies, they soon gave over the search for the cause of nostalgia to poets and philosophers. As Svetlana Boym notes in her book *The Future of Nostalgia*, this is a concept that belongs to no specific discipline, frustrating psychologists, sociologists, literary theorists, and philosophers: "Nostalgia tantalizes us with its fundamental ambivalence; it is about the repetition of the unrepeatable, materialization of the immaterial."[44] As kind of collective (or cultural) urge, nostalgia looks toward absences, and not directly toward the material present. But this search for the past is an impossible one, given that remembering is always a present-tense act: in looking backward, the nostalgist necessarily remakes history for the contemporary moment. Despite seeming to be a one-hit punch for pop culture criticism, then, nostalgia is a complex cultural invention that contains multitudes of meaning.

Nonetheless, Hofer may yet be of some use to us. As a yearning for home, as in Hofer's initial meaning, nostalgia makes more sense than in many of its contemporary applications that instead prioritize a fondness for the past. The most striking line (spoken by Han Solo) of the marketing campaign for *The Force Awakens* rests on this very idea: "Chewie, we're home," he says upon returning to the

Millennium Falcon. But of course, we, the audience, are home, too. Herein lies the fundamental ambivalence of Lucas's critique of *The Force Awakens* as "retro": although he himself had recognized the public's need for the nostalgic "home" of fairy tales and adventure serials in 1977, he had largely failed to provide such a return with his prequels, and further failed to recognize its return with *The Force Awakens*. Nostalgia as a marketing device for the new *Star Wars* films exploited this very sense of homecoming, as I show in chapter 2. Maybe *Star Wars* had gone away, or we had left it behind: either way, Disney's *The Force Awakens* represented the homecoming to cure this pain of absence. Yet it also provides *Star Wars* with its main line of criticism. There is more going on here than simple recapitulation or remaking. For *Star Wars*, nostalgia is both the disease and the cure.

THE LEFT WING OF THE FORCE

Whether stated outright or not, the nostalgic critique of *Star Wars* is also a political one. And indeed, both *The Force Awakens* and the first *Star Wars* were scolded for their politics: or perhaps, for their apparent lack of politics. The celebrated *New Yorker* film critic Pauline Kael famously eviscerated Lucas for his obsession with spectacle and surface. If Lucas "weren't hooked on the crap of his childhood—if he brought his resources to bear on some projects with human beings in them—there's no imagining the result," she wrote. "There might be miracles."[45] But there were never any miracles to be had: for many critics over the years, *Star Wars* was infantile and insubstantial, and possessed no cultural relevance whatsoever. If not distasteful nostalgia, it was pure escapism, disconnected from any important cause or reality of the day. Potentially, it was even worse—as I discuss in chapter 1, the original *Star Wars* trilogy was thought by some to have actually helped usher in a regressive political era for all of America.

Four decades later, and although the political content of *The Force Awakens* was widely thought to be a little more liberal (and more on that in chapter 4), the critique of nostalgia nonetheless paints this new film as similarly insubstantial. If *The Force Awakens* was simply a reheated version of the original *Star Wars*, then what hope could it have of making a meaningful intervention into today's politics? What relevance could this film possibly have? Again, the complaint of pure escapism was claimed. *The Force Awakens* might have been a breathlessly good time, but its nostalgic veneer allows us to bliss out for two hours and ignore our pressing social and political problems. Even worse: through its apparently slavish re-creation of the original *Star Wars* film, such blissing out is also coated in a sheen of reminiscence for the better yesterdays of a conservative past. *The Force Awakens* was both insubstantial and noxious, a kind of backward glance that stings.

Would that it were so simple. Far from being the tasteless corporate machine-work that it is often downplayed as, the post-Lucas era of *Star Wars* is complex and multifaceted. It is intelligent, it is concerned with the past and questions of legacy, and it is profoundly— yes, even politically—hopeful for the future. So far, we have witnessed a surprisingly thoughtful opening salvo in Disney's screen media future for the *Star Wars* universe: the first of the new "saga" films in *The Force Awakens*; the first of the "*Star Wars* Story" films in *Rogue One*; and the first of the small-screen series in *Star Wars: Rebels*. Each approaches the core concepts of *Star Wars* in a different way, and articulates the appeal of the series with a different accent. Yet each also presents a challenge for how *Star Wars* can be popularly understood and, as a decades-old media franchise, how it continues to adapt and respond to the times that it finds itself in.

This complex relationship between nostalgia, politics, and the new era of *Star Wars* is what this book hopes to explore. When Disney bought Lucasfilm and relaunched the *Star Wars* franchise, it also reinvigorated long-held debates about the significance of one of the most successful film franchises of all time. But what was to be different about this new Disney film, and the ones to follow? What was *Star Wars* to be, after Lucas?

Today, *Star Wars* has been so effectively returned to the heart of popular culture that it is almost difficult to remember what the ten years were like between 2005 and 2015, when it lay dormant. Beyond the films now released—*The Force Awakens*, *Rogue One*, *The Last Jedi*, *Solo*—and the *Rebels* television show, *Star Wars* continues to take up ever-expanding space in public life, be it as a political

insult, a joking meme, or critic's latest think piece. In 2019 Disney
will launch an extravagant new *Star Wars* area at its theme parks in
California and Florida, "Galaxy's Edge," which will include a full-
size Millennium Falcon and Cantina. Eventually, guests will also
be able to stay at a *Star Wars*–themed hotel, a "100% immersive"
experience that will "culminate in a unique journey for every person who visits."[46] Already, Disney has opened *Star Wars: Secrets of
the Empire* virtual reality experience locations in Orlando, Anaheim,
and London, where visitors wear headsets and walk around in real
(and virtual) space. Or perhaps you might enjoy "*Star Wars* Day at
Sea" on board one of Disney's Caribbean cruise liners, where guests
train to be Jedi, participate in scavenger hunts and remote-control
BB-8 races, and attend a *Star Wars*–themed stage-show spectacular.
Star Wars has escaped the screen in the Disney era, and constantly
picks away at the porous barriers between our screens and our lives.
This seems unlikely to end and, if anything, will only multiply. Dis-
ney has announced plans for a new trilogy of films to be created by
Rian Johnson, another new series written and produced by *Game of
Thrones* showrunners David Benioff and D.B. Weiss, and "not just
one, but a few"[47] *Star Wars* television series for a still-unlaunched
Netflix competitor. This is, with some back-of-the-envelope math,
more hours of *Star Wars* content than ever existed under Lucas by a
factor of at least two to one, without even speculating about future
"*Star Wars* Story" films or Indiana Jones sequels. Remember too
that it has only been half a decade since Disney took over Lucasfilm.

This is not necessarily to say that Disney has been careless in
its proliferation of *Star Wars* since 2012. In fact, as led by Kathleen
Kennedy, Lucasfilm has been decisive in guarding the *Star Wars*
brand. When rumors emerged of "erratic" behavior on the set of his
previous film, *Fantastic Four,* the director Josh Trank was removed
from an unannounced "*Star Wars* Story" film, and the project was
shelved.[48] After *Rogue One* was seemingly not coming together as well
as Lucasfilm had hoped, Tony Gilroy was brought in to direct reshoots over the film's actual director, Gareth Edwards. Colin Trevorrow was hired to write and direct Episode IX, but was fired after
Lucasfilm came "to the conclusion that our visions for the project
differ."[49] Most dramatically of all, *Solo* directors Phil Lord and Chris

Miller were fired and replaced with Ron Howard midway through production, with "deep fundamental philosophical differences" alleged.[50] When things have not proceeded to plan, the new Lucasfilm has been distinctly unafraid to be resolute.

All of this combines to make the period between 2015 and 2017 perhaps the most important in *Star Wars* history. It is a clear articulation point. During this time Disney renewed the franchise and recentered *Star Wars* within popular culture. There was the first new Skywalker film in a decade, the first stand-alone *Star Wars* film, and the rearticulation of *Star Wars* on the small screen with *Rebels*. This was the moment where Disney would make a case not just for *Star Wars* as a reinvigorated franchise back from the dead but for a world where *Star Wars* should never go out of fashion ever again. The new *Star Wars* films would be refined projects of the highest quality Disney could muster: star creatives and casts, beautiful cinematography, John Williams music, and state-of-the-art technology. Beginning with the renewal of *The Force Awakens* and ending with the revision of *The Last Jedi*, *Star Wars* after Lucas was in this period to undergo the most industrious change in its forty-year history. Under Disney and Kennedy, it was to become what *Wired* would call "the forever franchise,"[51] but was ultimately something even more than that. For Disney, *Star Wars* represented the keys to a dominion of popular culture that sat alongside Mickey Mouse, Marvel, Pixar, and their newly remade *Beauty and the Beast*, *Cinderella*, and *Jungle Book* films. Far from slowing down and diminishing, after Lucas, *Star Wars* was to be the franchise at the center of everything.

1

BEFORE THE EMPIRE

*The Politics of George Lucas
and the Critique of the Original Trilogy*

T wins you say?" tweeted the British actor David Ames in February 2017, following the announcement that pop superstar Beyoncé was pregnant. "During uncertain, tyrannical times? With a powerful dark lord and his senators corrupting the planet? Hmm . . ."[1] Variations on the same joke were everywhere at the time. The *Huffington Post* was less subtle. "*Star Wars* Is Pretty Much Happening in Real Life Because Beyoncé Is Pregnant with Twins" read their headline, with the writer imploring Beyoncé to "save us from the Dark Side."[2]

The jokes were pointed: yes, they were reactions to Beyoncé's pregnancy, but the real butt of the comparison here was the recently elected forty-fifth president of the United States, Donald Trump. Here was true evil, these jokes said: here was a man whose villainy can only be compared to the pure malfeasance of the fictional Emperor Palpatine. The shock and outrage that Trump's first month in office had created seemed to find solace in the thought that respite might come through popular culture.

This was in many ways unsurprising, as there was precedent here. Although *The Force Awakens* and *Rogue One* might have thrown

Star Wars back into the popular consciousness, *Star Wars* has long been one of popular culture's most enduring political analogies. During the first Gulf War in the early 1990s, the soldiers leading the strategy of the United States called themselves "Jedi Knights."[3] In the 2000s, George W. Bush's vice president, Dick Cheney, was so frequently likened to Darth Vader (particularly by Jon Stewart, who kept the comparison as a running gag on his *Daily Show*) that Cheney told reporters in 2007 that "I've been asked if that nickname bothers me, and the answer is, no. After all, Darth Vader is one of the nicer things I've been called recently."[4] In 2016, the conservative editor and commentator Bill Kristol was widely ridiculed for making a faux pas when he admitted that even as a child, he "was inclined to root for the Empire."[5] In Australia, the leader of the conservative government in the lower house, Christopher Pyne, featured in a widely shared parody where he smugly tells Darth Vader in the Death Star conference room scene in *A New Hope* that he's "fixed" the Rebel problem because "I'm a fixer" (comments that he'd made in an interview that week) before laughing at Vader's force choking of Admiral Motti.[6] "How will the Emperor maintain control without the bureaucracy?" asks one of the Imperials. "I want it to be a surprise for you," the digitally inserted Pyne replies.

It would be easy to suggest that it is simply *Star Wars'* popularity and ubiquity in popular culture over the years that has drawn out these political comparisons, as indeed some scholars have.[7] Yet the political uses for *Star Wars* are so enduring, so easily made, and so instantly meaningful that it feels like more is going on than a simple borrowing of popular culture. Heather Urbanski points out that these kinds of *Star Wars* analogies are often highly malleable, too: when one group from either end of the political spectrum wishes to satirize the other, they depict their enemies as the Empire; when another group wishes to valorize themselves, they paint themselves as coming from the noble tradition of the Jedi.[8] The same goes for objections to *Star Wars* in general: in 1979 Michael Pye and Lynda Myles report that French leftists saw the first *Star Wars* film as fascist, while the Italian right-wing thought it was communist.[9] Alyssa Rosenberg, a columnist for the *Washington Post*, says that it's precisely this malleability that gives *Star Wars* its enduring political power.

"The Emperor is the puppetmaster, Darth Vader is the one going out and causing trouble. The insurgent energy of the Rebellion, and the moral and intellectual purity of the Force—there's a role for almost anyone in any given conflict, even if the fit's not great."[10]

Some of these fits have endured longer than others. Most famously, in 1983 Ronald Reagan announced the Strategic Defense Initiative (SDI), an orbital missile defense system intended to intercept and destroy incoming nuclear missiles before they reached American soil. The initiative, announced a few months before the release of *Return of the Jedi,* was popularly nicknamed "Star Wars," first by its detractors and then, after realizing the power of the analogy, by its advocates. Finally, Reagan himself joined in: in a 1985 speech defending the program, after he had won the previous year's election in a landslide, Reagan claimed that SDI "isn't about war, it's about peace . . . and in that struggle, if you will pardon me stealing a film line, the Force is with us."[11]

This wasn't even Reagan's first invocation of *Star Wars.* Just a few weeks before his unveiling of the SDI initiative, Reagan gave perhaps his most famous speech, where he branded the Soviet Union an "Evil Empire." The language was perhaps a little vaguer than has been subsequently implied: in context, there's not much to suggest that Reagan wasn't referring to any of the other unpleasant empires that have existed in human history. Anthony Dolan, Reagan's speechwriter at the time, also emphatically denied intentionally making the *Star Wars* link.[12] Significantly, however, regardless of intention, it was *Star Wars* that the world heard: only a few days later, the *New York Times* reports that the speech had already become known as Reagan's "Darth Vader speech."[13]

Despite its political malleability, *Star Wars* has, for better or worse, gained a general whiff of cultural conservatism. Perhaps it is because of this Reagan link and the film's reputation as the biggest juggernaut to come from Hollywood. Or maybe this is simply to say that the most strident criticisms of *Star Wars* have traditionally come from the left. Indeed, the franchise's open nostalgia for the cultural products of the 1930s, 1940s, and 1950s has been a common point of disapproval for progressive critics. Yet the overall impression of *Star*

Wars as a conservative cultural force extends beyond the criticism of nostalgia to a broader claim of regressive social influence, particularly in American life. For some, it is not simply its backward glance that appears suspect, but seemingly its entire worldview.

Where this impression actually comes from is worth exploring. When I first encountered the impression of *Star Wars* as conservative, I assumed that this stemmed from the popular response to the film's overwhelming success in 1977. Although I was not alive in 1977, I had seen the way that similar criticisms of hugely successful films like *Titanic* or *Avatar* had accompanied their meteoric rise to the top of the box office. In Australia, we call this "tall poppy syndrome." When something is extraordinarily popular, it must be treated with suspicion—we compete to cut down the tallest poppies. After some research, however, my assumption proved incorrect. *Star Wars* was reviewed well in 1977 (in fact, all *Star Wars* films—including the prequels—have been reviewed quite well on first release). Audiences clearly loved *Star Wars* in 1977, and, not wanting to be left out, even the most curmudgeonly critics from the time seem happy to admit that the film is good fun. Famously, Vincent Canby's *New York Times* review claimed that "the story of 'Star Wars' could be written on the head of a pin and still leave room for the Bible," but even this jibe was actually meant very much as a compliment.[14] In fact, Canby doubled down on his enthusiasm for the film a few weeks after its release, noting that *Star Wars* "isn't about anything at all in any serious way, though it is so beautifully and cheerfully done and it is so full of references to the literature of one's childhood, that the escapism is of a particularly invigorating sort."[15] Perhaps, then, given this warm reception, we should be instead searching for critical dissent as the film became a cultural phenomenon over weeks and months in 1977, rather than just in its first days. Happily, 1977 was years before the practice of single global release days was instituted, so we can look at a range of reviews staggered over almost the entire year. When the film opened in the UK in December 1977, for example, there may well have been time for a more restrained critical appraisal to emerge. Yet six months after its positive American reception, the *Guardian*'s critic, Derek Malcolm, still saw *Star Wars* favorably: "It's an incredibly knowing movie," he wrote. "But the filching is so affectionate that you can't resent it."[16] Critics simply loved *Star Wars*.

It's also interesting to note that the political resonance of *Star Wars* was left fairly uncommented on in 1977. Contemporaneous film critics generally only make very brief mention of any political overtones in their reviews of *Star Wars*. Perhaps the closest to criticize the film along political lines at the time was an essay by Pauline Kael in the *New Yorker*, published almost half a year after the film was an assured success, where she criticizes it for promoting something that "goes way past nostalgia to the feeling that now is the time to return to childhood." Yet even Kael recognizes that the film is nonetheless "enjoyable on its own terms."[17]

So from where and how did the political critique of *Star Wars* emerge? Associations with Reagan aside, as far as I can tell, the clearest answer lies not in the popular press but in academe. Some of the earliest, but perhaps more importantly also the most enduring, critiques of *Star Wars* actually stem from academic sources. Writing in 2009, Will Brooker frames his review of the academic response to *Star Wars* bluntly: "Cinema scholarship seems embarrassed by *Star Wars*."[18] Writers such as Andrew Britton and Robin Wood memorably critiqued the film, and their line of argument has an enduring legacy even today, amounting to a general picture of distaste for the franchise particularly among academic work of the 1980s and 1990s. For these few scholars who seriously engaged with *Star Wars*, it was—its own merits aside as a film—largely seen as a force that had unraveled Hollywood and ushered in an era of simplistic blockbuster filmmaking. It had brought with it a renewal of good guys versus bad guys, and politically set the scene for what these critics saw as the shallow and infantilizing politics of the Reagan era.

The first—and possibly the most enriching to read—of these scholarly critiques arrived only a year after *Star Wars* did. In a dissection for *Jump Cut* in 1978, Dan Rubey provides an illuminating and original analysis of the film (and notably avoids the kind of narrative analysis based in Joseph Campbell's Monomyth structure that dominates much of later *Star Wars* scholarship) that nevertheless condemns the film for what Rubey sees as a conservative sanitization of modern warfare. "*Star Wars* uses an image of ourselves from the past as a defense against our more recent history," Rubey writes.[19] The Vietnam War had become a day-to-day horror for the American public in the 1970s. Rubey argues that by returning to the nostalgic imagery of the more morally favored combat of World War II, *Star Wars* essentially authorizes a reclamation of the imagery of the Vietnam War. The past is used to insulate against the present. Far from treating technology with the usual terror of the science fiction genre, Rubey argues that *Star Wars* sees speed and size as exciting new possibilities for conflict.

In 1986, in a percipient and influential essay, "Reaganite Entertainment," Andrew Britton expanded this critique to encompass a kind of national cultural psychoanalysis. Britton links *Star Wars* with *Rocky* and the proto-blockbuster disaster films (*The Towering Inferno*, *The Poseidon Adventure*) of the early 1970s, and suggests that they form a "general movement of reaction and conservative reassurance."[20] Key to this is their status as "entertainment" rather than art or any greater meaning: when watching this kind of film, Britton argues, we are encouraged to sit back and relax, to be "off duty." Britton's analysis here is quite true, of course, in many respects. Lucas *did* hope to make a film that was relaxing and entertaining in a way cinema had not been for decades. The producer Alan Ladd's comments about Lucas showing the audience that "it was all right to become totally involved in a movie again" are all we need here to agree with Britton. Where Ladd (and indeed Lucas) and Britton would disagree, however, is with the effect that such escapism has on audiences and on culture more broadly. Britton does not deny the pleasures of a film like *Star Wars* but argues that such entertainment films ultimately ask very little of their audiences: "We are not told not to think, but we are told, over and over again, that there is nothing here to think about."[21] The members of the audience, for Britton, are asked to relax but also to place little value in the work that they are consuming. The work is enjoyable but disposable. We are not asked to reflect on the world, we are not asked to value culture and the labor and work that goes into making it, and we are not asked to think about ourselves. Indeed, for Britton, such works of entertainment celebrate "the spectator as the consumer of spectacle."[22] It is a solipsistic activity, a kind of onanism that is about disconnected and momentary pleasure.

Of course, what Britton did not take into account here—and perhaps, given he was writing in 1986, the full ramifications of this point were impossible to foresee—was that when such works of entertainment enter the public sphere, they can become near-universal languages for articulating the political, our identities, and the quotidian. The uses of *Star Wars* as a political analogy actually counteract Britton's point: clearly, even if audiences are not thinking about contemporary politics while watching *Star Wars*, we frequently go on to use it as an apparatus to communicate in an immediate and articulate way about the world around us and ourselves. Paradoxically, *Star Wars*' minimal agenda greatly amplified its political utility.

Britton, in a defining move, also takes issue with the simplistic moral stakes of *Star Wars* and other films of its era, where ambiguity is replaced with tales of good versus evil. "There is a struggle, but no dialectic," Britton writes.[23] Luke Skywalker and the Rebellion stand for a goodness that is largely unarticulated by *Star Wars*. Part of this has to do with film history: John Hellman (among others) argues that *Star Wars* shifts the simplistic morality of the classical western into space.[24] Robin Wood also makes a similar argument in 1986 when linking *Star Wars* to the Reagan era. Like Britton, Wood suggests that *Star Wars* is inherently insubstantial and resistant to analysis. "To raise serious objections to them is to run the risk of looking a fool (they're 'just entertainment,' after all) or, worse, a spoilsport (they're 'such fun')," Wood writes.[25] The key problem for Wood seems to be that the pleasures of *Star Wars* are too immediately accessible: we do not have to "work" for them, and they are, "as all mindless and automatic pleasure tends to be," "extremely reactionary."[26] Wood identifies the similarity *Star Wars* has to the old adventure serials Lucas was inspired by, except to note that the serials "were not taken seriously on any level (except perhaps by real children, and then only young ones)," whereas *Star Wars* insinuated itself into a central position in popular culture to the point where it precluded the creation of different (and Wood suspects better) cinema.[27]

The heart of the argument here is that *Star Wars* more broadly—

as the most popular film franchise of its era in America—reflected and possibly to some extent anticipated the popular ideology of its time. If researchers and politically inclined critics saw in 1980s USA a nation with a simplistic political worldview of villains, heroes, and clearly drawn battle lines, and a general cultural preference for pleasure seeking over political consciousness, then they did not have to look far for a filmic inscription of these values. That a film like *Star Wars* is "fun," for these writers, is simply perhaps the greatest indication of the intrinsic alignment of the film's values with those of the era.

Star Wars' cultural and political regressivism, for these critics, also stems from what they see as its ideological incoherency. Here we can return to Rubey from 1978, who points out that Leia symbolizes this political confusion in her dual status as princess *and* senator, as an elite royalist *and* democratic leader. The Rebels, despite their aesthetics of liberation and freedom, are loyalists trying to preserve and restore the good old days rather than pursue any new or future-facing political emancipation. "They want to return to the old Republican days of the aristocratic Jedi knights (whatever sense that makes), and it is Tarkin and Darth Vader who are the rebels against the old order," Rubey writes.[28] In fact, argues Rubey, evil exists in *Star Wars* only to allow audiences to accept the violence of its protagonists. We do not mind Luke, Leia, and Han killing Stormtroopers on the Death Star because we know without thinking about it too deeply that the Empire is villainous. "By having no thought-out, consistent position on any of the issues he touches on, Lucas dooms *Star Wars* to repeat all the dominant ideological clichés of our society," Rubey concludes. "That distant galaxy turns out to be not so far away after all."[29] For Rubey, the dominant, conservative politics of the era is reflected—if not necessarily advocated for—in a dominant film such as *Star Wars*.

The film critic Karina Longworth sums up this kind of argument well in her book on the films of George Lucas:

> [*Star Wars*] anticipated the conservatism of the 1980s: patriotic and simpleminded, the series re-established movies as something the whole family could enjoy together, rather than just

another aspect of a generational war. Lucas's notion of "pure cinema" as based on image and feeling, rather than ideas and plot, invited viewers to experience cinema the way they did in the "old" days, rather than read it critically. There was no subtext to separate from the text; there was barely any text.[30]

For these critics, *Star Wars* is regressive because it is apolitical, insubstantial, easy, and enjoyable to watch, and ideologically confused, and because it nostalgically returns to and valorizes the media forms of the past. (Interestingly, Longworth is the partner of Rian Johnson, director of *The Last Jedi*—one wonders about any conversations they may have had about the franchise.)

This kind of political criticism of *Star Wars* also often overlaps with an industrial objection. For less ideologically predisposed critics, historians, and filmmakers, *Star Wars* instead represented an unwelcome shift in the industrial paradigm of American filmmaking. "*Star Wars* was the film that ate the heart and the soul of Hollywood," said the screenwriter Paul Schrader.[31] In this view of Hollywood history, filmmakers had in the late 1960s finally won the creative independence to make meaningful, impactful films that spoke to a new generation and embodied a kind of youthful spirit. This was the era sometimes described as "New Hollywood" or the "American New Wave," which was defined by films that stepped outside the usual Hollywood mold. These were films like *Bonnie and Clyde* (dir. Arthur Penn, 1967), *The Graduate* (dir. Mike Nichols, 1967), *Easy Rider* (dir. Dennis Hopper, 1969), and even Lucas's pre–*Star Wars* hit, *American Graffiti* (1973), all of which drew influence from European art cinema directors like Jean-Luc Godard and Michelangelo Antonioni and merged them with the American tradition. This American New Wave seemed to express an us-against-the-world attitude for the generation that came of age during the late 1960s—indeed, an intergenerational conflict was seen in the critical responses to *Bonnie and Clyde*, where older critics like Bosley Crowther derided it and younger critics such as Kael championed the film.[32]

In 1977 *Star Wars* came along and, with the films of Steven Spielberg (particularly *Jaws* in 1975), made serious inroads into reframing Hollywood as an industry of blockbusters. It became increasingly difficult for young and brash directors to make a film about youthful existential ennui (as in *The Graduate*) or the fear of an older generation (as in *Easy Rider*)—Hollywood now dealt exclusively in big budgets, big audiences, and big financial returns. In 1996, the critic David Thompson lamented that "the medium has sunk beyond anything we dreamed of, leaving us stranded, a race of dreamers," he wrote, "and I blame Spielberg and Lucas."[33] When the film scholar Wheeler Winston Dixon gave "twenty-five reasons why it's all over" in 2001, at number fifteen was "the malign influence of Steven Spielberg and George Lucas."[34] For Peter Biskind in *Easy Riders, Raging Bulls* (the popular Hollywood history that likely canonized this kind of interpretation), *Star Wars* and its ilk were "infantilizing the audience, reconstituting the spectator as child, then overwhelming him and her with sound and spectacle, obliterating irony, aesthetic self-consciousness, and critical reflection."[35] It might be fair in response to point to the longer history of Hollywood—its ebb and flow of creative control and conglomeration—and instead suggest that perhaps the American New Wave was an aberration, ripe for inevitable reversal at the hands of risk-averse corporations. If we take the American New Wave's end to be with *Star Wars*, as some critics contend, then it lasted just one decade. That is not the enduring narrative for *Star Wars*' contribution to the American film industry, however. It is barely an exaggeration to suggest that, in the eyes of some, the hopes of a progressive and creatively independent Hollywood lie murdered on the cutting room floor, with Lucas and a special effects team looking on and holding the bloodied knife.

LUCAS THE LEFTIST

Of course, almost all this analysis would be to the horror of Lucas himself. The irony is that Lucas hated Hollywood and the big studios, and with the success of *Star Wars* achieved the freedom to work without them. "I grew up in the 1960s," said Lucas. "I was very anti-corporation, and I was here in San Francisco, where anti-authority is even more extreme."[36] Lucas spent his fledgling career before *Star Wars* making every anti-establishment move he could have made. As a student, in 1969 Lucas had won a scholarship from Columbia Pictures to shoot a behind-the-scenes short during the making of *Mackenna's Gold* (a western directed by J. Lee Thompson).

Instead he produced *6-18-67*, a languid, five-minute portrait of the Utah filming location that focuses on the landscape of mountains and plains. The *Mackenna's Gold* crew appears only briefly, as insignificant specks in the distance, a move that paints them as an embarrassing intrusion amid the desert's natural beauty—hardly the glossy behind-the-scenes short that was expected.

Lucas always wanted to work outside the reach of the big studios, and as his career developed, he mostly got what he wanted. After cofounding the independent production company American Zoetrope with his friend and mentor Francis Ford Coppola, Lucas used his creative freedom (and almost a million dollars of Warner Bros. investment money) to direct the coldly dystopian science-fiction film *THX 1138* (1971), which was as political a film released by any major studio in the 1970s. "Modern society is a rotten thing, and by God, if you're smart, you'll get out now and escape" is the way that Lucas summed up the film's message.[37] *THX 1138* was a commercial flop and ended the relationship with Warner Bros., sending Zoetrope into significant debt (and Coppola off, reluctantly, to make a commercial film for Paramount called *The Godfather*).

Despite his first feature's failure, Lucas received directing offers for commercials and studio films but opted instead to pursue his own projects at great financial cost (Lucas and his wife, Marcia, borrowed thousands of dollars from his parents during this period, something he loathed).[38] After trying many studios and failing, Lucas eventually convinced Universal to finance and release *American Graffiti*, a period 1960s film about four small-town boys on their last night before leaving for the big city. In a prescient interview from 1974, Lucas agrees with a description of *American Graffiti* as a "nostalgia film"—those words precisely, eight years before Jameson used them—but adds that it's also "about the fact that you can't live in the past. . . . No matter how much you want things to be the same, they won't and can't; everything is always changing, and you have to accept change."[39] Despite Lucas's insistence that he wanted to make *Graffiti* as a "movie where people felt better coming out of the theater than when they went in,"[40] the film was ultimately another unpredictable turn. It had an odd, Italian-sounding name that the studio hated ("graffiti" as a term was not yet in common usage in English)[41] and was ostensibly structured around several decade-old pop songs. Coppola, fresh from his enormous success with *The Godfather,* was brought on as a producer as a surety for Universal, though Lucas knew Coppola had no interest in keeping him in line.[42] This didn't stop Universal cutting four and a half minutes from the final version of *Graffiti,* against Lucas's wishes and impassioned protests. An infuriated Lucas likened the cuts—which he viewed as spiteful rather than actually necessary—to "a crayon mark on my painting" and vowed never to give up creative control to the studios ever again.[43]

Nonetheless, *Graffiti* was a triumph. Lucas was a millionaire by the age of twenty-eight and, more important, had been gifted with the ability to forge the kind of creative freedom he had always wanted. Lucas and Universal's enmity also had another side effect. One month before *Graffiti* became the studio's biggest hit in years, it formally declined to option his next script—*Star Wars*—which Lucas took to Fox instead, using his newfound success in yet another independent move. "Lucas only wanted to make sure that *Star Wars* remained *his* movie," writes Dale Pollock: "He asked for control, not dollars."[44] Fox happily gave Lucas complete control over what at the time were considered "garbage" contract provisions with little financial potential: merchandising, music, and sequels. Of course, it is now common knowledge that it was these provisions that would make Lucas one of the most powerful people in Hollywood and allow him to reshape the industry. Lucas would go on to build Skywalker Ranch, his independent filmmaking retreat in Marin County, California, far away from Hollywood, and finance his five *Star Wars* sequels himself, effectively making them semi-independent films in economic terms if not spiritual ones. The conglomeration of Hollywood, for which Lucas is so routinely accused of pioneering, was in fact born out of an extreme distaste for the studios and a burning need for creative control.

Lucas's own politics—and his political motivations in making *Star Wars*—is equally at odds with the cultural legacy of the film argued for by critics like Britton, Wood, and Longworth. Of course, there is no straight line between the political intent of a director, his or her film, and its cultural impact, and it is not unreasonable to

think that if Britton et al. are correct, Lucas himself might be morti-
fied. As a young college graduate, Lucas claimed to be an activist
and was strongly opposed to the Vietnam War. "I was angry at
the time, getting involved in all the causes," he said.[45] His student
films, if not directly politically inclined, do also share a clear anti-
authoritarian and anti-establishment bent. Nonetheless, Lucas was
never publicly politically active, at least not during his Lucasfilm
years, though he remained politically left-wing. (We may still raise
an eyebrow at Lucas's professed leftist politics given his many en-
tanglements with filmmaking unions while making *Star Wars*; Lucas also bitterly complained about not being able to cross a picket
line on *American Graffiti*.)[46] Yet as an older man, the influence of his
partner, Mellody Hobson, saw Lucas take a more active interest
in politics—including supporting Hobson's friend, the then Senator
Barack Obama and his presidential campaign.[47]

It is nonetheless fair to say that Lucas could hardly be described
as a dissident or a political influencer in Hollywood (in a sharp assessment, Biskind describes him as "essentially apolitical"[48]). Yet all
of Lucas's films do contain fairly clear political elements and sub-
texts, *Star Wars* included. *THX 1138* contained a strong political
message, and despite *American Graffiti*'s nostalgia, it too was intended
to be a politically motivated portrait of small-town America on the
verge of the loss of innocence. *Graffiti* ends, quite strikingly for an
upbeat teen film, with an abrupt title card that reveals the fate of the
film's four young men. "John Milner was killed by a drunk driver in
December 1964," we learn. "Terry Fields was reported missing in
action near An Loc in December 1965." The idyllic past is brutally
disrupted by the degraded present. Vietnam intervenes.

Indeed, in *How Star Wars Conquered the Universe*, Chris Taylor
argues that Lucas was set to make a trilogy of films about Vietnam
and its effect on the American psyche.[49] There was the past: *American Graffiti* and its nostalgic embrace of a time before the violence of
Vietnam and its wrecking of American unity. There was the present: Lucas had been planning to make *Apocalypse Now* for American
Zoetrope and had worked with the writer John Milius to develop a
story directly about the war in Vietnam. Only one thing was certain at this point: the film would show the reality of the war on

the ground. Finally, there was the future: Lucas would draw on the Vietnam conflict in an allegorical mode for his new science fiction film, *Star Wars*.

The relationship between Lucas, *Apocalypse Now*, and *Star Wars* is a contested one. In his biography of Lucas, Pollock claims that *Apocalypse Now* was the result of a long-standing ambition on Lucas's behalf to make a film "about the bizarre media circus the Vietnam War had become." It was to be "an updated *Dr. Strangelove*, a case of trying to kill an ant with a sledgehammer, only to discover that the ant is winning."[50] According to Pollock, Lucas tried several times to negotiate with Coppola to get the film made, but Coppola financially leveraged Lucas to the point that Lucas gave up *Apocalypse Now*.[51] Longworth characterizes *Apocalypse Now* as having been "robbed" by Coppola from Lucas,[52] but Milius disagrees. "George had nothing whatsoever to do with it, other than the fact that he was going to direct it," Milius is quoted by Biskind as saying. "Francis gave George ample opportunity to make the movie. George never did. He was too good for it."[53]

Whatever the case, Lucas claims that his interest in making a film about Vietnam carried over from *Apocalypse Now* into *Star Wars*. "I figured that I couldn't make that film because it was about the Vietnam War," he said, "so I would essentially deal with some of the same interesting concepts that I was going to use and convert them into space fantasy, so you'd have essentially a large technological empire going after a small group of freedom fighters."[54] Older science fiction had featured colonialist themes from a different perspective: this is a genre so often about traveling to new and exotic locations, and subjugating them. As Jessica Langer puts it, the science fiction trope of the "dangerous planet whose inhabitants dare to fight back against the lantern-jawed colonial hero" is all too often a replaying of the European mythos of the era of Empire.[55] Indeed, the idea that science fiction broadly has its roots in colonialism is so uncontroversial that John Rieder dryly notes that it "has strong foundation in the obvious."[56] Yet the motif of scale and conflict is crucial to *Star Wars* in a reversal of science fiction's usual colonialist overtones, and it is the most obvious element of the film derived from Vietnam. The Empire attempts to kill an ant with a sledgehammer, only to discover that the ant—in the form of the Rebel Alliance—is winning. Although Longworth argues that the opening battle of the first *Star Wars* simply presents "two types of never-before-seen aircraft, both shooting lasers, before we've met a single character,"[57] the economy of scale—one tiny starship being pursued by an enormous one—tells a very intelligible story, and one clearly inspired by this line of thought from *Apocalypse Now*.

Lest we suspect that Lucas's Vietnam allegory was cynically devised after the fact to give *Star Wars* some defense, there are several direct mentions of Vietnam in Lucas's early script treatments and interviews that he gave well before *Star Wars'* release. In one early two-hundred-page rough draft of *Star Wars*, Lucas toys with the idea of a location called Aquilae, which is "a small independent country like North Vietnam threatened by a neighbour or provincial rebellion, instigated by gangsters aided by empire."[58] He continues with a mind clearly focused on the twentieth century:

> The Empire is like America ten years from now, after Nixonian gangsters assassinated the Emperor and were elevated to power in a rigged election: created civil disorder by instigating race riots. . . . We are at a turning point: fascism or revolution.[59]

By the time of *Return of the Jedi*, where Lucas apparently jovially pointed out the oval-office shape of the Emperor's throne room to the actor Ian McDiarmid,[60] the ongoing allegory, this time made in the form of the pre-industrial Ewoks, was clear enough. Even Biskind, who otherwise credits Lucas with having ushered in the era of mindless blockbusters, agrees: "What was subtext in *Star Wars* became text in the Moon of Endor sequence in *Return of the Jedi*, where the furry little Ewoks deep in the forest carry on guerrilla warfare with sticks and stones against Imperial Walkers."[61]

Star Wars, plainly, was at least partly intended by Lucas as political allegory. It was also seemingly received as such by many, even if the political legacy of the original trilogy is still contested. Why, then, are the accusations against the film of apolitical spectacle so persistent? Perhaps the allegory is poorly made, or is so buried underneath special effects and action that it is difficult to discern. Or it could reflect Lucas's own political uncertainty, as well as the basic incompatibility between many of the ideological messages he tried to build *Star Wars* on. In interviews, Lucas speaks of his opposition to Vietnam and his critique of Nixon and imperialism, and fear of the atomic bomb and environmentalist issues; in a 1981 interview he goes on to describe all his films as his version of the "Horatio Alger" myth: "The fact that if you apply yourself and work real hard, you can get what you want accomplished."[62] This Alger myth is usually associated with conservative American ideology—Ella Shohat and Robert Stam go as far as to suggest that its prevalence has "served to weaken any popular, working class movements in the United States."[63] It is difficult to reconcile Lucas's use of the Alger myth with a progressive worldview. Nonetheless, Lucas also appears to have been horrified by the conservative uses of *Star Wars*. In 1985 he even went as far as to seek, unsuccessfully, several restraining orders to stop political groups from calling Reagan's Strategic Defense Initiative "Star Wars."[64] Lucas has also clearly been stung by the various claims of racism and sexism in his films over the years. That said, it wasn't until 2012 and *Red Tails*, his passion project about the African American Tuskegee airmen during World War II, that he meaningfully followed through on his protests (he also said that it took twenty years to make *Red Tails* "because it's an all-black movie" and that studios wouldn't touch it).[65]

Perhaps an explanation for the chasm between *Star Wars*' political origins and its apolitical critical legacy actually lies in this very confusion. Just as *Star Wars* succeeded as a reworking of a vast array of filmic influences, perhaps Lucas also drew on a similarly wide range of political ideas. This would explain both why *Star Wars* frustrates close analysis and how it can effectively serve as a symbol for all ends of the political spectrum. There is certainly no doubt on this point: there is *something* political about *Star Wars*. The details, however, are less clear.

POLITICAL PREQUELS

Sixteen years away from *Star Wars*, and Lucas had had plenty of time to consider the franchise's politics and its reception. In this time, too, global politics changed significantly: the Berlin Wall fell, the Cold War ended, and the USA shifted from being *a* superpower in global affairs to being *the* superpower. The Reaganite rhetoric of evil empires and good versus bad of the original trilogy made less practical sense in the 1990s than it ever had. The first prequel, *The Phantom Menace* (1999), was made under a Democrat president, Bill Clinton, and a period of relative prosperity for the United States. The next two, however, *Attack of the Clones* (2002) and *Revenge of the Sith* (2005), were made during the Republican leadership of George W. Bush, and the American invasion of not one but two foreign countries, Afghanistan and Iraq, and the long-lasting wars that accompanied them. The result of all this was that Lucas's three *Star Wars* prequel films are marked by a wholly different geopolitical universe that disturbs the series' otherwise uncomplicated moral center and plays—however successfully—with political complexity. Could this be Lucas's artistic response to political critique?

Even in *The Phantom Menace,* the lightest and most child-friendly of the three prequels, the political universe is much less straightforward than in the earlier *Star Wars* films. We are immediately introduced into a world of trade and taxation disputes, unsanctioned blockades that turn into invasions with unclear motivations, and hidden agendas. Though *The Phantom Menace* has its heroes and villains, we are not given a clear protagonist to hold the majority of the film together (Anakin only turns up halfway through), and as Anne Lancashire argues, "the large ensemble cast of characters features different kinds of doubles who metaphorically indicate opposing sides of human nature and/or the potential of any one individual to move in either direction."[66] The stakes of good and evil in this *Star Wars* are far more contested and unstable than ever before in the franchise, in other words.

This mode of storytelling only continues to intensify throughout the other two prequels. Despite the ever-present "light" and "dark" sides to the force, the prequels nonetheless offer a political arena where motivations are unclear, where good people act badly, and villains sometimes appear to be advancing the cause of good. "There are heroes on both sides," reads the opening crawl for *Revenge of the Sith*. The original trilogy was set against a galactic conflict with clearly drawn factions: for Stephen McVeigh, "war was a given," and an expected part of the story.[67] For the prequel trilogy, the narrative thrust was much less conclusive and attempted to untangle the forces and events that lead to war and the collapse of peace. "The issue was: how does a democracy turn itself over to a dictator?" said Lucas. "Not how does a dictator take over but how does a democracy and Senate give it away?"[68] This necessitated a dramatic change not just in storytelling but in the political and moral setting of the *Star Wars* universe. As Lancashire points out, by the end of even *The Phantom Menace*, "all main characters have been revealed to be significantly flawed": Anakin fears losing his mother; Queen Amidala has been politically outmaneuvered by Palpatine; Qui-Gon Jinn, who was defeated in battle at the film's climax, has been shown to be obstinate, and his apprentice, Obi-Wan, too loyal in following his dangerous dying command.[69]

Indeed, and though perhaps Lucas's abilities as an effective storyteller got in the way of his ambitions, as the prequels unfold, the Jedi Order's orthodoxy is shown to have led to their own destruction. This was a bold move for a filmmaker who had, in the original trilogy, virtually created a real-world religion of the Jedi, so stirring was their aura. In Lucas's prequels, he instead plays an audacious double game with the Jedi—depicting them as spectacular martial artists, on the one hand, and failing philosopher-kings with an overemphasis on discipline and hierarchy, on the other. "Throughout the prequels, various Jedi, including Yoda, fail to recognize their hubris and overestimate their abilities to control the situation," writes Douglas M. Kellner.[70] Their list of mistakes is long and shocking: the Jedi fail to notice or avert the rise of Palpatine, a Sith lord, in the guise of someone they do business with daily; they alienate their strongest young ally in Anakin Skywalker and allow him to be mentored by the Sith lord; and perhaps most egregiously, the Jedi accidentally cause the creation of a secret, monumental army and, on discovering this, decide to use the army despite not knowing anything about its origins. That same army eventually massacres them. In other words, Lucas deliberately chose to show the Jedi at their peak as arrogant, dogmatic, and fatally short-sighted to a seriously impressive degree.

Lucas chose to add nuance to his *Star Wars* universe and to

answer his self-imposed questions of how a democracy becomes au-
tocracy by analogizing the United States of the early 2000s and President George W. Bush. "All democracies turn into dictatorships—
but not by coup," Lucas told *Time* magazine in 2002. "The people
give their democracy to a dictator, whether it's Julius Caesar or
Napoleon or Adolf Hitler."[71] This idea is hardly engaged with in an
oblique manner, too, and if anything the prequels can be faulted for
being too direct in their political analogies. Anakin advocates dicta-
torship in conversation with Padmé in *Attack of the Clones,* and then
in *Revenge of the Sith* directly paraphrases Bush, who in his post-9/11
warning to the world claimed that "either you are with us, or you
are with the terrorists." Anakin Skywalker, at this point well on his
way to becoming Darth Vader, puts it even more simply: "If you're
not with me, then you're my enemy," he says. Obi-Wan Kenobi's
reply seems almost to rebuke Anakin, Bush, and the political landscape of the original trilogy in one sweep: "Only a Sith deals in
absolutes."

This is a long way from the straight lines of good and bad in
the original trilogy. As the *New York Times* critic A. O. Scott rightly
noted in his review for *Revenge of the Sith* in 2005, "You may applaud
this editorializing, or you may find it overwrought, but give Mr. Lucas his due. For decades he has been blamed (unjustly) for helping to
lead American movies away from their early-70's engagement with
political matters, and he deserves credit for trying to bring them
back."[72] By the time of the prequel trilogy, Lucas has had time to
reflect on his critics and reappraise the politics of the galaxy far,
far away. "Hence, one of the major blockbuster series of all time
provides prescient warnings against the assault on democracy in the
US during the Bush-Cheney era and the dangers of militarism,"
concludes Kellner.[73] If there was something political about Lucas's
original trilogy, then there is something rather more partisan about
the prequels.

THE FALL OF THE EMPIRE

Though critics at the time quite liked each of Lucas's new *Star Wars*
films (an "astonishing achievement in imaginative filmmaking,"
read Roger Ebert's rave review of *The Phantom Menace*),[74] popular

opinion quickly turned sour after each installment. Despite box office success and critical praise, the *Star Wars* prequels fairly quickly
found a place among the most publicly reviled films in popular
memory. From Jar Jar Binks to clunky dialogue and the overuse of
chroma key effects in lieu of sets, almost every aspect of the prequel
trilogy has been widely criticized in the years following their release.
Yet for all their obvious failings, we can also see in the prequel trilogy three films that introduce political nuance to the *Star Wars* universe. Lucas may frequently complain about his critics, but, if his
surely ironic wearing of a "Han Shot First" T-shirt on the set of
Indiana Jones and the Kingdom of the Crystal Skull indicates anything,
he is obviously also deeply aware of them. Jar Jar Binks also all but
disappeared from *Star Wars* after *The Phantom Menace*. In 2015 an
uncomfortable Lucas spoke of the criticism he faced while making
the prequels as acting like a creative straightjacket: "You go to make
a movie and all you do is get criticised, and people try to make
decisions about what you're going to do before you do it."[75] He
was done directing *Star Wars*. God, to return to Gareth Edwards's
analogy, had retired.

I suspect that the *Star Wars* prequels are films that were made
at least partly in response to the critiques of the original trilogy. It's
important to notice this, because I want to argue that *Star Wars*
films both respond to the era they were made in—their politics,
their films, their technology—but *also to other* Star Wars *films* and the
discourse that surrounds them. The outright rejection of the prequel trilogy by popular culture is already significant if only for its
influence on the Disney-era films, as it became a legacy—a burden,
even—that was impossible to ignore. Yet could it be that part of that
rejection was fueled by the viewing public encountering a galaxy
whose unfamiliar moral relativism was actually a creative response
to the critique of the original films? Gone is the simple, black-and-
white politics of *Star Wars,* and in its place we find a complex (and
often convoluted) story of a republic being destabilized from within.
It feels likely that, for better or worse, to some degree each *Star Wars*
film is in dialogue with the last—and with contemporary politics.

All of this formed a crucial context for *Star Wars,* after Lucas.
The rejection of the prequels, the criticism of the politics of the

original trilogy, the impact that *Star Wars* had on the mechanisms of the Hollywood moviemaking industry—the new Disney films had to follow all of this, and have been made in an era where *Star Wars* had otherwise won. *Star Wars* had become the model—almost, in some respects, the only model—for big-picture filmmaking, in an industry whose contemporary corporate paradigm could almost be described as having pre–*Star Wars* and post–*Star Wars* epochs. More than that, *Star Wars* was now to be handled by Disney, one of the biggest omnipresent entertainment corporations of our times. Lucas's independent individualism—which had funded all the *Star Wars* sequels and Skywalker Ranch, as well as enabled his obdurate and sometimes unfathomable artistic decisions—no longer even slightly mitigated the cultural dominance of the franchise. Thomas Schatz describes the history of Hollywood as being driven by the dual impulses of consolidation and independence, and with *Star Wars*, "Conglomerate Filmmaking" became once again ascendant and has largely stayed that way since.[76] With the sale of Lucasfilm to Disney, one of the largest remaining independent entertainment corporations in America had finally found its parent company. If there was ever any doubt, it was now wholly expunged: *Star Wars* was corporate culture. But how would the franchise's concerns with politics and nostalgia play out in this new era?

2

IT CALLS TO YOU

Selling Star Wars *in 2015*

'm freaking out," laughs the woman on the screen in front of me. She takes a deep breath. "Okay," she says quietly, and her eyes widen in anticipation. In a small inset in the bottom right corner of the screen, the first full trailer for *The Force Awakens* starts to roll. As John Williams's "force theme" begins to play, she lifts her hands, clasped, to her face, and I notice that I'm automatically doing the same.

This is YouTube user Lauren Stardust's reaction video for *The Force Awakens* trailer, and by now it has almost a quarter of a million views. As an acquaintance of Lauren's, I had a different perspective on this video than most—to me, it was a familiar face charting familiar emotions, while to most others it was just one of many such reaction videos to become popular online after the release of the trailer in April 2015. I have seen this video a dozen times by now, yet I still cannot help but become swept up in Lauren's emotions. Her overwhelming joy at the trailer is totally infectious, her response possibly even more affective than the original promotional clip itself.

Stardust begins to well up quietly from the first shot of the downed Star Destroyer on Jakku, with a clear emotional escalation coinciding with Poe Dameron's whoop of joy as he pilots his X-wing

Lauren Stardust's reaction video to *The Force Awakens* trailer.

in a daring move one minute in. By the time we get to the end of the trailer, with Han Solo's sentimental "Chewie, we're home" line, Lauren is a sobbing mess. I am, usually, too, in a kind of strange sympathetic emotional vortex.

The reaction video was, by the time of the trailer for *The Force Awakens*, a well-understood genre of internet video, and they came thick and fast for this new generation of *Star Wars*. Though Lauren Stardust's was perhaps one of the more successful of its kind, hundreds of reaction videos were created to mark the release of the first trailer (and all subsequent trailers), often with views into the many hundreds of thousands.

By the time of the final, three-minute-long trailer in October 2015, the creators of *The Force Awakens* appear to have noticed the power of these reaction videos, as both John Boyega and Daisy Ridley's final trailer viewings were filmed and uploaded online. In reaction to the hero shot of Finn brandishing a lit lightsaber, Boyega falls backward off his couch, while Ridley pushes tears away with her hand ("It's amazing," she says) on its conclusion. Such *Star Wars* reaction videos were familiar enough to be quickly parodied: uploaded in April 2016, a clip that imitated such videos using a scene from *Interstellar* (dir. Christopher Nolan, 2015), where Matthew McConaughey plays a space traveler breaking down while watching videos from Earth, went on to be viewed more than ten million times. Fan-made reaction videos were eventually compiled into segments for the official *Star Wars* YouTube channel.

Reaction videos are, of course, all performances of some kind. In their study of the genre, Julia Kennedy and Clarissa Smith point out that the "reaction video" genre necessarily includes "individuals or groups who are demonstrably aware that what will be shown is a representation which requires a dramatic reaction at the same time as seeming to respond entirely spontaneously."[1] It is not, in other words, necessarily an unfiltered observance of a natural reaction. Those reacting to the trailer for *The Force Awakens* are performing their response for us, the viewer, while seemingly being caught in the moment. Indeed, the reaction video as a genre of the internet era is remarkably stable across types and topics of content. Originating largely as a cultural phenomenon aligned with jump scare videos such as the "Scary Maze Game" from 2006 and "gross out" videos such as "2 Girls 1 Cup" in 2007,[2] the reaction video has expanded to include reactions to iconic pop cultural moments, tests of new technologies, sporting events, pranks, and even medical scenes such as a deaf person having a cochlear implant turned on.[3] The stability of the reaction genre is anchored not to its content, however, but to its intended affective response. The key factor in reaction videos is not necessarily what is being reacted to but the reaction itself, which can range from humor to amazement, horror, and disgust.

In the case of *Star Wars,* and *The Force Awakens* in particular, the reaction video as a genre serves as the public face—literally, in most cases—of nostalgic affect. These videos reflect and embody the way that *The Force Awakens* was created and marketed to *Star Wars* fans by Disney and Lucasfilm as both an articulation point for the franchise and a moment in time for popular culture.

What is it, exactly, that these fans are reacting to, then? They are reacting to a return to a style of filmmaking and an aesthetic, as well as a carefully pitched reassurance that a particular kind of *Star Wars* film has been made and an authorization to embrace a new film in a Hollywood franchise deeply at the center of contemporary culture. Such fans are also reacting to the end of an absence: not just of *Star Wars* more broadly, but of a particular type of *Star*

Wars that many in *The Force Awakens* audience would have grown up with.

Lauren Stardust's video encapsulates the success of this strategy in an affect-centric sense free from both cynicism and critical reflection. We feel as viewers that we are not just witnessing a pop culture event, or even witnessing an emotional moment in someone else's life, but that we are witnessing it together, as a community of sorts. The reaction video in its profusion creates communality as well as simply a sense of shared occasion. This is why no amount of co-option by official Lucasfilm channels or the parody of the form can truly dilute its core appeal: there is no central text or idea to unsettle here except a sense of shared affect and the observance of an event. For one commenter on Stardust's video, at least, the appeal of the reaction itself is clear enough: "I loved this video," writes 220volt74. "Escapism, imagination, emotions and nostalgia used to its fullest. . . . To me this video is as good as the trailer itself."

REVIVING A FRANCHISE

Despite the eventual success of the new generation of *Star Wars* films, it's important to remember just how strong the public reaction was to Lucasfilm being purchased by Disney in 2012, and the then-surprising news of plans for the future of *Star Wars*. After *Revenge of the Sith* in 2005, *Star Wars* was widely thought to be finished. The general response to the news that it was not was, in turn, negative, dismissive, cynical, and in some quarters, quietly optimistic. The *Atlantic* reported at the time that the news had sent "a tremor of panic down the spines of hard core *Star Wars* fans,"[4] while the comedy website Funnyordie.com joked that the sale surpassed Hurricane Sandy (which killed 233 people) as the biggest disaster of the week. Jibes about Leia becoming a Disney princess circulated widely on social media (including one from the English actor Simon Pegg, who went on to have a role in *The Force Awakens*), as did photoshopped images of Darth Vader with Mickey Mouse ears.[5] "It remains to be seen if they revive the characters," said Leonard Maltin. "There are a lot of unanswered questions."[6] On the day after the announcement, Disney stock actually fell by 2 percent.

This new generation of *Star Wars* films would have to confront a Hollywood landscape radically different from that faced by either the original films or the prequel trilogy in previous decades. Although in 1977 *Star Wars* played a significant role in shaping the modern Hollywood franchise, by the time of the first prequel film in 1999, the now-prevalent franchise logics of reboots and cinematic universes had not yet taken hold to anywhere near the same degree. In 1999 *The Phantom Menace* competed with original hits like *The Sixth Sense* (dir. M. Night Shyamalan), *Notting Hill* (dir. Richard Curtis), and *American Beauty* (dir. Sam Mendes), as well as sequels following established franchise logics such as *Austin Powers: The Spy Who Shagged Me* (dir. Jay Roach) and *Toy Story 2* (dir. John Lasseter). In particular, Pixar's enormous animated success in *Toy Story 2*, taken as an example of the era, follows the previously accepted template for sequels closely—even going so far as to parody *The Empire Strikes Back* at one point.

In 1999 the renewed *Star Wars* franchise was an unusual and stand-alone case. This was before *Harry Potter*, before *Twilight*, and before the Marvel Cinematic Universe. *The Matrix* would go on to spectacularly pioneer contemporary franchise-making with its sequels, spin-off animated short films, parallel-produced video games, and webcomics ("No film franchise has ever made such demands on its consumers," wrote Henry Jenkins in his famous exploration of *The Matrix*'s transmedia aspirations).[7] In 1999 such far-reaching textual extensions were still a dream, as the first *Matrix* film beat *Phantom Menace* to release by only two months.

Perhaps its closest existing model in a franchise sense was the then nineteen-film strong James Bond series, which for decades had pioneered entire logics of franchising, rebooting, and serial storytelling for English-language cinema. As Tony Bennett and Janet Woollacott point out, the Bond series always followed its own framework for remaking and recasting: "Bond is always identified with himself but is never quite the same—an ever-mobile signifier."[8] Bond had been resurrected several times already: from the revolving door of actors between 1967 and 1973 (Sean Connery to George Lazenby, to Sean Connery again, before ending with Roger Moore) to the then-recent six-year break between *Licence to Kill* (1989) and *GoldenEye* (1995) that saw the Bond series forced to reinvent itself after the end of the Cold War. Yet the Bond series' resilience was always something of an outlier, and in 1999 its rival for *The Phantom Menace* was *The World Is Not Enough* (dir. Michael Apted), a competent and unremarkable Bond that reflected the series' ability to evolve while remaining rigid. Though significant, the idiosyncrasy—and obvious nonreplicability—of the Bond series meant that before the *Star Wars* prequel trilogy, there was not much in the way of a contemporary Hollywood model for the wholesale revival of a dormant franchise or of the plotting of a serialized narrative over many decades and many films.

The *Phantom Menace* and the *Star Wars* prequels were therefore not only tasked with forming their own frameworks (indeed the word *prequel* only entered popular culture through these three films), but they were more easily able to stand alone as franchise films of note in the process. A new *Star Wars* film, in this era, was an event—regardless of what audience members thought of it. The revival of the *Star Wars* brand was enough.

By 2015 and *The Force Awakens*, however, this had changed. The superhero film craze, as the dominant force in contemporary Hollywood, had blended the logic of the "new sincerity" film with the franchise reboot, beginning with Christopher Nolan's *Batman Begins* in 2005. Jim Collins introduced the term *new sincerity* (a term also used in literature and music) in film studies to discuss a kind of cinema that, in the "rewriting of the classic genre film that serves as their inspiration, [attempt] to recover a lost 'purity,'" such as *Field of Dreams* (dir. Phil Alden Robinson, 1989) and *Dances with Wolves* (dir. Kevin Costner, 1990).[9] Heather Urbanski also points out that reboots are often seen as attempts to appeal to a cynical contemporary viewer whose tastes are not matched to the excess of well-developed franchises, yet in practice also have to balance contemporization against veteran fan expectations.[10] *Batman Begins* proposed a defamiliarized superhero universe unconcerned with the spectacle and excess that had dominated the genre in the 1990s, and instead embraced an aesthetic of credibility and authenticity. "Everything about *Batman Begins* was carefully worked out . . . to be believable," notes the comic book writer and Batman expert Grant Morrison.[11] This was taken as a deliberate marker of difference—both as an aesthetic and as a statement of intentions—from the previous Batman films. The slate was wiped clean. In the process, the reboot model of franchising became a linchpin of the Hollywood blockbuster.

The success of *Batman Begins* and its sequels (2008, 2012) created a dominant model for the reentry of once-dormant Hollywood franchises into everyday culture that many other franchises keenly exploited. *Casino Royale* (dir. Martin Campbell, 2006), *Star Trek* (directed by future *The Force Awakens* director J. J. Abrams, 2009), *Sherlock Holmes* (dir. Guy Ritchie, 2009), *Rise of the Planet of the Apes* (dir. Rupert Wyatt, 2011), *Teenage Mutant Ninja Turtles* (dir. Jonathan Liebesman, 2014), and *Godzilla* (directed by future *Rogue One* director Gareth Evans, 2014) all had success in one way or another from this model. Also faithful to this approach, though less successful, were films like *The Omen* (dir. John Moore, 2006), *The Wolfman* (dir. Joe Johnston, 2010), *Conan the Barbarian* (dir. Marcus Nispel, 2011), and *RoboCop* (dir. José Padilha, 2014). As Urbanski notes, the reboot has many progenitors that predate this era, from *The Wiz* (dir. Sidney Lumet, 1978) to *The Fugitive* (dir. Andrew Davis, 1993) to the various iterations of *Fame* (dir. Alan Parker, 1980). However, the last two decades have seen a particular flourishing of this strategy: this has coincided with a thirst for, and the technological enabling of, complex narrative and franchise memory. The reboot continues to proliferate today as one of the major modes of Hollywood franchise filmmaking, but Urbanski makes the crucial distinction that this is less a singular model than a continuum of "increasing separation from their inspiration franchises."[12] Some reboots are more faithful than others, in other words.

The crucial strategy for this post–*Batman Begins* reboot model was the balance between nostalgia and contemporary relevance: the most successful of these films offered audiences a return to what they remembered enjoying most in the past, articulated for the present. *Casino Royale* offers the James Bond audience a homecoming to the first novel in Ian Fleming's series, rearticulated to respond to, and keep up with, the unembellished action of the Jason Bourne era. *Rise of the Planet of the Apes*, on the other hand, retained and amplified the dystopian tragedy at the heart of the 1968 film while furnishing it with contemporary computer-generated effects and performances.

Equally important for the franchise reboot is its iconography. As Robert Arnett argues, this kind of film selects various visual and narrative elements from the aggregate of the previously existing franchise "that negotiate multiple intertextual connections while challenging the aura of the original brand." Accordingly, the reboot serves as a "franchise re-activator by rescuing [the series] from self-parody and necessitating additional installments of the franchise."[13] The reboot therefore contains a double logic—as well as usually illustrating the origins of the franchise heroes, the reboot also aims to rearticulate the nub of the cultural appeal of the franchise.

This logic came to encompass seemingly every tent-pole Hollywood blockbuster. By the time of *The Force Awakens*, the reboot model was so entrenched that even before the seventh *Star Wars* film's opening weekend in December 2015, the year had already seen big hits in the form of *Jurassic World* (dir. Colin Trevorrow), *Mad Max: Fury Road* (dir. George Miller), *Terminator Genisys* (dir. Alan Taylor), and *Creed* (dir. Ryan Coogler). Though not all are strict reboots (in that franchise continuity is maintained), all clearly aim to recapture something of the spark of the original film in their franchise after a lengthy absence. Just over the horizon, and with already humming marketing machines, also lay *Ghostbusters* (dir. Paul Feig, 2016), *The Jungle Book* (dir. Jon Favreau, 2016), and *Independence Day: Resurgence* (dir. Roland Emmerich, 2016). That *Star Wars* should reenter a popular sphere so dominated by the logic of the reboot is ironic, given George Lucas's own frustrated attempts to remake *Flash Gordon* before *Star Wars*, and the self-parodic version of *Flash Gordon* that followed in 1980 on *Star Wars*' coattails. Yet the contemporary ubiquity of the reboot and the restored franchise is crucial for understanding the context within which *The Force Awakens* was made and sold.

I'll look at the relation of *The Force Awakens* to the reboot/remake/remix model in the next chapter, but for now, the sheer prevalence of this kind of film as the context for new *Star Wars* endeavors is crucial to note. Combined with the general cynicism surrounding the purchase by Disney, it is possible that a new *Star Wars* film could have arrived with significantly less cultural cachet than Lucasfilm's new owners would have liked. Consider that in 2015, only *Inside Out* (dir. Pete Docter) and *The Martian* (dir. Ridley Scott) made it into the ten highest-grossing films in America without being part of an established franchise. In 1999, on the other hand, *The Phantom Menace*'s mode of franchising was hardly going to be mistaken for that of *Austin Powers*. Yet *The Force Awakens* was in 2015 one of many resurrected 1970s, 1980s, and 1990s Hollywood franchises, along with new *Rocky, Terminator,* and *Jurassic Park* films, the last of which had set an intimidating all-time-record $500 million opening weekend, and had gone on to become the third-highest grossing film of all time. Though it was impossible to imagine *The Force Awakens* as a complete failure, there were no guarantees that a new *Star Wars* film would look sufficiently different to film audiences now significantly more exposed to event franchise films than they had been in either 1977 or 1999.

It is not only possible to imagine a less successful *Star Wars* film than *The Force Awakens* eventually proved to be—there was precedent. On the heels of the maligned *Phantom Menace,* in 2002 *Attack of the Clones* was the first *Star Wars* film to not be the highest grossing of its year. That year, as it happens, was another year for well-considered franchise films: Episode II was fourth behind *The Lord of the Rings: The Two Towers* (dir. Peter Jackson), *Harry Potter and the Chamber of Secrets* (dir. Chris Columbus), and *Spider-Man* (dir. Sam Raimi). To multiply things further, 2015 was a spectacular year for Hollywood's bottom line: just behind the record-breaking *Jurassic World* was *Furious 7* and *Avengers: Age of Ultron* (which before *The Force Awakens* were the fifth- and sixth-highest grossing films of all time, respectively). It would have been easy, in such a supercharged year, for *The Force Awakens* to make only a relatively minor impact on global cinema behind such titans.

So how did we go from cynicism and franchise fatigue at the news of Lucasfilm's sale to tears of joy at new trailers for *The Force Awakens?* The answer lies in a clever marketing campaign of carefully pitched nostalgia from Disney and Lucasfilm that completely reshaped the public discourse surrounding the film and readied the world for its positive reception. This was the specter of a nostalgic homecoming, one that, as Svetlana Boym poetically puts it, "gives us the same sensation of returning to where we have never been."[14]

The campaign for *The Force Awakens* prepared the ground for a new era of *Star Wars* films—and the revival of a once-dormant franchise. It was Disney's first move.

THE PREQUEL PROBLEM

The Force Awakens had a bigger problem than competing franchises, anyway. How do you make a new *Star Wars* film in the shadows of the loathed prequels? By this point, each *Star Wars* prequel had its own infamous RedLetterMedia review on YouTube, which lasts in excess of seventy minutes each and is presented in character by "Harry S. Plinkett," a caricature of a lonely internet pop-culture obsessive. The RedLetterMedia review of *The Phantom Menace* begins with Plinkett describing the film as "the most disappointing thing since my son . . . and while my son eventually hanged himself in the bathroom of a gas station, the unfortunate reality of the *Star Wars* prequels is that they'll be around forever." The first video in the series has today more than seven million views.

The vehement rejection of the prequels across large sections of the moviegoing public meant that selling *Star Wars* in 2015 meant weaponizing nostalgia. This may be unsurprising—the preexisting *Star Wars* fan base was still huge, and by 2015 was approaching an age ripe for a rose-tinted return to the media of their youth. The same goes for other franchises involved in reboots and reworkings at the same time: the *Terminator* and *Ghostbusters* franchises in particular both date back to 1984, just one year after *Return of the Jedi*. That nostalgia would be involved in some capacity was not surprising. Even the early announcements about the movie—that Lawrence Kasdan, *Empire* and *Jedi* writer, was working on the script, John Williams was involved, and that Mark Hamill, Carrie Fisher, and Harrison Ford would return—indicated a preference for not moving too far from the original formula.

What was more surprising was the way that nostalgia became a totalizing, mythologizing marketing force for *The Force Awakens*. Even the name, when it was announced, suggested as much. Today, years after the film's release, it's still not entirely clear what specifically is awakened in *The Force Awakens*, aside from a few cryptic comments from Snoke and one possible interpretation of Rey's character arc. At least in part, then, we can understand the title as being a coy reference to the reentry of a pop culture behemoth into the entertainment industry. It is *Star Wars* that has awoken as much as anything else.

More tellingly, visual references to previous *Star Wars* films were clear and unequivocal from the first frame the public saw of *The Force Awakens*. Such an aesthetic deliberately called on the lexicon of *Star Wars* moments that had become staples of popular culture both obliquely and obviously. When Han Solo and Chewbacca made their reentry to the Millennium Falcon and public discourse at the end of the 2015 teaser trailer, it didn't take anyone very long to notice that the shot was seemingly intentionally framed to recall a well-used promotional image of the two of them from 1977.

Similar visual cues featured throughout the trailers. In the teaser trailers, theatrical trailers, and television spots used prior to *The Force Awakens'* release, we see sunsets over desert planets specked with moisture equipment, ships in hyperdrive tunnels, pilots in jumpsuits prepping for action, and characters overlooking remote outpost cities. In one shot, clearly intended to evoke the short-lived rebel surrender outside the shield generator at the battle of Endor from *Return of the Jedi*, Han and Chewbacca turn, hands on heads, to look in surprise at something off-screen. In both *The Force Awakens* and *Return of the Jedi*, the shot is framed from below, with Han to the right of screen and Chewbacca to the left. In both cases, they are surrounded by Stormtroopers. We see Leia, once the princess and now the general, resting her head on Han Solo's chest, while Han holds her reassuringly—just like he did in *Return of the Jedi* ("Hold me," Leia says in *Return of the Jedi*, and though wordless in the trailer, such a line could just as easily work for this moment in *The Force Awakens*). In another scene, we see Rey firing angrily toward something off-screen. We now know that this is Rey defending herself from the First Order invasion force on Takodana, but it is framed almost identically as Luke is in *A New Hope* as he fires in anger toward Stormtroopers after Ben Kenobi's death. Both are dressed in white rags and placed in the center of the eyeline-level frame, with their weapon-brandishing right arm extending into the foreground to the image's left side. We see Kylo Ren in silhouette as

Han, Chewbacca, and Leia are captured in *Return of the Jedi*.

Han, Chewbacca, and Finn are captured in *The Force Awakens*. These images are deliberately designed to evoke a visual, perhaps semiconscious memory of the original trilogy films and place *The Force Awakens* as their rightful heir.

he gazes on the galaxy from the bridge of an enormous starship with triangle viewports, just as we saw numerous shots of Darth Vader in the same pose, and with the same viewports, in *The Empire Strikes Back*. We also see Finn, a young and inexperienced man, wielding a blue lightsaber against the red-sabered Kylo Ren, his much more capable foe. They begin to fight in a dark and dramatic landscape of a snowy field, surrounded by tall thin trees. In *Empire*, of course, we have a comparable scene, as Luke and Vader square up in a similarly shot, dark and dramatic environment—no snow this time, but smoke—framed in a similar way by tall, thin metal pylons.

Critics of *The Force Awakens* later attacked these kinds of images and the overall plot structure of the film as merely derivative of the original trilogy, and of adding nothing while simply replaying the original trilogy's greatest moments (and such criticisms are discussed in the following chapter). It would therefore be possible to argue that since much of the film itself holds these visual similarities, then there is nothing particularly special about the marketing campaign—that it is simply advertising *The Force Awakens* using imagery from *The Force Awakens*. Yet this argument would be unconvincing: despite the criticism, there are a great many visual elements in *The Force Awakens* that mark departures from, rather than a return to, the original trilogy. A potential *Force Awakens* trailer, for example, might have instead focused on the in-atmosphere dogfights, the escape from the Star Destroyer, the crashed TIE fighter, the Jakku starship graveyards, Han Solo's freighter, or the night-time Jakku village fight—none of which have such straightforward visual parallels in the original films. Or indeed such a teaser might have focused more on the new protagonists, who in both casting and narrative role (not to mention gender and ethnicity) have no straightforward analogue to Han, Leia, and Luke. Indeed, the very first *Force Awakens* teaser trailer from late 2014 does exactly this, with its brief focus on Finn, Rey, Poe Dameron, and Kylo Ren in turn, with a far less nostalgic effect as a result.

That 2015 saw a deliberate strategy of targeting nostalgia is reinforced by the music of both trailers. It's no coincidence, for example, that the major musical theme of the full-length trailer released in October 2015 is "Han Solo and the Princess" from *The Empire Strikes Back*. This is, of course, the only major musical theme from the whole original trilogy that did not make a return in any form in the prequels. Audiences had not heard that particular piece of music in *Star Wars* since Han, Leia, and Luke disappeared from the big screen in 1983. Even relatively minor themes, such as Jabba the Hutt's theme, had reappeared more recently in the prequels: "Han Solo and the Princess" was a direct musical line straight to the original trilogy.

This is a more precise form of nostalgia, then—one that invokes some *Star Wars* films but not others. In the marketing for *The Force*

Awakens, it was almost as if the prequels did not exist, such was their exclusion from the nostalgia invoked. Yet the prequels served as another kind of presence, too, as part of the nostalgic power of the prospect of these new *Star Wars* films was that in the general public's mind, they might go some way to righting the wrongs committed by Lucas's second trilogy. This was a difficult balance to strike: such a marketing campaign needed to invoke the quality of the original films and provincialize the prequels, all the while not mentioning them directly.

Such a campaign came down to selling *The Force Awakens* as the *Star Wars* that audiences used to like. This was reflected in the few lines of dialogue selected for these trailers. When Han Solo tells Rey and Finn, "It's true—all of it. The Dark Side, the Jedi—they're real," he's less making an in-world revelation to the characters standing in front of him than talking to nostalgic audience members who long for the era of their childhood where the events of the original trilogy seemed so mythical. Han Solo cannot speak directly to members of the audience themselves, so he speaks to them in the mode of his own wistful recollection. He is authorizing a reembrace of a kind of *Star Wars* film that the audience had perhaps thought gone forever.

This was even reflected in behind-the-scenes material used to market *The Force Awakens* prior to release. The emphasis on "real" sets and props in particular clearly rejected the approach of the prequels, which had been widely criticized for an overreliance on computer-generated imagery. A behind-the-scenes reel released at Comic-Con in 2015 best embodies this approach: we are shown concept art of a crashed TIE fighter, translated into a miniature model of the crashed TIE fighter, translated into a full-scale set of the crashed TIE fighter. Clapper boards appear in front of meticulously dressed sets and elaborate costumes and alien animatronics. "Real sets," we hear Mark Hamill say in voice-over, "practical effects . . . nothing's changed. I mean, everything's changed, but nothing's changed. That's the way you want it to be." We hear the crew talking about the challenges and the excitement of going on location and building life-size spaceships. "We're getting back to the old ways of doing things," says Peter Mayhew in his Chewbacca costume. The prequel trilogy is not mentioned by name, but it does not have to be, so clear is the inference.

It's also important to note the subtle incorporation of Ralph McQuarrie concept art, created for the original films but never used. McQuarrie played a significant role in developing the look of the *Star Wars* universe, and a number of unused designs familiar to *Star Wars* enthusiasts through coffee table *Star Wars* artwork books and older making-of material resurfaced in realized form in *The Force Awakens*. A large arch originally intended to be part of Jabba's Palace from *Return of the Jedi* became part of the Jakku set. R2-D2's original design involved him rolling on a large ball-bearing—an idea that influenced the look of BB-8. The humble X-wing fighter also received an update in *The Force Awakens,* with its engines now neatly split at the wing instead of extending over it in a circle—something originally in McQuarrie's concept art that was not possible in 1977 due to technical limits. It's also worth wondering whether a significant moment of the plot—a former Stormtrooper wielding a lightsaber—was inspired by a piece of McQuarrie concept art featuring a Stormtrooper with a drawn saber. These small connections were used to signal subtly to fans that the DNA of the original films had been retained and repurposed by experts and enthusiasts alike. Such repurposing is also a strategy of nostalgia.

I use the term *weaponized* nostalgia here, not just because nostalgia is wielded as a tool to appeal to audiences' emotional drives, but because it is aimed like a weapon, too. "Remember these sets of memories," this form of nostalgia says, "and not these other ones." Of course, all nostalgia involves the selective editing and correcting of the past. But as Fredric Jameson points out, nostalgia also involves a yearning for an alternative present, too.[15] For Carly Kocurek, "This idealized form of the past often points not to the superiority of the past but to the shortcomings and disappointments of the present. That is, nostalgia often expresses a displaced desire for a better present."[16] This reinforces the strength of *The Force Awakens'* targeted nostalgia: not only does it use the idealized love of the original *Star Wars* films to build its prerelease hype; it does so by subtly pointing to the shortcomings of the prequel trilogy, which we can understand in this instance as aligned with the "disappointments of the present."

Nothing sums up this carefully calibrated nostalgia as clearly as perhaps the most significant shot from all of *The Force Awakens* marketing material: the very first from April 2015's teaser trailer, the ultra-long shot of Rey making her way across the Jakku landscape in her speeder. To understand the significance of this shot, we have to turn to what is uncontroversially the most iconic shot in the original *Star Wars* trilogy—the first. After the giant logo and the opening crawl, in 1977 *Star Wars* reaffirmed that this was a film about escapism and scale by giving audiences a tiny rebel ship, followed by an enormous Imperial Star Destroyer overhead. For all that critics have disparaged Lucas's perfunctory visual style, this is a remarkably economic visual strategy. It tells the audience everything about the conflict at the heart of *Star Wars* in a single shot: we have an impossibly tiny yet determined force up against an enormous, impersonal killing machine. The way that the two ships echo the movement of the opening crawl—by falling forward into endless space, daring the audience into pursuit—was a literal entry point into the *Star Wars* universe. This was reinforced by the triangular, perspectival lines of the massive Star Destroyer aiming toward a vanishing point far in deep space. As Angela Ndalianis argues, the Star Destroyer seemed to "invade the screen from the space of the auditorium. The frame dissolves, as the spaceship appears to move from the real space of the auditorium into the representational space within the screen."[17] *Star Wars'* first image was also its biggest. In a way, this breakdown between diegetic and audience space also signaled the multitude of coming franchise futures, too. This was pure escapism into a galaxy far, far away, but this was also an impossibly large universe that could be opened up and explored in many conceivable directions through sequels, merchandising, and spin-offs. This opening image told audiences about the possibilities of *Star Wars* as much as its spectacle.

The first shot from the April 2015 *Force Awakens* teaser trailer performs a similar move—while turning it on its head, literally. While Rey's speeder moves at speed in the distance, we see the wreckage of a long-ago battle, featuring similar, if long-gone, protagonists. In the midground of the shot, we see a tiny Rebel ship—a crashed X-wing—followed into the frame by another enormous

Rey's moving speeder frames the downed Rebel ship
and Imperial Star Destroyer in a sideways movement.

The first shot of *A New Hope* has an Imperial Star Destroyer
chase a Rebel ship into the frame.

Star Destroyer that takes up the majority of the previously empty
image. Unlike *A New Hope,* however, both ships are destroyed
wrecks on a planetary surface, and the camera is moving sideways
instead of gazing into space. Unlike *A New Hope*'s opening, the action of the scene is animated by the camera itself as it tracks Rey
moving in the distance, yet the spectacular effect of briefly captur-
ing the monumental is still present. We're playing the same game in
this moment as audiences did in 1977, but with a new set of rules—
maybe even someone else's rulebook. Rey's indifferent movement
between both Rebel and Imperial wrecks also reframes the setting.

We have returned to the same galaxy, and it is in some ways like we remember—but, as the wreckage illustrates, time has passed, and behemoths that once set the galaxy alight are now just detritus, waiting to be scrapped, like J.M.W. Turner's famous painting *The Fighting Temeraire* (1838). This is a universe of consequences.

This image is precisely aimed. Consciously or not, it gives us a narrative for understanding the relationship between this new *Star Wars* film and the nostalgia for the original trilogy in just a single shot. Like the opening shot of *A New Hope*, it provides audiences with an entry point into the *Star Wars* universe, one that offers both the familiar as well as a literalized promise that things will now move in a different direction.

Yet what this marketing campaign also did was articulate a relationship between this new era of *Star Wars* and a broader sense of cinematic history. Just as *The Force Awakens* found itself in a highly concentrated environment of reboots and franchise nostalgia, these trailers also acknowledged the passing of cinematic time. Through locating *Star Wars* within the history of cinema, the marketing campaign crucially allowed audiences to acknowledge that times have changed—but that we can go back to this world, too.

Much has been made of Lucas's voracious borrowing of elements that made up the original *Star Wars* film, including the B-movie serials of his youth (*Flash Gordon, Buck Rogers*), war films (*The Dam Busters, 633 Squadron*), samurai films (*The Hidden Fortress, Seven Samurai*), and westerns (*The Searchers; The Good, the Bad, and the Ugly*). Lucas was not alone in this referential style: it was a hallmark of sorts for the American film school generation that he belonged to. Noël Carroll described the approach of Hollywood directors of the time—including Francis Ford Coppola, Peter Bogdanovich, Brian De Palma, and Martin Scorsese—as being defined by allusion as "a major expressive device" that incorporated "practices including quotations, the memorialization of past genres, the reworking of past genres, homages, and the recreation of 'classic' scenes, shots, plot motifs, lines of dialogue, themes, gestures, and so forth from film history."[18] When Scorsese shows a wordless Travis Bickle mesmerized by a dissolving Alka-Seltzer in *Taxi Driver*, he gives us psychological insight into the character as well as providing an intertextual allusion to Godard's *Two or Three Things I Know about Her* (1967), where a character discusses social isolation over a close-up of a stirred mug of coffee. Bickle is not intellectual enough to make this commentary himself, so Scorsese makes it for him for a film-literate audience through the allusion to Godard.

With Lucas, allusion was less about making a point than about just illustrating an aesthetic love of style. He took inspiration from where he could find it. To give one well-trodden example,[19] in the final scene of the original *Star Wars*, we're shown a medal ceremony that bears a striking resemblance to Leni Riefenstahl's infamous Nazi propaganda film, *The Triumph of the Will*. Is Lucas trying to tell us that the Rebel Alliance is secretly fascistic? Certainly not: it's just a striking visual image that he has appropriated for effect. Lucas has taken the aesthetic and is counting on the intellectual association not coming with it.

For *The Force Awakens*, Abrams seemed less interested in such allusions to a broader film history. "The world is a different place now than it was when [the first *Star Wars*] movie came out, we can't come out with the same thing and expect people to react as if they hadn't seen it before," Abrams told *Vanity Fair*. "I'm not sure we could count the movies that have, since 1977, tried to embrace a similar mythic quality and in some cases a similar aesthetic or even humorous approach to a space adventure."[20] Yet even in the marketing material there were still certainly some deliberate visual links: *The Force Awakens* was clearly revisiting the Nazi imagery for the villainous First Order, while one trailer shot of TIE fighters flying into a sunset clearly paid homage to *Apocalypse Now*—another 1970s war film once set to be directed by Lucas.

Ultimately, *The Force Awakens* does diverge from the rest of the *Star Wars* films in that its clearest cinematic touchstones are not genre classics but other *Star Wars* films. It is this strategy that gifts *The Force Awakens* with its strongest ammunition for its carefully aimed weapon of nostalgia. Crucially, it allows *The Force Awakens* to recenter the original *Star Wars* films at the mythological heart of the series—both in-universe and without.

The makers of *The Force Awakens* accordingly perform this double move. By the time of the events of *The Force Awakens*, in-universe, the stories of the original trilogy have entered folklore in the galaxy far, far away. Rey is not certain whether Luke Skywalker or Han Solo are real people or just legends ("there are stories about what happened"), while Finn, who has only encountered their story through First Order propaganda, views them warily. The force itself, once explained through the pseudo-science of midi-chlorians in *The Phantom Menace* (the "one word [that] ruined *Star Wars* for me, and probably for a generation of fans, too," wrote Evan Narcisse in *Time*[21]), was once again a mystical and unknowable power. Han Solo, once the cynic, has the role of explaining to Rey that the Jedi were real: "I used to wonder about that myself," Han says.

The links with the original trilogy are, again, not without precedent. Lucas himself made heavy reference to his original trilogy in the prequels and is sometimes mocked for it. For some critics, this looked like lazy storytelling, with a fleet of reoccurring characters, planets, and iconic moments making the galaxy far, far away seem like a very small place indeed. The furious array of retroactive narrative expansion of the *Star Wars* films now means that when Darth Vader boards the Tantive IV at the beginning of *A New Hope*, he is in fact taking his daughter hostage in orbit above the planet on which he grew up, and where the droid he built as a child will shortly encounter his son and his childhood mentor—and Vader (and the audience at the time) knows none of this.

Yet these links to the logic of the prequels are unescapable, as much as Disney and Abrams might have liked to avoid them. *The Force Awakens* was, as discussed, not the first time that the *Star Wars* franchise had been renewed after a period of dormancy. Sixteen years elapsed between *Return of the Jedi* (1983) and *The Phantom Menace* (1999), six more than the decade between *Revenge of the Sith* (2005) and *The Force Awakens*. There were lessons to be learned from this first attempt at guiding *Star Wars* back into the popular imagination: and looking back, it is surprising how effective the first trailer still is for *The Phantom Menace*. Though it obviously does not make the same appeals to the nostalgia for physical sets and "material" filmmaking that *The Force Awakens* does, it nonetheless performs a similar move to Abrams's film by mythologizing the *Star Wars* franchise as both a fictional world and a cultural artifact.

"Every generation has a legend . . ." reads the first title card for the first *The Phantom Menace* trailer. In 1999, still the early days for the internet, I vividly remember downloading the trailer as a boy in rural Australia over a dial-up 56k modem. The pace of downloading was not quick, and I had a new five-second section of the trailer to contemplate every ten minutes or so. Yet it is this first title card that still has the most impact. To which generation does it refer? Is it the generation who grew up with the original films in the 1970s and 1980s? Is it instead grandiosely announcing its mythological aspirations for the then-current generation—that *The Phantom Menace* would be the legend to my generation as *A New Hope* was to my parents'? Perhaps instead it refers to the in-world generation of the prequels—that as we have gone even longer ago in a galaxy far, far away, we will now be told the legend of the generation that preceded Luke, Han, and Leia's. Such multilayered mythmaking is not unlike *The Force Awakens'* most powerful marketing trick. Both displace the iconography of the *Star Wars* franchises into our world and blur the boundaries between universes in the process. The one major difference between *The Phantom Menace* and *The Force Awakens* here is that the latter is using this technique to silently signal to *Star Wars* fans that this mythmaking allows us to bypass the prequels and aim our nostalgia squarely at the original trilogy.

This, ultimately, is how *The Force Awakens'* targeted nostalgia gains such potency. The acknowledgment of the passing of time only gives greater power to the possibilities of looking back. By consciously framing *The Force Awakens* as a moment in history, audiences are encouraged to recognize Harrison Ford's gray hair and aging jowls, and also the long and dark shadow of the prequels. This acknowledgment actually authorizes, rather than diminishes, the audience's nostalgic return to the golden era of *Star Wars*. It allows the audience to reminisce on what it felt like to be young again, and to feel the rumble of that Star Destroyer overhead both in their bones and in their memories. Such love at last sight allows us a tremor of recognition as we feel the nostalgic emotion inherent in simply identifying the flow of time. The central lines of dialogue in all the trailers speak to this reassurance: "Chewie, we're home," "There are stories about what happened," "It's true—all of it. The

Dark Side, the Jedi—they're real," "The force, it's calling to you."
Star Wars is reinforced both as myth and as part of its audiences'
own lives. This is again the specter of the impossible homecoming,
the nostalgic return to a time that truly can be returned to. As with
the Star Destroyer of *Star Wars'* opening moments, the line between
diegesis and audience has been blurred, and the reassurance that
there are many more stories to tell in this galaxy has been offered.

According to Chris Taylor's account, when the first *Star Wars*
was released, the beat poet Allen Ginsberg saw the words "A Long
Time Ago, in a Galaxy Far, Far Away . . ." on-screen and turned to
his cinema-going companion. "Thank goodness," he said, "I don't
have to worry about it."[22] That reaction—the pure escapism of the
Star Wars films distilled into one wry quip—was not too far away
from the entire marketing strategy for *The Force Awakens,* and the
master plan for selling new *Star Wars* films after Lucas. Disney's entire proposition was one of telling its audience that it didn't have to
worry about *Star Wars* anymore. The audience didn't have to worry
about more prequels, or a Disney Princess Leia, or a Darth Vader
with Mickey Mouse ears. All the audience had to do was return to
the warm, nostalgic embrace of the original *Star Wars* undertaking.
After all, it's true. All of it.

LET IT IN

Nostalgia is a deeply emotional project. That the success of it as
a strategy can in some ways be measured in YouTuber tears is
hardly surprising. When Fredric Jameson wrote about the original
Star Wars film as nostalgic, he shrewdly identified the ways that "far
from being a pointless satire of [Saturday afternoon serials, it] satisfies a deep (might I even say repressed?) longing to experience them
again."[23] For media-literate viewers, at least, the original *Star Wars*
trilogy allowed a kind of emotional access to a media moment from
another era. For some, this cast them back to filmgoing memories of
their youth; for others, it permitted the retrieval of a cultural memory previously only experienced indirectly.

In either case, however, nostalgia blends with emotion "as way
of thinking that arises from a deeply felt encounter between our personal continuities and discontinuities."[24] What is emotional, then,

for someone filming a reaction video, or for someone such as myself who is totally and somewhat pitifully subject to the nostalgic pull of Lucasfilm's marketing strategy, is the encounter between the personal and the mediated. We remember not just the media franchise in question (in this case, either the first *Star Wars* film or even the idea of the original films), but our relationship to it, who we were at the time it entered our lives, and perhaps even who we have become, where we are, and when we are. In her discussion of the video game arcade, Kocurek notes that toys and other objects of childhood can, through a nostalgic lens, stand in not just for "youth" but also for far "more specific emotional states or even for more abstract values associated with youth, such as 'innocence' or 'ambition.'"[25] This is certainly the case here: the nostalgia of *The Force Awakens* is not so clumsy as to simply target a sense of recalled youngness. Its approach is far more targeted.

The kernel of this strategy is best summed up by the Maz Kanata line (which is ironically not actually in the completed film) that concludes the full trailer from October 2015: "The force is calling to *you*. Let it in." Let what in, though? In the context of the trailer, are audiences really meant to understand this to be solely referencing the force? Clearly, in this sense, the force is, like the film's title, at least partly being conflated with the appeal of *Star Wars* more generally. Maz Kanata addresses us, the audience, as much as any character in the *Star Wars* universe. Sixty-five thousand people at the 2011 Australian national census identified as Jedi; this is a real, if tongue-in-cheek phenomenon that gives some level of indication of the personal relationship that some people have to the *Star Wars* mythology.[26] Through this lens, this line—and I am reading this line as emblematic of the whole campaign here—is almost nostalgia-as-interpellation, in the Althusserian sense, as a hail that renders "concrete individuals as concrete subjects."[27] The marketing campaign for *The Force Awakens* uses nostalgia to target a mass audience as individuals as well as communities, asking us to recall the specifics of our previous encounters with *Star Wars* as a way to reframe the entire context of the prospect of new films. *The Force Awakens* calls to me, Dan Golding, in Melbourne, Australia, just as clearly as it calls to any particular individual, anywhere.

Nevertheless, however we view the marketing strategy, it was a dramatic success. The overall public mood regarding new *Star Wars* films went from an air of distrust to uninhibited public displays of emotion. The 2015 teaser trailer has received seventy-nine million views, while the full trailer has seen ninety-six million. *The Force Awakens* itself went on to make over two billion dollars at the global box office—which makes it one of the highest-grossing films of all time, even adjusted for inflation. The critical response to the film was nearly universally positive. Not only was the strategy successful at chaperoning the notion of new, quality *Star Wars* films, but the overwhelming success of *The Force Awakens* by most metrics set the bar for subsequent *Star Wars* films at considerably high levels. Should every new *Star Wars* film break box office records to be considered a success? Could nostalgia be so precisely wielded multiple times, and is there a ceiling for its use?

Indeed, as I show in the next chapter, quickly after its success was assured, *The Force Awakens* faced criticism for merely retreading the selling points of the original films. Had nostalgia, so vital in providing a marketing strategy for *The Force Awakens* and an emotional point of connection for a skeptical returning audience, been taken too far?

3

LOOK HOW OLD
YOU'VE BECOME

The Force Awakens *as Legacy Film*

y the end of 2015, by almost any measure *The Force Awakens* was a success. Financially, the film had lived up to the wildest box office analyst's predictions and looked set to exceed them: there was even talk at *Forbes* that *The Force Awakens* might surpass *Avatar*'s all-time global box-office record of $2.78 billion.[1] Critically, the renewal of the *Star Wars* franchise had also hit the mark: the aggregator Rotten Tomatoes found 93 percent of 376 film reviews to be positive, while Metacritic's averaged review score placed the film at 81 out of 100. "That giant wheezing sound you hear is a collective sigh of relief, heaved by now-legion generations of 'Star Wars' fans, from toddlers to their grandparents, who can rest assured that the Force is still with the franchise they grew up on or grew old with," wrote Ann Hornaday for the *Washington Post*.[2] Audiences also loved the film: according to the market research firm CinemaScore, audiences graded the film as an A. There was even some hopeful Oscar buzz of a degree unusual for a genre blockbuster, and the following February *The Force Awakens* was nominated for five awards (original score, sound editing, sound mixing, film editing, and visual effects), though it won none.

More than simply a good film, *The Force Awakens* had revived the *Star Wars* franchise and recentered it in popular culture. The largely unloved prequels from the previous decade were a thing of the past, as was the nerdy image of the *Star Wars* fanatic. John Boyega, Daisy Ridley, and Harrison Ford were photographed by Annie Leibovitz and placed on the cover of *Vanity Fair*; the ensemble cast chatted with Ellen DeGeneres and Jimmy Kimmel, and Carrie Fisher befuddled breakfast television hosts with Gary, her dog; Ridley won "Breakout Star" at the Teen Choice Awards, rubbing shoulders with Zac Efron, all of One Direction, and YouTube superstar Lilly Singh. *Star Wars* was cool again.

Yet for many, a nagging feeling remained, fueled by the apparent similarities between *The Force Awakens* and the original *Star Wars* trilogy—*A New Hope* in particular. Had nostalgia, the crucial weapon in Disney's arsenal for reviving *Star Wars* and reconnecting it with a skeptical audience, been taken too far? This was the central, and most enduring, criticism of *The Force Awakens*, and it arrived quickly after the film itself: that it was too similar to the first *Star Wars* film, and perhaps even broadly a remake of sorts. "*The Force Awakens* is practically a beat-by-beat reworking of the original," wrote *Vox*, while *IndieWire* proclaimed it the "Biggest Fan Film Ever Made," and the *Washington Post* argued that it "succumbs to the worst parts of remix culture."[3] This kind of censure proved persistent among both critics and fans alike, and would even go on to frame the promotional campaign for *The Last Jedi* in 2017, with the director Rian Johnson having to respond to comparisons to *The Empire Strikes Back* before *The Last Jedi* was even released.[4]

So what, exactly, are these alleged similarities, and why do they matter? In broad strokes, and with the help of a little deliberate fuzziness, one can fairly clearly compare the plots of *A New Hope* and *The Force Awakens* in a single stroke. In both films, we open with our heroes under attack from Stormtroopers searching for some secret information. Before being captured, a key hero conceals the secret in a droid and sends it on a mission across a desert planet, where the droid encounters a parentless waif. With the droid and the secret information in tow, the waif escapes the Stormtroopers on the Millennium Falcon, and, with the help of an aged mentor figure, tries to return the droid to the forces of good. At this point, however, a powerful weapon that the evildoers have developed is unleashed on the galaxy, killing many millions in the process. The goal for our heroes is now twofold: destroy the powerful weapon, and rescue the captured hero. Our heroes successfully perform the rescue, but the mentor figure is tragically killed in the process. Then, X-wings dog-fight with TIE fighters (monitored from a situation room by Leia) and eventually fly through a trench in order to destroy the powerful weapon and avert disaster. The day is saved, and the film is over.

There are also isolatable scenes that echo across both films, but out of order: Han Solo encounters someone he owes a debt to; our heroes travel to a space cantina filled with exotic aliens who take a moment to stare in silence; there is a briefing scene at a hidden hero base about how to destroy the powerful weapon; someone in a Stormtrooper uniform breaks our hero out of prison. The list goes on: a few days after the release of *The Force Awakens*, *Entertainment Weekly* listed eighteen major points of similarity.[5]

The question of why such similarities are automatically a prob-lem for *The Force Awakens*, however, is less clear. After all, the simi-larities were certainly intentional: J. J. Abrams later spoke of "em-bracing the history that we know to tell a story that is new—to go backwards to go forwards," and the wild success of the film suggests that this approach was a good idea.[6] Most often, the critique of rep-etition and recycling stands alone without much interrogation, but a few critics provide deeper explanations. Andrew O'Hehir at *Salon* argues that the similarities reveal that *The Force Awakens* is otherwise meaningless: "This is the work of a talented mimic or ventriloquist who can just about cover for the fact that he has nothing much to say."[7] Geraldo Valero, for RogerEbert.com, on the other hand, suggests that the problem with the film's borrowings is "that it never provides them with a worthy, original story to justify going back to this universe."[8] In other words, the commitment to homage and revival leaves *The Force Awakens* without a meaning of its own.

This is an interesting objection to take seriously. If nothing else, the many slavish points of similarity between *A New Hope* and *The Force Awakens* also starkly and helpfully reveal its points of dif-ference and discontinuity, not just with the first film but for *Star*

Wars generally. After all, despite the claims of some critics, *The Force Awakens* is not actually a beat-for-beat remake, and the choices as to what has been retained and what has been changed can tell us a lot about this new era of *Star Wars*.

Most obviously, the central difference for *The Force Awakens* lies in its casting along gender and racial lines: the new protagonists of the *Star Wars* universe are a woman, a black man, and a Latino man, in clear contrast to the original and prequel trilogies. There are other significant differences as well, including major plot points, such as the defecting Stormtrooper, the failed parent figures of Leia and Han, the contrast and antipathy between a child who yearns for a parent (Rey) and a child who kills his (Kylo), the lightsaber-induced flashback and visions, and the centralized search for a disappeared and mythical Luke Skywalker. *The Force Awakens'* gestures to seriality are also much more transparent than *A New Hope*. *The Force Awakens* ends with the most barefaced cliffhanger ending since *The Empire Strikes Back* and makes a point of theatrically introducing its returning cast members. Han and Chewbacca, Leia, and Luke all reappear in showstopping scenes that otherwise disrupt the film's narrative flow—culminating, of course, in Luke Skywalker's wordless and climactic introduction that acted for viewers as a dramatic suspension of narrative for two years. Like the marketing campaign that so cleverly tapped into fan yearning for a renewal of *Star Wars'* mythology, *The Force Awakens* stands alone in the *Star Wars* oeuvre as a film that makes the effort to mark the real-world passing of time and the homecoming of characters, actors, and worlds.

Yet the most significant point of divergence for *The Force Awakens* is a thematic one: transferal. *The Force Awakens* is very clearly a film about handing over the baton in a way that *A New Hope* (or any other *Star Wars* film) plainly is not. The thematic resonance of *The Force Awakens* is built on the foundations of the transferal of protagonist status between generations, from Han and Luke and Leia to Rey and Finn and Poe. It is a film, as Abrams argued, for "going backwards to go forwards," for establishing future heroes by rekindling and building on the past. Yet *The Force Awakens'* returning characters, these older heroes, are not quite the eccentric and good-natured mentors of *Star Wars* past, like Obi-Wan Kenobi and Yoda. They have regrets, and sorrows, and fears of their own, mistakes they don't want to see repeated. They want to pass the baton, but they're also concerned with what they're passing on. In other words, these characters and this film face one central concern: legacy.

THE LEGACY FILM

The Force Awakens is not alone in this concern: in fact, a preoccupation with legacy has become one of the defining features of blockbuster sequels in recent years. Into the 2010s, film franchises established in the 1970s, 1980s, and 1990s have gained significant nostalgic currency and have been frequently revived by studios looking for financial dependability and predictability. Jason Mittell argues that post-2000 serial and episodic storytelling has become ever more complex, "with a heightened degree of self-consciousness in storytelling mechanics and demanding intensified viewer engagement."[9] In the era of reboots, quality television, online streaming, and the renewed importance of established franchises, the familiar modes of franchise making have been reinvented. New models have been created. Chief among these is what I call the legacy film.

The ideal scenario goes something like this: a Hollywood studio has the rights, or has recently acquired the rights, to a popular and successful franchise from the 1980s, but this franchise has, for whatever reason, become dormant. Perhaps the iconic actors or creatives associated with the franchise moved on to other projects, or maybe the last installment in the story was poorly received or was too clearly an endpoint, a finale, for the series to go on. However, financial volatility in today's age of increasing competition for entertainment other than cinema-going (the internet, streaming, video games, quality television) has made studios increasingly interested in reliable products. Nostalgia has long been a reliable tool for Hollywood, and targeting older generations for the cultural capital of their youth has time and again proved an irresistible proposition for risk-averse studios. So, one of these once-popular-yet-dormant franchises is selected for revival: the original actors and possibly creatives (directors, composers, scriptwriters, producers) are engaged for the new film and rolled out in a saturation marketing campaign. It's possible that these once-famous actors have declined into relative obscurity since the last franchise entry, and their sudden reappearance on chat shows and film junket runs is fascinating enough to start building buzz: "Look how old they've become," the press might as well be exclaiming, to paraphrase Kylo Ren. But while the thrill of the return can sustain a temporary revival, it won't hold out for multiple films (and that deeply desired financial reliability), and so, crucially, some younger actors are also thrown into the mix. These younger actors can be either unknowns ready to be wholly identified as the new face of a franchise or a big name of the moment used to multiply the star factor. These younger stars can also more convincingly carry the action scenes and keep awkward illustrations of the effects of age to a minimum (unless the point of the film is to play into the subgenre of "geri-action," focusing on aged action stars).[10] At the start of the film, the new faces are naive and in need of tutelage. Happily, however, the older, returning heroes step in to play mentor to the younger faces and authorize a handing off of the franchise to these newer stars. By the end of the first film, the new heroes have been given their own quests and storylines to fulfill, and the older heroes have anointed them as their successors, with the returning characters either dying or returning to the margins in smaller roles. The baton has been passed, and the event-spectacle of renewal has guaranteed box office returns. The dormant franchise is revived for at least several sequels more.

This mode of franchise storytelling has become widespread, and by now has seen numerous stratospheric successes as well as some dismal failures. Matt Singer was one of the first to identify this trend in an article for *ScreenCrush* in 2015: "Welcome to the age of the Legacyquel," he wrote. "Actors retire, but their franchises don't; at least not anymore. And so new heroes have to be invented to restaff them."[11] The year 2015 was indeed replete with legacy film examples and was perhaps the central year for the approach, with not only *The Force Awakens* but also *Creed, Terminator Genisys, Vacation,* and *Jurassic World*. This moment of popularity for the legacy film approach came after several years of franchise tinkering from major studios, particularly after the era of the reboot that accompanied *Batman Begins* and *Casino Royale*. The straight reboot can take on creative risks, however, some of which can miss the mark with older fans: losing the proverbial baby with the bathwater that can turn off a significant segment of a franchise's built-in fan base, as Heather Urbanski notes.[12] On the other hand, a simple late-sequel (where no attempt at transferal is made, such as *Zoolander 2* or *xXx: The Return of Xander Cage*) makes no real attempt to engage a new audience and generate longevity: the parameters of success are too well defined. Only the returning audience is engaged.

On the other hand, the legacy film's authorization of transferal from one franchise era to another, rather than the sharp break of the traditional reboot or the restrictions of the late-sequel, offers a more elegant solution to franchise fatigue or dormancy. Older audiences are asked to remember, while newer audiences can claim the cultural capital of an older franchise for their own and for the future. As a long-term strategy, the potential gains are nearly limitless. Singer suggests that through the model of the legacy film, franchise fandom becomes a kind of family heirloom, passed down between generations: "Even as older characters hand down these stories, older fans in the audience should do the exact same thing. Parents pass down old family stories and sports loyalties; now they can pass down *Star Wars* as well."[13] Nonetheless, parents were already passing down *Star Wars*: the idea of a parent sketching out the ideal viewing order to introduce *Star Wars* to their children (or other newcomers) was already so ingrained that entire fan debates have taken place about their comparable merits.[14] What is different today, however, is that the narrative structure of the entire franchise is designed to stage this generational transference. *The Force Awakens* is therefore about legacy in more than one sense.

The goal of the legacy film—to extend the life of a film series and renew it for a new era—might well define it, but there are also several key ingredients to contend with. The clearest examples of the legacy film, and the most successful instances of the model, contain at least five common elements:

1. An original actor or actors reprise a key role from an earlier film as an aged version of that character. Lucasfilm president Kathleen Kennedy refers to these roles as "legacy characters."[15] This role is ideally one heavily associated with the

actor in popular culture: Harrison Ford in particular has been part of many legacy films via his *Star Wars, Indiana Jones,* and *Blade Runner* roles. This may, of course, have nothing to do with any sense of nostalgia from the creatives themselves. Ford considers these legacy roles as a professional opportunity rather than anything affectionate: "I'm not nostalgic," he told the *Telegraph* in 2017. "I'm a little sentimental from time to time, but that's not enough to get me to do something."[16] The legacy character will usually have changed somehow to account for the period of dormancy or absence: Luke Skywalker has vanished because of his failure to create a new generation of Jedi; Rocky Balboa has retired from boxing and no longer wants to be involved in the sport. These characters are often reluctant returning heroes or mentors and have to be convinced to reclaim their roles in the franchise. An interesting outlier to this criterion can be found with *Jurassic World.* Although *Jurassic World* features the return of B. D. Wong as Dr. Henry Wu, he is the only returning character and a relatively minor one at that. Instead, the legacy character function is taken up through two different avenues: a physical space (the original and dilapidated visitor center) and a monster (the original Tyrannosaurus rex). Both ultimately aid the new characters despite their aged state.

2. New characters are introduced who are in some way primed, or who are primed over the course of the legacy film, to take up the mantle of older characters. We may encounter these characters—we might call them "successor characters"—as naive newcomers requiring the mentorship of the legacy characters in order to grow into or accept their roles. Often, these characters share some traits with the legacy characters (such as Rey's aptitude with the force and piloting in *The Force Awakens,* or Adonis Creed's raw boxing ability in *Creed*). However, one of their most important traits is usually a kind of optimistic hope, or drive, which can be played against the reluctance of the legacy character to reinvigorate the franchise. This hope is naive and unchecked by the pessimistic experience of the "real world" possessed by the legacy character but is used to remind

the legacy character of the hope and drive they possessed in their youth (and in the franchise's original installments).

3. In the legacy film, new narrative concerns repeat and revise old narrative concerns, following the reboot model. This might be plot similarities as close as in *The Force Awakens* and *A New Hope,* or *Creed* and *Rocky,* or it might be an extension of that narrative, as in *Blade Runner* and *Blade Runner 2049* or *Tron* and *Tron: Legacy.* However, unlike the reboot, the shared narrative concerns here allow legacy characters to pass on specialized knowledge or skills that the audience is already familiar with. It also allows for the dormant franchise's appeal to be rearticulated and renewed in a more complicated way than straight repetition: the legacy character recognizes the familiar plot beats along with the audience (recall Han Solo's comment about Starkiller Base being similar to the Death Star).

4. There will be a handover moment, or a series of handover moments, between legacy characters and successor characters. Sometimes these are consciously recognized as handover moments by the characters passing the torch (such as a time-traveling Kyle Reese giving his younger self the mission he has just completed at the end of *Terminator Genisys*). These moments are sometimes also literalized, as the legacy character gives the successor character a quest, or an object, or a role to perform. The object-giving legacy character is perhaps the most literal icon of the legacy film: in *Tron: Legacy,* Kevin Flynn sacrifices himself and saves his son, Sam, in one movement by giving him his identity disc; in *The Force Awakens,* Luke Skywalker's lightsaber is literalized as a totem of heroism and the call to adventure, with characters lusting after it (Kylo Ren), rejecting it (Rey, initially), taking it on for the benefit of others (Finn), and virtuously accepting it and the mission it connotes (Rey, the second time). This handover moment is consciously averted in *Indiana Jones and the Kingdom of the Crystal Skull* as Mutt Williams reaches for his father's iconic fedora, which is calmly snatched away just before he places it on his head. "Not yet," *Crystal Skull* seems to be saying

to its audience: "wait until the next Mutt Williams-Indiana Jones adventure for the full transferal to occur" (this second Williams-Jones film ultimately did not transpire and seems unlikely to, given the critical failure of *Crystal Skull*).

5. By the conclusion of the legacy film, the narrative impetus will have shifted from the legacy characters to the successor characters. This is achieved in two ways. First, the successors should no longer require blessing or authorization to proceed in their roles or take up the narrative drive of the franchise. They will be shown to be, if not perfect, then at least capable enough to drive the franchise narrative from this point on: usually this means taking the lead in the (somewhat) success-ful final battle and playing an irreplaceable role in saving the day. Second, and most importantly, the legacy character will in some way have clearly withered. This is often achieved via the death of the central legacy character, similar to the way that mentor figures in Hero's Journey–style narratives often sacrifice themselves to allow the hero to stand alone (Ben Kenobi's death in *A New Hope* is a good example of this).[17] However, the decline of the legacy character doesn't actually need to be fatal. It can be achieved via retirement or domes-ticity (similar to Will Wright's analysis of the classical western gunfighter hero rejoining society via marriage).[18] Perhaps the legacy character declares an intent to move on to a lesser but important off-screen challenge (perhaps to help rebuild what has been destroyed during the climactic battle, for instance). In all these scenarios, however, it is made explicitly clear that the legacy character has withered to the point that although they might still play a role, they will be on the margins of the ongoing franchise storyline.

A further comparison to Joseph Campbell's Hero's Journey mono-myth is in some ways instructional. In 1949 Campbell published *The Hero with a Thousand Faces,* a book that argues that mythological stories from around the world often follow an identifiable arche-typal template. Campbell's work has had lasting influence, often via secondary sources such as *Star Wars* (the influence on which is contested),[19] or Christopher Vogler's later simplified and adapted version, *The Writer's Journey*,[20] which explicitly targeted screenwriters. Broadly speaking, the Hero's Journey involves an ordinary person being called to adventure, an encounter with a mentor who helps them along the way, a number of trials and tests, before the final ordeal, which, once overcome, leads to a great reward and resurrection for their return to normalcy.

With the rise of the legacy film, we can identify a new variation of this that builds on Campbell: the legacy's journey. Although for the most part, legacy characters are not the protagonists of these films, they still undergo their own reliable character arcs—made all the more compelling because many of these legacy characters have already undergone their own version of the Hero's Journey in the original franchise films. In the legacy film, the legacy character begins the story as experienced, but reinitiated to everyday life instead of continuing their adventuring ways. Han Solo has returned to smuggling rather than fighting for justice; Indiana Jones is poking around in the dirt in Nevada rather than chasing supernatural objects; Rocky Balboa has retired from boxing and now runs an Italian restaurant, Adrian's. The legacy character's call to return to adventure usually comes in the form of meeting the successor character, who might ask them for help or guidance, which they may initially refuse. Here, we can think of Adonis asking Rocky for boxing training, which Rocky refuses; Finn and Rey asking Han Solo for his help in getting BB-8 back to the Resistance, a responsibility he tries to offload to Maz Kanata; K tracking down the exiled Rick Deckard for assistance in *Blade Runner 2049*, where they fight upon meeting, such is Deckard's resistance to returning to society; or Spock Prime's insistence to Kirk in *Star Trek* that he cannot meet the young Spock, which later is revealed to have been a ruse. The legacy character reluctantly rejoins the fight and offers mentorship to the successor character, sometimes on the successor's insistence (*Creed, Crystal Skull*), or as the result of events that necessitates them to alter course (*The Force Awakens, Blade Runner 2049*). The legacy character eventually finds purpose in this mentoring role, and realizes the fated nature of their relationship to the successor character during the film's finale. In this moment, they fully give themselves

THE ELEMENTS OF THE LEGACY FILM

Film	Legacy characters	Successor characters	
Blade Runner 2049 (2017)	Rick Deckard (Harrison Ford)	K (Ryan Gosling)	
Creed (2015)	Rocky Balboa (Sylvester Stallone)	Adonis Creed (Michael B. Jordan)	
Independence Day Resurgence (2016)	David Levinson (Jeff Goldblum), Thomas J. Whitmore (Bill Pullman), Dr. Brakish Okun (Brent Spiner)	Jake Morrison (Liam Hemsworth), Dylan Hiller (Jessie Usher), Patricia Whitmore (Maika Monroe)	
Indiana Jones and the Kingdom of the Crystal Skull (2008)	Indiana Jones (Harrison Ford), Marion Ravenwood (Karen Allen)	Mutt Williams (Shia LaBeouf)	
Jurassic World (2015)	Dr. Henry Wu (B. D. Wong), the original park, the original Tyrannosaurus rex	Owen Grady (Chris Pratt), Claire Dearing (Bryce Dallas Howard), the Velociraptors	
Ocean's 8 (2018)	Reuben Tishkoff (Elliott Gould), The Amazing Yen (Qin Shaobo)	Debbie Ocean (Sandra Bullock), Lou (Cate Blanchett)	
Star Trek (2009)	Spock Prime (Leonard Nimoy)	Spock (Zachary Quinto), James T. Kirk (Chris Pine)	
Star Trek: Generations (1994)	James T. Kirk (William Shatner)	Jean-Luc Picard (Patrick Stewart)	
Terminator Genisys (2015)	The Terminator "Pops" (Arnold Schwarzenegger)	Sarah Connor (Emilia Clarke), Kyle Reese (Jai Courtney)	
The Force Awakens (2015)	Han Solo (Harrison Ford), Leia Organa (Carrie Fisher), Luke Skywalker (Mark Hamill)	Rey (Daisy Ridley), Finn (John Boyega), Poe Dameron (Oscar Isaac)	
Tron: Legacy (2010)	Kevin Flynn (Jeff Bridges), Alan Bradley (Bruce Boxleitner)	Sam Flynn (Garrett Hedlund), Quorra (Olivia Wilde)	
Vacation (2015)	Clark Griswold (Chevy Chase), Ellen Griswold (Beverly D'Angelo)	Rusty Griswold (Ed Helms), Debbie Griswold (Christina Applegate)	

Narrative concerns revised	The handover	Legacy's withering
Is our protagonist a replicant or a human? (Flipped from the original)	The origami animals	Averted: K dies, while Deckard approaches Stelline (Carla Juri)
Training an aspiring boxer into greatness	Rocky admits that Creed has taught him to fight again	Rocky has non-Hodgkin's lymphoma
Save the world from alien invasion on July 4	Not present	Whitmore's sacrifice
A mysterious archaeological object must be returned to its resting place from evil foreigners	The fedora at the wedding (hinted but averted)	Jones is now married (i.e., domesticated)
Corporate greed leads to the costly destruction of a dinosaur theme park	The old destroyed visitor center is used by the kids to help escape the new dinosaur	The new Velociraptors ally with the returning Tyrannosaurus rex to defeat the hybrid dinosaur
A freshly released thief forms a gang to pull off a once-in-a-lifetime heist and get personal revenge	Debbie visits Danny's grave and toasts him with a martini	Danny Ocean is dead; Reuben Tishkoff warns the new crew against the heist
Boldly going where no one has gone before, saving the galaxy from alien threat, time travel	Kirk is promoted to Captain of the USS Enterprise	Spock Prime leaves to rebuild Vulcan and persuades younger Spock to stay in Starfleet
Boldly going where no one has gone before, saving the galaxy from alien threat, time travel	Two captains of the USS Enterprise work together to save the day	Kirk's death
Time-traveling cyborgs try to change a future war	Kyle tells his younger self about Genisys	Pops sacrifices himself
Saving the galaxy from a totalitarian group with a super weapon	The passing of the lightsaber	Han Solo's death
Miniaturized heroes navigate a world on a microchip and defeat a totalitarian regime	Kevin's disc passed to Sam	Kevin's sacrifice to stop CLU
A family man attempts to create the perfect holiday by journeying to "Walley World"	Clark Griswold gives Rusty the family Wagon Queen Family Truckster to get to Walley World	Clark and Ellen have retired to run an appalling bed and breakfast

to the successor's cause, perhaps through sacrifice (*The Force Awakens, Independence Day Resurgence, Terminator Genisys, TRON: Legacy*) or through total commitment to a supporting role (*Creed, Star Trek*). The legacy character has therefore undergone their own identifiable journey, from normalcy and reluctance to total support of the successor hero, and a withdrawal from the protagonist role.

There are, in some ways, progenitors for this model. The seventh film in the Star Trek series, *Star Trek Generations* (1994), is perhaps the earliest clear instance of a legacy film. Intended to mark the passing of the torch between the original Star Trek cast and the *Next Generation* ensemble, *Generations* fulfills all the elements of the legacy film. Late in the film, the central successor character, Jean-Luc Picard, encounters a disoriented James T. Kirk in a timeless, dream-like place called the Nexus. Kirk is reluctant to leave, but Picard convinces him to return to his time period to make a difference and avert disaster. Kirk agrees, and later sacrifices himself to save the day, acknowledging the handover between characters in the process ("The least I could do for the Captain of the Enterprise," he says while dying). *Star Trek Generations* thus deliberately marks a moment of transition between legacy and successors in the unusual context of a feature film being used to articulate a moment of transition for a television series. This mode of seriality, signaled via *Generations*, would prove prescient given Hollywood's embrace of reviving and passing on franchises two decades later.

Another antecedent of the legacy film is found in literature, in the way that *The Chronicles of Narnia*, by C.S. Lewis, deliberately shift between generations of protagonists. For example, in *The Lion, the Witch, and the Wardrobe* (1950), the Pevensie children are the protagonists, but are subtly enabled by their uncle, Digory Kirke, whose time in Narnia as a child is later explored in *The Magician's Nephew* (1955). The Pevensies, in turn, become too old to return to Narnia by the time of *The Silver Chair* (1953), whereupon characters encountered in previous books as youths are now greatly aged (such as Prince Caspian). Characters age and tasks are passed on between generations as a matter of routine in the Narnia series: this is especially interesting given that unlike the filmic examples discussed so far, Lewis had no ageing actors to contend with to drive these decisions. If Lewis had instead wanted to keep the Pevensies as the heroes of Narnia for the entirety of the series, there would have been nothing to stop him in the same way that Harrison Ford cannot be the hero of the *Star Wars* series infinitely across multiple decades.

Instead, Lewis elected to shift the protagonists across generations for several reasons. First, it allows the Narnia books to retell a story of coming of age and maturity. Once the children protagonists become mature enough, usually in their midteenage years, they no longer require the experiences that the secret world of Narnia has to offer and accordingly cannot return.[21] Only children on the verge of their teens can find a place in Narnia. We can see obvious parallels here for the legacy film, which frequently returns to and revises the narrative concerns of the original film franchise. Legacy films do not simply hand over a franchise; they also renew their fundamental and familiar appeal, and it is the new generation of heroes that allows that rearticulation to occur. Han Solo cannot have the same adventure and character arc that he had in 1977, but a character under his guidance can. Relatedly, the transition between generations allows audiences to grow into the world of Narnia. Sam McBride argues that Lewis had Lucy Barfield, his goddaughter, in mind as the specific audience for the first Narnia novel, *The Lion, the Witch, and the Wardrobe*.[22] Barfield grew and matured as Lewis did as an author, and both alongside the changing generations of the Narnia books themselves.

"There are stories that we have to grow into," writes Stratford Caldecott, "stories that deal with the way the world is made, and the way the Self is made."[23] This illustrates the way that Lewis's goals with the shifting generations in Narnia were perhaps not quite so removed from the apparently commercial motives of the legacy film. These too are stories for different generations to grow and mature into, to be passed down from parent to child. They act a way into the franchise, certainly, but they also retell similar stories for different ages. The central mythos of the franchise is rearticulated, not just as a way to remind nostalgic audiences of past successes, but to open the series up to a new generation of viewers. All this is perhaps to note that there's an echo in the legacy film of that line from *The Phantom Menace*'s initial trailer: "Every generation has a legend . . ."

This detailed legacy film model tells us a lot about the prevailing uses of seriality in Hollywood, and it also gives us a set of criteria to evaluate shifts and variations from the norm. For instance, we might wonder whether *Independence Day Resurgence* is actually a legacy film given that no clear handover between generations occurs: instead, audiences are promised a third adventure featuring the legacy and successor characters on equal footing (such a film is unlikely to eventuate given the poor box office performance of *Resurgence*). We can also use this model to illustrate how films that otherwise follow a logic of franchise nostalgia are in fact not legacy films, such as *Zoolander 2*, *T2: Trainspotting*, *xXx: The Return of Xander Cage* (which feature no handovers to successors or withering legacies, and are therefore late sequels), *Ghostbusters* (which seems to take place in a brand-new narrative timeline and is therefore a reboot, despite a number of cameos from legacy actors), or *Wall Street: Money Never Sleeps* (which repeats the success of the legacy characters rather than handing off to successors, for thematic reasons). The legacy film is but one method of franchise nostalgia and is hardly all-encompassing: it is as important to note which franchise films do not take on the logic of the legacy film as those that have done so with success.

We can also identify reoccurring themes across these legacy films. Indeed, though clearly driven by a financial imperative, the legacy film has created a selection of franchise films with some interesting preoccupations, many of which are epitomized in *The Force Awakens*. Chief among these is time: again and again in the legacy film we see questions of temporality, particularly the passing of time, take a central focus. This ties in with the chief goal of the legacy film itself as an industrial model, which allows audiences to position each franchise film in time, both in terms of the series' narrative but also in terms of the actual years passed between each film. *The Force Awakens* certainly marks time passed in both senses: as in the years between 1983 and 2015, which separate Ford's performances as Han Solo, and also the in-world time passed in the *Star Wars* universe, which ultimately mark him as an aged character. "You're Han Solo?" an excited Rey asks. "I used to be" is his response. Although Solo has returned to the smuggling of his youth, it is clear in *The*

Force Awakens that he's not doing as well as he once did. "Your game is old," Guavian Death Gang member Bala-Tik tells Solo, "there's no-one in the galaxy left for you to swindle." There's also an emphasis on the changes wrought by time passing as well as the similarities. When Han and Leia reunite for the first time in the film, they trade fond barbs on just this topic: "You changed your hair," Han tells Leia. "Same jacket," she responds. "No, new jacket," he replies, though the audience could be forgiven for thinking otherwise.

The legacy film's obsession with time began as early as *Star Trek Generations,* which features a time-travel plotline and a villain, Soran, who wants to travel to an extra-dimensional, time-free space called the Nexus so he can reunite with his dead wife. "Aren't you beginning to feel time gaining on you?" Soran taunts Picard. "It's like a predator. It's stalking you." This is especially resonant in the context of *Star Trek Generations* because Picard has earlier discovered that his brother and nephew have died, meaning that his family line will end with him. Instead, however, it is the other Enterprise captain, James T. Kirk, who meets his death in *Generations,* passing on the mantle of look to Picard. *Generations,* perhaps unsurprisingly given its name, is a film about legacy in three senses: family lineage, Enterprise captaincy, and *Star Trek* protagonists. The 2009 *Star Trek* film is similarly interested in time travel and lineage: by the film's end, due to time travel, two versions of Spock exist (an aged and a young version), yet both are progenitors of a dwindling legacy, given that most Vulcans died during the film.

"Time takes everybody out, it's undefeated," Rocky Balboa tells his young protégé, Adonis Creed. Legacy characters are deeply aware of their own mortality: just as they have aged out of the possibility of continuing as the hero of the franchise narrative, their own death also approaches, whether to be shown on-screen or not. In *Indiana Jones and the Kingdom of the Crystal Skull,* Jones and his elderly colleague, Charles Stanforth (Jim Broadbent), reflect on the deaths of franchise regulars Henry Jones Senior and Marcus Brody: "We seem to have reached the age where life stops giving us things and starts taking them away," remarks Stanforth. Yet what is left, after death? The legacy film is also concerned with inheritance, and what will be left behind. In this instance, *Crystal Skull* is instructive, as it is narratively focused on the passing on of knowledge, belief, and power. We see this transferal through the titular Crystal Skulls, which serve as a gateway to an extreme form of knowledge ("I want to know!" exclaims the villainous Irina Spalko before she dies), but also in the way that Indiana Jones mentors his son, Mutt Williams, during the film. Though the returning audience knows to expect unbelievable and even supernatural occurrences in the Indiana Jones franchise, Williams plays a disbelieving foil to Jones's more experienced tutor. The Crystal Skull plotline is also about the need to return: a plot point that revolves, in fact, around the translation of the word *return* across multiple languages. Just as the Skull needs to be returned to its resting place, the legacy film itself represents an attempt at a return to vitality for the franchise, a revival of what can be then passed on. Nostalgia, if we remember, was originally meant to provide a welcome emotional homecoming. *The Force Awakens* skews this through its repositioning of the hero's journey as the legacy's own bequest-oriented character arc. Its own concern with history and myth, in this context, reveals a Han Solo and Leia Organa who are filled with angst over whether they did the right thing in the past (in their conversation over who is to blame for Ben Solo's fall), as well as a Han Solo who wonders whether he really did perform all the heroic feats the successor characters have heard about (it was twelve parsecs, after all, he notes).

Importantly, the legacy film also uses the passing of time as an access point for authenticity, or even reality. In *Blade Runner 2049,* Deckard is taunted by Niander Wallace with a re-creation of his lover from the original film, Rachel (with a digital likeness of the original actress, Sean Young). "Is it the same now, as then?" asks Wallace. "The moment you met her. All these years, drunk on the memory of its perfection." In the audience, we are invited to marvel at the CGI perfection of the 1982-era Sean Young, as though no time had passed at all. "I know what's real," responds Deckard, before dismissing the re-creation as flawed. Equally, in *Tron: Legacy,* Sam Flynn is initially presented with two versions of his father, both played by Jeff Bridges, returning from the original. The first is a CGI-perfect re-creation of Bridges from 1982, as though he has not aged a day from the last time Sam saw him. The other is a gray-haired, sagely figure whom Sam immediately identifies as his real father. "Long time," says Sam. "You have no idea," responds his father. The passing of time therefore provides a sense of authenticity in the legacy film, and setting this sense of "genuine" aging against the fakery of timelessness only enhances this type of film's fascination with the interchanging of eras.

There is, clearly, also an interest in the mixing of old and new— and not just in the way legacy characters pass protagonist status to their successors. *Jurassic World*, for instance, is clearly preoccupied with a hybridizing of eras. The film's plot is driven by just such an urge: the new Indominus rex has been created via genetic splicing, an amalgamation of many dinosaurs, but most importantly for the franchise, the Tyrannosaurus rex and the Velociraptor, the dinosaur icons of *Jurassic Park*. This monstrous new foe is eventually defeated at the film's climax by the surprising alliance of the first *Jurassic Park*'s Tyrannosaurus rex with *Jurassic World*'s intelligent and well-trained Velociraptor pack. This is, of course, also a revision of the first film's climax, which saw Velociraptors versus Tyrannosaurus rex as humans escaped; in *Jurassic World*, they ally to fight the Indominus rex while the humans escape to safety. Timelines are mixed and matched, in genetics, in loyalty, in audience memory, and in franchise homage.

J. J. ABRAMS: LEGACY FILM AUTEUR

Of course, all of this is to say nothing of the fact that *The Force Awakens* not only is perhaps the linchpin example of the legacy film but that it is directed by surely its foremost proponent in J. J. Abrams. Although frequently the butt of "lens flare" jokes, Abrams has a distinct authorial style that has nothing to do with his on-set lighting. As director of *Mission Impossible III, Star Trek, Super 8, Star Trek into Darkness,* and *The Force Awakens,* Abrams has worked within the contemporary Hollywood system to produce a body of work concerned with history, nostalgia, and transferal. Although not all his directorial works are legacy films, they all contain key elements for the development of the legacy model and how it has subsequently been implemented. Accordingly, instead of simply understanding *The Force Awakens* as some form of simple remake, we must come to terms with Abrams's role as a legacy film auteur of sorts and his oeuvre, which clearly pivots on franchise legacies.

While Abrams started his career in the 1990s as a scriptwriter (*Regarding Henry, Forever Young, Armageddon*) and television producer (*Felicity, Alias, Lost*), his first feature film was not until 2006, with *Mission Impossible III*. This was the third film in the *Mission Impossible* franchise, and one intended to revive the series' fortunes after the poorly received (57 percent on Rotten Tomatoes) second install- ment directed by John Woo.[24] For *USA Today*'s reviewer, Claudia Puig, Abrams "achieved the nearly impossible: taking a predictable, tired franchise and putting his signature style on it so that it feels fresh and cool."[25] Part of that style, in retrospect, echoes that of the legacy film. Although there is no straightforward legacy/successor model, at the beginning of *Mission Impossible III*, we find our hero, Ethan Hunt, looking to move into retirement and domesticity (via an impending marriage) and away from fieldwork. Instead, he is caught up averting an international conspiracy with a twist—the film's climax sees Hunt needing to electrocute himself in order to deactivate a bomb located inside his head. To do so and survive, the finale involves Hunt training his wife—a nurse—to defend herself and revive him while he is unconscious from the electrocution ("I'll die unless you kill me!"). Accordingly, even in this early Abrams franchise film there is a climactic instance of transferal and legacy: in this instance, undertaken within a framework that aims to revive both the franchise (in the audience's terms) and the hero (in the film's narrative).

Abrams's next film, released in 2009, was another franchise revival project of even greater significance. *Star Trek* would be the first Trek film since the critical and commercial failure of *Nemesis* in 2002, and a clear attempt at reviving the franchise, which had been a diminishing box office prospect for decades. As already dis- cussed above, Abrams's *Star Trek* is one of the template films for the legacy model, clearly featuring a legacy character (a time-traveling Spock Prime), successor characters in the young, alternative time- line Kirk and Spock, repeated and revised narrative concerns from the original television series and films, a clear handover moment in Spock Prime aiding Kirk to take command of the Enterprise, and a withering of the legacy character in Spock Prime electing to leave to rebuild Vulcan at the film's conclusion. Yet there are further similarities to *The Force Awakens*. As with Finn and Rey, there are not one but two origin stories in play in *Star Trek* with Kirk and Spock. Much of the film's narrative drive is concerned with the interplay between each character's family traumas—the death of Kirk's father and his need to prove himself, and Spock's half-Vulcan, half-human childhood combined with the death of his mother and the destruction of the planet Vulcan. This mirrors the fundamental family drama that underscores *The Force Awakens*: Rey feels lost without the family she never knew, while Finn finds purpose in escaping the First Order after they kidnapped him from his family as a child. There's even a shared visual motif across both films, as Abrams has both Kirk and Rey drive bikes across the horizon in extreme long shots. In both instances, it is used to illustrate each character's contemplation of their call to adventure and their fate: Kirk has been challenged to join Starfleet, while Rey dreams of a life less ordinary on Jakku. In Abrams's hands, Kirk and Rey, as successor characters, literally search the horizon for clues for their future, and for inspiration to become the story's hero.

As with *The Force Awakens,* in Abrams's hands, the legacy model was a success with *Star Trek*. Ty Burr in the *Boston Globe* praised the film for its *Force Awakens*–like mixing of audience and franchise, in

Kirk drives his motorcycle across the horizon in
Star Trek in a motif recalled in *The Force Awakens.*

the way that the film functions "as a family reunion that extends across decades, entertainment mediums, even blurring the line between audience and show." The legacy model applied to *Star Trek* also rearticulated the fundamental appeal more clearly than a straightforward reboot might have: for Burr, "It reminds us why we loved these characters in the first place."[26] The legacy film logic was being perfected.

Abrams's next film, *Super 8,* remains his only nonfranchise directorial project and is based on an original Abrams script. That said, it is difficult to conceptualize *Super 8* as anything but deeply related to dormant filmmaking practices and nostalgia, given it is unmistakably a homage to a swathe of 1980s blockbusters. In particular, *Super 8* is a fond pastiche of several Amblin Entertainment films (Steven Spielberg's production company, which also produced *Super 8*), particularly *E.T. The Extra Terrestrial* and *The Goonies,* as well as other Spielberg films such as *Close Encounters of the Third Kind* and *Jaws. Super 8* features mysterious night skies above rural towns, a gang of dorky youths who get about on bicycles, an overworked small-town cop, and of course an alien and his spaceship, all elements tied to this genre of 1980s blockbuster filmmaking. Echoing Jameson's comments about *Star Wars,* Roger Ebert suggested in his review that *Super 8* represented "nostalgia not for a time but for a style of film-making,"[27] and that style is present in *Super 8* through much more than its plot elements. Although Abrams's directorial work has always been influenced by Spielberg, *Super 8* represents a broader imitation of the latter's kinetic and visually inventive style. "The typical Spielberg identification-figure is a spectator, often also a surrogate director," writes Nigel Morris.[28] *Super 8*—a film that conflates the childlike joy of filmmaking with special effects–driven science fiction—contains a highly active camera that dollies and pans to guide the spectator's attention in a direct way, frequently using visual puns and optical shorthand to tell the story. Even the film's opening shot feels particularly Spielberg-esque in its visual concision: it is a crane shot inside a factory, with a sign in the foreground that reads "Safety is our Primary Goal! Days Since Last Accident: 784." A man on a ladder slowly takes the "784" off and replaces it with a single number: "1." Like Spielberg in *Jaws* or *Jurassic Park,*

Abrams is also highly selective about how and when he reveals the film's monster to the spectator: in one night shot, the alien wreaks destruction just behind a rotating and brightly illuminated "Kelvin Gasoline" sign; in another, a small white cube flies through a wall, leaving an aperture that the inquisitive camera moves to look through, revealing the film's iconic water tower, where the alien is hiding. "[Spielberg] spent hours with me in the editing room," said Abrams. "He'd say, 'What I would do is . . .' and give a suggestion. It would always make me laugh inside, because I can't tell you how many times I would work on something and wonder, 'What the hell would Spielberg do here?'"[29]

The influence of this kind of spectator-driven visual style translates into *The Force Awakens*, too. At the point of its release, it was certainly the most visually active *Star Wars* film ever released. Taking the opening sequence alone—the village scene on Jakku—almost every shot either dollies, pans, zooms, or shifts focus in some way. Some are ornate, such as the introductory shot of BB-8, which swivels around him 180 degrees, going from an over-the-shoulder shot to a close-up on his eye. Others are subtle, such as the final exchange between Poe Dameron and Lor San Tekka, where Lor tells Poe to flee: the shot begins with Poe and Lor facing the camera and pulls focus between each as they trade dialogue, before finally dollying subtly on Poe as he realizes the grimness of the situation and turns. The camera continues to dolly, but this time shifting in on Lor as he takes command of the conversation. The reverse shot on Poe is also a dolly.

Although George Lucas included some camera movement in *A New Hope* and his prequel trilogy, Abrams's relentlessly energetic camera is a stylistic departure for *Star Wars*, and one that can be traced back to the influence of Spielberg via *Super 8*. Yet it is likely the broader logic at work in *Super 8*—one of stylistic emulation of a cinematic idol—that is most important of all. It was in this film that the stylistic elements of the legacy film began to solidify through the lens of visual nostalgia, and Abrams's directorial style along with it.

Stylistic emulation took a concerted turn with Abrams's final pre–*Force Awakens* film. Returning to the *Star Trek* universe, Abrams's *Star Trek into Darkness* extends the homage-logic of *Super 8* into a conscious and intricate reworking of a specific franchise film. Although *Into Darkness* spends at least half of its runtime as its own project, significant portions of the latter sections of the film are spent in conversation with *Star Trek II: The Wrath of Khan,* widely considered the best of the *Star Trek* films. This includes the return of Khan Noonien Singh (Ricardo Montalbán in the original and Benedict Cumberbatch in *Into Darkness*), as well as an inversion of the climax of *The Wrath of Khan,* where Kirk sacrifices himself in the Enterprise's radioactive reactor chamber instead of Spock. The section goes as close to the first film to include direct lines of dialogue, though sometimes given to other characters (given the inversion of the situation). Though the use of *The Wrath of Khan* found a mixed reception among *Star Trek* diehards, the practice of reworking franchise cinema was clearly on Abrams's mind.

In these four films—*Mission Impossible III, Star Trek, Super 8, Star Trek into Darkness*—we can see a clear lineage both for the Abrams flavor of legacy film and for *The Force Awakens.* These four films illustrate in turn franchise renewal, a concern for transferal and legacy, movement between legacy and successor characters, the emulation of an older filmic style for nostalgia purposes, and the emulation of a beloved franchise film, respectively. All these ingredients can be found in *The Force Awakens.* Far from a simple borrowing of *A New Hope,* through the lens of the legacy film, Abrams was clearly building up to this kind of film as a major concern of his directorial style. This, above anything else, defines him as a filmmaker.

Yet if all this discussion fails to convince that *The Force Awakens* is no simple remake, then perhaps in the next chapter, we can take a moment to look at something genuinely new for the franchise: its politics.

4

AN AWAKENING

Diversity as the Politics of The Force Awakens

he *Star Wars* universe was, in one way or another, always a political one under the yoke of George Lucas. The risk-averse corporate ethos of Disney suggested a different tack might be taken with the franchise under its new lease of life. Lucas had no corporate overseer to disapprove of Darth Vader's borrowing of George W. Bush's vocabulary, or the use of the Ewoks as Viet Cong stand-ins; allegories of American imperialism might not sit so well with shareholders eager to see a return on Disney's big Lucasfilm investment. Nonetheless, any doubt that *The Force Awakens* would be seen in a political context was quickly extinguished on its release. "Spread my warning across the galaxy, Padawans," wrote David G. Brown, an "intellectual rebel" for the right-wing men's rights website Return of Kings, "*The Force Awakens* is spectacularly replete with the handiwork of the avowed Social Justice Warrior JJ Abrams."[1] The litany of complaints from far-right viewers like Brown was long: *The Force Awakens* had cast too many people of color, and too many women, so they claimed, for diversity's sake and not for their acting abilities. They were put up against the evil First Order, a largely white organization led by two young, angry white men. Then, and this criticism applied especially in the case of Rey, these new women and people of color were made far too powerful and competent, relative to their white male counterparts. Rey was frequently described as a "Mary Sue," a term that emerged from fan fiction where the written protagonist was supposedly a wish-fulfillment stand-in for the fan-ish author: in the hands of far-right critics of *The Force Awakens*, it became an incoherent critique that revealed dramatic prejudice against stories featuring capable women. For these viewers, left-wing social justice warriors (SJWs for short) had taken over *Star Wars*. Whether Disney planned it or not, it seemed *Star Wars* could not escape political ends.

Yet put plainly, *The Force Awakens* was not made with the same direct political intent that the original trilogy—or even the prequels—was. As I showed in the previous chapter, the film has to some degree a borrowed and augmented narrative structure. With that, of course, comes borrowed themes: the insurgency-and-rebellion narrative of *The Force Awakens* could be just as easily applied to the politics of the 1970s as Lucas's original trilogy, such is the similarity in the way the galactic conflict is drawn. *The Force Awakens* is hardly a contemporary allegory of Iraq or Syria or North Korea, which it may well have been in the hands of Lucas. Despite the complaints of far-right columnists, J. J. Abrams did not intend *The Force Awakens* as any kind of political parable to the degree that Lucas hoped viewers would see a bit of Richard Nixon in the Emperor, or George W. Bush in Anakin Skywalker. In 2015 Leia, Rey, Finn, and the Resistance were not taking on an allegorical Taliban or fighting for the success of a proxy Arab Spring. *The Force Awakens* is simply too bound up in the franchise itself and in commercial considerations to comment in such a direct way.

Despite this, *The Force Awakens* is still clearly a political film— perhaps even more so than Disney hoped or intended it to be. Despite the obvious partisanship of critics like Brown and their radically out-of-step views (just 3 percent of viewers in a Morning Consult poll in December 2017 agreed that the politics of *Star Wars* had stopped them watching the films),[2] these kinds of complaints nonetheless are illustrative of both *The Force Awakens* and the media landscape it was released in. This is the fundamental tension for the *Star Wars* franchise and its political contexts. The stuff of *Star Wars* is the stuff of politics: allies, antagonists, war, belief, ideology, mysti-

cism, individualism, martyrdom. The political uses of *Star Wars* are
accordingly invariably of greater and wider significance than any
creative intent. As Dan Hassler-Forest points out, "Our immersion
in imaginary storyworlds takes place not within, but *across* media."[3]
Each new film finds itself in a new political moment and is both
reflective of and a new implement for the congealed soup of context.

In 2015—and indeed, for much of the entire period that Disney
has been in control of *Star Wars*—the central debate of the media
and entertainment industries has surrounded diversity of representation and opportunity for creatives. Molly Fischer, writing for *The
Cut* in 2017, sums up the key questions of this era clearly:

> A new set of concerns—a self-conscious moral duty in
> matters of identity, of inclusion and representation—had
> come to dominate discussions among creators, critics, and
> consumers alike. A fundamental question (perhaps the first
> question; sometimes the only question) to ask of a work was
> how well it fulfilled these ideals. In what ways did it engage
> with the values of a pluralistic society? Who got the chance
> to make mass culture, and about whom did they get to
> make it?[4]

It would almost be disingenuous to select a grouping of work that
best embodies this kind of discussion, such was the depth and uni-
versality to which popular culture has been framed along these lines.
From the obvious (*Dear White People, Master of None, Wonder Woman,
Girls, Transparent, Orange Is the New Black,* Netflix's *She's Gotta Have It*
series, *The Handmaid's Tale, Get Out, Moonlight, Black Panther*) to the
indirect (Katy Perry and Taylor Swift's debated feminism, *Game of
Thrones, Stranger Things,* Disney's remake of *Beauty and the Beast, La
La Land*), virtually all of pop culture discourse has been realigned
toward questions of identity, inclusion, and representation. This did
not happen overnight, accidentally, or as the result of some kind of
cosmic coincidence. Young women and people of color have powerfully advocated and collectivized for inclusion and diversity, using
new platforms and social media to make space for these kinds of
discussion in popular culture, and the powerful expectation that, if
you are making culture in the late 2010s, you will at least consider
representation. Sara Ahmed notes the momentum that feminism

built in the 2010s, charting its spread in classrooms, on social media, in global protests, and its instrumentalization by popular artists
like Beyoncé. "Feminism is bringing people into the room," Ahmed
writes.[5]

In some respects, this shift in the media industries is hardly surprising. As the cultural critic bell hooks wrote in 1996:

> Whether we like it or not, cinema assumes a pedagogical
> role in the lives of many people. It may not be the intent of
> a filmmaker to teach audiences anything, but that does
> not mean that lessons are not learned. . . . Movies not only
> provide a narrative for specific discourses of race, sex, and
> class, they provide a shared experience, a common starting
> point from which diverse audiences can dialogue about these
> charged issues.[6]

The dialogue between the popular, the personal, and the political
has always occurred: "A feminist movement is not always registered
in public," writes Ahmed.[7] It is the ease of these specific cultural
conversations to be had in public that has shifted and dramatically
intensified: social media and self-publishing enabled by the internet
has greatly multiplied the reach of already existing diverse voices of
cultural criticism; newspapers and traditional publishers have published from a wider pool of people, sometimes as a direct result of
such online intervention and visibility; and more generally, media
critics have taken a profound notice of the renewed and widespread
interest in these kinds of perspectives to the point where discussion of
identity, inclusion, and representation is no longer an outlier but the
norm. "In many ways, this is a remarkable moment," write Sarah
Banet-Weiser and Laura Portwood-Stacer in the journal *Feminist
Media Studies*, noting the way that feminism has "undeniably *become*
popular culture." Yet this did not happen without force: what is
crucial about Banet-Weiser and Portwood-Stacer's argument is that
popular feminism is "a terrain of struggle, a space where competing
demands for power battle it out."[8] Not only did feminist critics have
to battle to force space within popular culture, but feminism itself
contains multitudes and is itself a site of struggle as competing forms
of popular feminism write and rewrite discourse.

It is in this context that Disney was to revive *Star Wars*. The science fiction genre in particular has long been celebrated for its ability to help audiences imagine the future, in what Brooks Landon has called "science-fiction thinking,"[9] and Istvan Csicsery-Ronay "science fictionality."[10] Usually this kind of analysis is focused on the technical impact of technology on our day-to-day lives, and the way that science fiction films have themselves driven technological advancements, such as *Minority Report*'s work in rejuvenating interest in touch screens and haptic computer interfaces. However, the power of science fiction cinema to explore the trajectory of culture is broad. "In their own way, science-fiction films attempt to come to grips with the radically changing world around us," writes Angela Ndalianis.[11] It is hardly surprising, then, that a *Star Wars* film might be perceived by audiences of all stripes as political, regardless of the filmmaker's intent. *The Force Awakens* might not build toward a critique of the Republican Party or the war in Afghanistan, but by engaging in diversity of representation, it profoundly engages with the politics of today's world.

The other major shift in the contemporary media landscape has been the intensity of publicized backlash against progressive voices in the media. Jason Ward runs MakingStarWars.net, a popular online location for spoiler-filled reports and plot leaks for the Disney-era *Star Wars* films. "The difference between the email I get today versus the email I got five years ago is that certain keywords like "feminazi," "snowflake," "libtard," "SJW," and "cuck" are in these messages often," he told Syfy Wire. "When you see those things, you know they're consuming a certain type of media in conjunction with *Star Wars* media."[12] These kinds of media might be websites like Return of Kings, which led a conservative boycott of *The Force Awakens*, or Breitbart, which described it as "an extended propaganda promo for women in the military,"[13] or the social media users who posted racist, antisemitic, sexist, and transphobic bile to the twitter hashtag #BoycottStarWarsVII.[14]

Such a venomous conservative response to *The Force Awakens* was perfectly placed in a year of sexist and racist responses to popular films. In May 2015, *Mad Max: Fury Road* had received a similar reaction for its inclusion of a variety of roles for women, including one of the film's protagonists in Furiosa (Charlize Theron), and the playwright and feminist Eve Ensler's involvement as a consultant on the film.[15] Men's rights activists again (and again unsuccessfully) called for a boycott of *Fury Road,* while the far-right conspiracy theory website Infowars called it "a trojan horse to dupe guys into watching feminist propaganda."[16] A year later, and in May 2016, Paul Feig's *Ghostbusters* reboot starring Melissa McCarthy, Kristen Wiig, Leslie Jones, and Kate McKinnon faced ongoing conservative reprisal for daring to cast four women in the original all-male roles. An organized online campaign saw the film's trailer become the most disliked in YouTube history,[17] while then presidential hopeful Donald Trump reacted with a video blog where he exclaimed "What's going on?"[18] *Ghostbusters* also became notable as the inciting force behind Breitbart writer Milo Yiannopoulos's campaign of racist, sexist, and transphobic tweets targeting Leslie Jones, for which he was eventually permanently banned from the site.[19] For *The Force Awakens* to be released at this time guaranteed that it would become part of a triumvirate, with *Mad Max: Fury Road* and *Ghostbusters,* as the cinematic harbingers of the current moment's widespread popular culture wars. Yet this moment is not just about the interfacing between *Star Wars* and popular culture: *The Force Awakens* also played a crucial role in responding to and providing a much-needed correction to the very white and very male legacy of the *Star Wars* franchise.

RACE AND GENDER IN
GEORGE LUCAS'S *STAR WARS* FILMS

The Force Awakens was hardly the first *Star Wars* film to provoke discussion surrounding questions of gender and racial inclusion and representation. In 1977 Carrie Fisher's Princess Leia was genre- and stereotype-busting, but other women were few and far between for the original trilogy. Leia aside, just four women have dialogue in the entire original trilogy: Aunt Beru, Mon Mothma, an unnamed Rebel in *Empire,* and Oola the dancer in Jabba's Palace in *Return of the Jedi,* who begs for her life before dying. This did not go unnoticed by critics. "Women," wrote Dan Rubey in one of the first scholarly analyses of *Star Wars* in 1978, "exist primarily to provide motivations for male activity, to act as spectators, or to serve as mediators between different levels in the male hierarchy."[20] He points out that along with their lack of presence in the film, the women who do exist in *Star Wars* serve minor roles with little agency. Aunt Beru mediates between Luke and his uncle and performs domestic duties; Princess Leia has "attractive spunkiness and toughness" but nonetheless is still "dependent on her male rescuers."[21] If we consider the weaknesses of each central character in *A New Hope*, Rubey argues, Han is disempowered through his cynicism, Luke through his naïveté and youth, but of the three, Leia's stems not from a lack of competence, experience, or belief but from her gender. "Power in *Star Wars* is male power," writes Rubey, "the patriarchal power of fathers and sons."[22]

To some extent, this is both problematized and reinforced by the revelation that Lucas wrote an early *Star Wars* draft script where the protagonist hero was to be a girl, before changing his mind and splitting the character into Luke and Leia.[23] One can only imagine what the history of filmmaking might have been had he persisted. Clearly, such a thought was possible, even in 1977 where women-led action films had become nearly invisible after their rampant popularity in the 1910s.[24] *Star Wars* would have been a very different universe in 1977 if the fate of the galaxy had been bestowed on daughters rather than sons, and surely on some level Lucas would have understood the decision in front of him. Yet it would be a mistake to read too much political enlightenment into Lucas's considerations here. Twenty years later, when making *The Phantom Menace*, he caustically downplayed the film's romantic subplot: "Well, it's not *Titanic*," Lucas said. "This is a boy movie."[25] (One wonders, if perhaps he had made it less a "boy movie," then *The Phantom Menace* might have more forcefully challenged *Titanic*'s unassailable box office takings, falling almost $200,000 short in America alone.) Despite the many women and girls who love and have always loved *Star Wars*, Lucas left minimal space for them to be represented on-screen in all six of his films. As Will Brooker notes, "The main roles for women in the *Star Wars* saga are, of course, Princess and Queen."[26] Though they may have led the rebellion against the Empire and the fight against Palpatine, they never led Lucas's films.

Race was also an obvious issue for Lucas's original films. As

Andrew Howe writes, "The *Star Wars* franchise has never been able to escape the gravitational pull of contemporary racial politics."[27] Even Carl Sagan, the well-known American astronomer, made this point when interviewed by Johnny Carson about the film in 1978. While critiquing *Star Wars* for overfeaturing humans in the galaxy far, far away, he also notes that "they're all white . . . not even all the colors represented on the Earth are present, much less greens and blues and purples and oranges."[28] The only actor who isn't white in the whole first film is James Earl Jones, who of course acts in voice only in all his *Star Wars* appearances (leading Melissa Harris Perry to observe that Vader is played by a black man while evil, but when he is redeemed at the end of *Return of the Jedi*, his unmasking reveals him as white[29]). Instead, for much of the original trilogy, the Rebel Alliance's diversity is communicated not by including characters or actors of color but by aliens and droids, which for Adilifu Nama are "exotic beings symbolically proxy for blacks and other people of color."[30] The Rebel Alliance seems to value difference in all respects, except among its humans.

The major character of color in the original trilogy is of course Lando Calrissian, played by Billy Dee Williams. Though beloved by many, Lando is not without his issues. In his debut in *Empire*, as seemingly the only black man in the galaxy, Lando is introduced as a scoundrel, a swindler, and a sexual threat to Han and Leia's budding relationship. He's someone whom Han Solo is genuinely impressed with once he learns Lando's latest business is legitimate—upon which Lando promptly betrays Han. Lando is shown as a criminal in need of redemption, and in *Return of the Jedi*, as Kevin Whetmore Jr. argues, he is first made ineffectual (in the rescue of Han) and then reduced to the leader of a "B team" of Rebels (Admiral Ackbar, Nien Nunb, Wedge Antilles) in the destruction of the Death Star.[31] It is also perhaps worth noting that Lando's contribution to the plot of the original trilogy was insignificant enough that his character is yet to make a return—or even be mentioned at all—in Disney's sequel trilogy, though he has been announced as cast in *Episode IX*.

As far as race goes, Lucas's *Star Wars* prequels are more of a mixed bag. The concentrated whiteness of the lead characters remains, as does the maleness. Padmé Amidala is the one major female character in the prequels, and her merits as a feminist character oscillate wildly. In *The Phantom Menace*, she is quiet and restrained, yet she also drives, plans, and enacts the military liberation of her home planet of Naboo, including ascending over her palace walls with grappling guns. Despite a meaningful career as a democratic-inclined senator through the other two prequels, and becoming an early leader of the resistance to Palpatine's autocratic rule, Padmé eventually dies an undignified death in *Revenge of the Sith*. She expires in childbirth, having "lost the will to live," and is martyred as a disappointing plot point, a woeful piece of character motivation for her husband, Anakin Skywalker. Diana Dominguez likens Padmé's fall from adventurous and independent ruler to secretive and isolated wife as "disturbingly symbolic" of domestic abuse, and "alarmingly analogous to the countless stories of women who lose their voices, independence, and their very souls in order to 'keep' their lovers or husbands."[32] Despite over two decades of day-to-day political progression and improvements in broader cinematic representation, Padmé is certainly a step back from her daughter's feminism in *Star Wars*.

However, women generally populate the galaxy a bit better in the prequels than in the originals, with small speaking roles for Shmi Skywalker, Padmé's handmaidens, one Nubian pilot in *The Phantom Menace*, and some of young Anakin's friends on Tatooine (including Jira, the old lady), among others. Nonetheless, it's worth noting that Padmé is quite literally the only woman with dialogue in all 140 minutes of *Revenge of the Sith* (Genevieve O'Reilly was to have a few lines as Mon Mothma—a role she would reprise in *Rogue One*—but they were cut in editing). A senator, former queen, action heroine, mother, and leader of the proto-rebellion, yes, but Padmé is also the only woman in the galaxy with a voice. That she expends almost all her dialogue in *Revenge of the Sith* either discussing Anakin or talking directly to him hardly improves matters.

The racial stereotypes in the prequel trilogy's aliens have also been consistently commented on and criticized since *The Phantom Menace*'s release in 1999. The Neimoidians, the frog-like aliens who run the nefarious Trade Federation, speak with strong accents (which many have described as variously built on Japanese or "Asian" stereotypes, perhaps drawing on Japanese villains in American World War II films[33]), have greenish-yellow skin, and have slanted pupils. Their roles as the leaders of the villainous Trade Federation, an explicitly corporate imperialist organization, were for some reminiscent of racist imagery of Japanese *zaibatsu* or the growing dominance of Chinese businesses in the 1990s. For Vincent Law, "The choice of Chinese-sounding accents for merchant characters caught in the middle of a nefarious plot of corrupt bargains and political intrigue is a dangerous one."[34] Watto, the Toydarian junkyard alien who keeps the young Anakin Skywalker and his mother as slaves, has also variously been interpreted as playing on Jewish, Arabic, or Italian stereotypes. With his comprehensibly stereotyped hooked nose, pot belly, obsession with profit and gambling, and his gravelly accent, Patricia Williams writes that Watto is "comprehensively anti-Semitic—both anti-Arab and anti-Jew."[35] Things are hardly improved when, in *Attack of the Clones,* a derelict, fly-covered Watto returns with a stubbly beard and a circular, brimmed hat, like a *Der Stürmer*-era antisemitic cartoon.

Finally, and perhaps most infamously, Jar Jar Binks has long been held by critics to be a racist amalgamation of Jamaican and Caribbean stereotypes. In fact, in his analysis of contemporary reviews, Brooker goes as far as to suggest that the reading of Jar Jar as a racist caricature was "the dominant interpretation" from film critics at the time of *The Phantom Menace*'s release.[36] As a lanky, dim-witted alien with long ears that some identified as dreadlock-like, Jar Jar's accent and speaking voice have commonly been criticized as "pidgin" or "patois"-like. Jar Jar's role is as the comic relief in the film: he is stupid and contains no real moment of vindication, instead pratfalling and unintentionally lucking his way to victory. "The ability to speak does not make you intelligent," Qui-Gon Jinn tells him early in the film. Many reviewers[37] likened Jar Jar to the actor and comedian Stepin Fetchit, who according to the historian Donald Bogle was the "arch-coon" of shambolic comic relief of 1930s Hollywood: "His grin was always very wide, his teeth very white, his eyes very widened, his feet very large, his walk very slow, his dialect very broken."[38]

An irritated Lucas pled innocent to these charges. "It really reflects more the racism of the people who are making the comments than it does the movie," he told the BBC.[39] This attempt to reverse culpability, of course, is a classic example of what Robin DiAngelo has called "white fragility," where the person who objects to racism is deemed racist for breaking the unspoken expectation of "racial comfort" where such difficult topics are politely left unraised.[40] Yet as Brooker argues, such critiques of racism are complicated by *The Phantom Menace* creatives most directly responsible: the concept artist Doug Chiang for the Neimoidians (who is Taiwanese American) and Ahmed Best as the motion capture and voice actor for Jar Jar Binks (who is African American).[41] Best himself vocally defended his performance as Jar Jar in the media at the time: "I can't even begin to explain the ridiculousness of this," he told the *New York Daily News*. "My family comes from the Caribbean—Barbados and St. Thomas—and I don't know anybody from the Caribbean who talks like that."[42]

Of course, the obvious answer is that such stereotypes can be unintentional and still problematic, especially when working within genre and pulp movie histories in the ways that *Star Wars* does. Science fiction as a genre has a long history of replaying racist and colonialist tropes in space. For Jessica Langer, "A mutual central focus of science fiction and (post)colonialism is that of *otherness*":[43] the interplay between extraterrestrials/aliens, xenophobia, and racism is tightly wound. Obnoxious tropes of first contact, the noble savage, or the orientalized other are easily unintentionally reproduced without careful attention to them. It is entirely possible to understand Chiang, Best, and even Lucas to have had absolutely no malicious intent yet still have reproduced harmful ideas through inattention.

Despite these widely perceived stereotypes, however, and the incontrovertible whiteness of the core cast, Lucas's prequels are, unlike the original trilogy, replete with smaller and background roles for people of color. Mace Windu, played by Samuel L. Jackson, is certainly the most prominent of these. However, though the Jedi Master is in all three prequels and features in key action scenes, including Anakin's betrayal of the Jedi, he has no character arc to speak of and is simply the most significant supporting character of the prequels. Unlike Lando Calrissian, however, Mace Windu is far

from the only person of color in the second *Star Wars* trilogy. Tem-
uera Morrison, a Māori actor from New Zealand, was cast as Jango
Fett, which accordingly made all of the Republic's Clone Troopers
as well as his son Boba Fett (played by Daniel Logan in *Attack of
the Clones*) ethnically Māori. The two queens of Naboo, following
Padme, are both played by women of color: Queen Jamilla in *Attack
of the Clones* who is played by Ayesha Dharker, and then Queen Apa-
ilana in *Revenge of the Sith,* played by Keisha Castle-Hughes. Similarly, Padmé's heads of security are both played by men of color:
Hugh Quarshie in *The Phantom Menace* (Captain Panaka), and Jay
Laga'aia in *Attack of the Clones* and *Revenge of the Sith* (as Captain Ty-
pho). The Alderaanian senator Bail Organa—Leia's eventual adoptive father—is played by Jimmy Smits, an actor from Puerto Rico,
and other background Jedi, including Masters Depa Billaba and
Eeth Koth, are played by actors of color. Despite its focus on white
protagonists, the prequel galaxy is not as overwhelmingly white as
the original trilogy.

The Lucas-era legacy of gender and race for *Star Wars* is accordingly mixed, with both clear progress and inexcusable nega-
tives. For Brooker, *The Phantom Menace* "offers countless instances
where Lucas draws on diverse cultural influences and loads them
with either 'negative' or 'positive' connotations,"[44] and much the
same could be said about the other Lucas-era *Star Wars* films. Diversity in these films is usually endorsed as a positive in the abstract, yet
in the original trilogy actual human diversity was limited exclusively
to the presence of one visibly black character. While the supporting
cast of the prequel trilogy was genuinely much less white, the core
cast members remained white and were accompanied by an assort-
ment of aliens who are all too easy to read as racial stereotypes.
And, although it can be keenly debated as to whether both Leia
and Padmé are positive representations of women in the galaxy,
what cannot be contested is their anomalousness. The Lucas-era
Star Wars universe is monotonously male.

Accordingly, there was some expectation that any new *Star
Wars* film in the 2010s might spend some effort correcting this. Disney was hardly the most progressive corporation in Hollywood—it
would take until the eighteenth film in Disney's Marvel Cinematic

Universe for a black superhero to take the lead, and twenty-one for a woman—but as an astute money-making company, Disney should clearly have been able to read the winds of change afoot in the entertainment industries. "Close your eyes, for a moment, and imagine a version of the *Star Wars* universe full of rich female characters who play diverse roles ranging from Jedi warriors to military leaders to bounty hunters," wrote Laura Hudson for *Wired* in 2013.[45] Against a backdrop of cultural change and the largely white and male *Star Wars* franchise, what would Lucasfilm do?

A NEW GALAXY AWAKENS

For all the discussion that has followed *The Force Awakens,* it's easy to forget that when the film's cast was initially announced, it was widely criticized for its lack of diversity. On April 29, 2014, Lucasfilm announced that not only would *Star Wars* veterans Harrison Ford, Carrie Fisher, Mark Hamill, Anthony Daniels, Peter Mayhew, and Kenny Baker return to the galaxy far, far away, but they would be joined by John Boyega, Daisy Ridley, Adam Driver, Oscar Isaac, Andy Serkis, Domhnall Gleeson, and Max von Sydow. Alongside the announcement, a now-famous black-and-white photo by David James was released of the cast at the first read-through of the still-untitled Episode VII script. Take a look at that cast lineup again, however. In hindsight, knowing that Driver, Gleeson, and Serkis were all villains with varying screentime, and that von Sydow would only appear in the film for a few minutes, makes this cast seem less contentious; at the time, however, none of this was known. In 2014 persistent rumors suggested that Gleeson would be Luke Skywalker's son, for example, while the *Guardian* described Isaac, von Sydow, and Serkis as "shock additions" to the cast.[46] It was certainly possible at this point for many observers to think that Ridley, Boyega, and Isaac could end up as the supporting cast. It seemed like business as usual in the white male–dominated *Star Wars* universe.

"This is the only new woman to join the *Star Wars* cast so far" was how *Time* magazine introduced Daisy Ridley to the world.[47] "Today's news hints that *Episode VII* may not do much to improve the old films' famous gender gap," wrote the *Atlantic.*[48] "There's still time to fix this, Disney," wrote Rebecca Pahle at the feminist pop culture site *The Mary Sue*. "Come back to me when you have a *Star Wars* movie with more than two women in it."[49]

That was, happily, precisely what happened. Rumors rapidly emerged that Disney was still casting at least one more role—and that that role would be filled by a woman.[50] In the end, the final major cast announcement for *The Force Awakens* was for two women: Lupita Nyong'o (who had been the subject of casting rumors since meeting with Abrams earlier in 2014) and Gwendoline Christie. The announcement was a relief to many and indicated that *Star Wars* might finally shift beyond its previous white male dominance. For *Entertainment Weekly*, the addition of Nyong'o and Christie was "certainly a substantial and necessary improvement for a traditionally boys-heavy franchise entering the post *Hunger Games* universe."[51] Behind the scenes, although Nyong'o had been targeted for some time, it appears that Phasma had been written as male and was changed only weeks before shooting. Interestingly, the fan response to the lack of women in the initial announcement pushed Abrams and Lawrence Kasdan to rethink the Phasma character to be instead played by a woman. "When the idea came up to make Phasma female, it was instantaneous: Everyone just said, 'Yes. That's great,'" Kasdan recalled.[52] Thus, *The Force Awakens* would have four major roles for women: Rey, Leia, Phasma, and Maz Kanata (though admittedly the last two, of course, would never be seen in person in the film). Phasma would also be the first major female villain of the *Star Wars* saga, following the short-lived appearance of the shapeshifting bounty hunter Zam Wesell in *Attack of the Clones*.

Perhaps just as important as the broader cast was the composition of the lead trio for this new *Star Wars* trilogy. In contrast to the original trilogy and the prequel trilogy, which had both featured one white woman and two white men (Luke, Han, and Leia, and Anakin, Obi-Wan, and Padmé, respectively), the sequel trilogy's heroic leads would be Rey (Daisy Ridley, a white woman), Finn (John Boyega, a black man), and Poe (Oscar Isaac, a Latino man). With days to go before the worldwide release of *The Force Awakens*, Susana Polo proclaimed this as an achievement for diversity: "For the first time in Star Wars history, a franchise will be built around the adventures of the sort of people that Hollywood routinely over-looks."[53] Indeed, between *The Force Awakens, Rogue One,* and *The Last Jedi,* there was not a single new central white male hero in the *Star Wars* universe.

This was no accident. Behind the scenes, Lucasfilm has made deliberate and concerted attempts to tell diverse *Star Wars* stories. Abrams, who was already known for writing and directing strong women characters in his television work (*Felicity, Alias, Fringe*), commented at the time of *The Force Awakens'* release that he had consciously hoped to expand the *Star Wars* audience through casting. Almost evoking Lucas's "boy movie" comments about *The Phantom Menace* (not to mention the generational inheritance implicit in the legacy film), Abrams argued that *Star Wars* had always been "a movie that dads take their sons to," but that "I was really hoping this could be a movie that mothers could take their daughters to as well."[54]

Yet this strategy was more comprehensive than just one director's preferences or just one single film. Since taking over the day-to-day running of Lucasfilm, Kathleen Kennedy has shifted Lucasfilm toward diversity in casting, production, and perhaps most unusually for Hollywood, leadership. In 2016 Kennedy announced that Lucasfilm now had women making up more than half of its executive leadership, including Lynwen Brennan as executive vice president and general manager, Janet Lewin as vice president of production, Kayleen Walters as vice president of franchise marketing, Jacqui Lopez as vice president of animation production, and Lori Aultman as vice president of finance. "In the creative community, there's no excuse for not making a more equitable environment," said Kennedy. "It literally comes down to companies that just aren't trying hard enough."[55]

Indeed, one of Kennedy's earliest, and perhaps most defining, moves at Lucasfilm was to appoint Kiri Hart, a film and television writer, as the founding head of the new Lucasfilm Story Group. Before the Disney acquisition, all *Star Wars* story decisions were made by a single person: George Lucas. "George *was* story," says Lucasfilm executive Diana Williams.[56] With Lucas's departure, however, Kennedy handed off that power to the Story Group, to be led by Hart. This effectively made Hart the person with the greatest creative control at Lucasfilm, and though she doesn't have the same industry profile, she is regularly compared to Marvel's Kevin Feige as the creative leader of a multifilm franchise.[57] Hart's first two appointments to the Story Group were women (Rayne Roberts and Carrie Beck), and as of 2017, the expanded group maintained a diverse makeup: of eleven total members, four are women and five are people of color.[58] In a sense, this marks both a shift from a single authorial voice for the *Star Wars* saga to a team approach and also a behind-the-scenes embrace of the power-through-difference ethos that the films have ostensibly always championed.

It is quite clear that the contemporary political agenda for Lucasfilm and the Disney-era *Star Wars* films is a broad approach of diversity in most facets of production and casting. Unlike the original or prequel trilogy films, *The Force Awakens* is not directly allegorical or politically embellished, yet it is still fundamentally political. This is a *Star Wars* film that is political through filmmaking practice instead of plot or drama alone. Again, we can see the *Star Wars* franchise as both engaging with and reflective of the cultural moment. Megen de Bruin-Molé argues that *Star Wars* has in fact "not become fundamentally more or less feminist over the past 40 years. Instead, its engagement with feminist discourse has constantly shifted, shaped by the radical changes that both the transmedia franchise and the political movement have undergone."[59] Accordingly, *The Force Awakens* is a film that takes on the important questions of casting, what roles are diverse and what function they perform within the plot, and whose stories are being told and by whom. This is, however, still a new development: *Star Wars* under Lucas did not quite take such a keen or public interest in these questions. As a renewable franchise, the key to *Star Wars* is malleability and the capacity to observe the contemporary moment.

Certainly, in promoting *The Force Awakens,* Abrams frequently returned to the power of representation as a narrative thread for the newness of this latest *Star Wars* film. "I think it's important people see themselves represented in film," Abrams said at Comic-Con 2015. "I think it's not a small thing."[60] Much has been made of this kind of impact of Rey and Finn in particular on young fans: heartwarming stories featuring young girls cosplaying as Rey and young black boys taking on Finn as a role model are easy to find and were a common part of the marketing buzz building to *The Force Awakens'* release.

The power of modeling is clear enough, but what is also important about representation is the power to see others, or rather, "the other." In his most famous work, *Orientalism,* Edward Said argues that representation is a powerful and formative tool for creating entire frameworks for how those with little power are perceived by those with greater power, and ultimately how they can act and be acted on. "From the beginning of Western speculation about the Orient, the one thing the Orient could not do was to represent itself," Said writes.[61] Instead, as a concept, the Orient (what today we might call the Middle East) and those who lived there were fixed by Western thought within certain roles that could not easily be escaped. It is important, in other words, that Rey and Finn are shown to be heroes not just for the girls and black boys who might see in these characters a shadow of themselves drawn into possibility but also for white male audiences who might otherwise only see these "others" as represented as inferior. The power of representation therefore also lies in breaking apart limiting views of those whose experiences we do not share.

This kind of identification is not particularly difficult: after all, it has been regularly illustrated that it is hardly necessary for audience members to share traits with on-screen characters in order to identify with them (underrepresented demographics have been doing this for decades). Carol J. Clover, in her classic study of exploitation cinema, concludes that "I will never again take for granted that audience males identify solely or even mainly with screen males and audience females with screen females . . . we are truly in a universe where the sex of a character is no object."[62] I do not need to be a woman or to be black to identify with Rey and Finn, to share in their struggles and rejoice in their victories. In fact, perhaps it is of help to me as a white man to see the other not represented as "the Other" but instead in the kinds of broadly heroic terms usually reserved for those characters on-screen who I am most like. Through Rey and Finn in *The Force Awakens* I can see nuance and complexity and inner life represented in the kinds of characters who, in a mainstream Hollywood blockbuster—and hitherto in *Star Wars* at least—might otherwise have simply been a superficial stereotype.

Diversity is "incredibly important to *Star Wars*," Kennedy later said when promoting *Rogue One*, but "I think it's more important to the film industry in general. I think having casts that represent the world today and having characters that people can relate to all over the world. This is very much a global industry. Films mean something to people all over the world."[63] Indeed, it is difficult to imagine how the diverse cast of the Disney-era *Star Wars* films and the women and people of color-filled executive team at Lucasfilm could *not* constitute a political statement in an entertainment industry where in 2015, 29 percent of films released had women as lead actors, while 13.6 percent featured people of color; 10.1 percent of films were directed by a person of color, while 7.7 percent were directed by a woman.[64]

Indeed, it is worth asking why, at this point, no *Star Wars* film has been directed by a woman or a person of color or is currently planned to be. "We have every intention of giving someone an opportunity," said Kennedy in 2016 of the challenge to hire a woman director.[65] But the closest any woman came to directing *Star Wars* in Disney's first three films was Ava DuVernay's helpful suggestions to Abrams regarding tweaks to the climactic Rey and Kylo fight in *The Force Awakens* (which is to say, not very close at all, unless you count Abrams's subsequent enthusiasm for DuVernay to direct a future *Star Wars* film).[66] Kennedy has suggested a few times that first, she has not been approached by many women to direct a *Star Wars* film, and that second, there is a certain kind of experience necessary as a precursor to directing a large blockbuster of this kind (a rather self-fulfilling prophesy). These explanations are in line with what Martha M. Lauzen identifies as a trend in Hollywood for executives to "suggest that women self-select out of directing high-budget studio blockbusters and films in certain genres," in contrast with the actuality of "women directors [who] express an interest in pursuing a wide range of projects."[67] Squaring Kennedy's comments about "companies that just aren't trying hard enough" to hire women executives with her lack of movement on hiring a woman director is puzzling, to say the least.

Yet the up-front-and-center diversity of the new era of *Star Wars* is, more than any other factor, actually what marks it most clearly as new and different to the Lucas era. These films *have* changed. Diversity is its primary political agenda and also its most effective rebuttal against accusations of unadorned nostalgia. We can almost place Rey, Finn, and Poe against any combination of Luke, Han, and Leia, or Anakin, Obi-Wan, and Padmé, and let the favorable comparison make the argument alone. "With Rey the *Star Wars* series managed to finally foreground a female hero who is neither limited nor defined by her gender," writes Jeffrey A. Brown, and we must note that it took seven whole films to get to this point.[68] *The Force Awakens* accordingly presents a narrative of progress in two distinct senses: the political one, of course, but also in the way that *The Force Awakens* prompts a conversation with the older *Star Wars* films by improving on such an anterior aspect. With *The Force Awakens, Star Wars* has progressed. The combination of progressive feminism with nostalgia (which we can remember was argued by Janice Doane and Devon Hodges to be inherently antifeminist[69]) is complicated, but uniquely *Star Wars*–esque.

All this is not to say that *The Force Awakens* was perfect in terms of diverse representation. There were plenty of lost opportunities or chances not taken to improve on the film's representation. BB-8, for example, began life in *The Force Awakens* creature design shop as female but reverted to male—the apparent default for all *Star Wars* droids until L3-37 in *Solo*—during production.[70] The role of Korr Sella, played by Maisie Richardson-Sellers, was almost entirely cut—despite a scene in the film with Leia that would have seen *The Force Awakens* pass the Bechdel-Wallace test much earlier in its runtime than it does in its released form (with Maz Kanata and Rey's discussion after her lightsaber flashback at the film's midpoint). The British actress Christina Chong was also cast in an unknown role in *The Force Awakens* and had all her scenes cut from the released film—she would have otherwise been one of *Star Wars*' only on-screen characters of Asian descent.[71] Many scenes in *The Force Awakens* are still dominated by men: every member of Kanjiklub and the Guavian Death Gang appears to be male, leaving Rey as the only woman in the sixteen-person (counting BB-8) showdown scene on

Han Solo's freighter. *Star Wars* is still yet to have a clearly identi-fied queer character on-screen, and even just on the terms of 2015's blockbusters, *The Force Awakens* was a distant runner-up to *Mad Max: Fury Road*'s positive depiction of disability.

Of course, *The Force Awakens'* approach to diversity also proved to be a flashpoint for *Star Wars* fandom and the continuing discus-sion about representation in entertainment. When the very first *Force Awakens* teaser trailer was released in 2014, some fans im-mediately questioned whether a black man like Boyega could be a Stormtrooper, citing everything from obscure *Star Wars* lore to plain and simple racism. Boyega's response to these fans was sim-ple and direct: "Get used to it," he posted on Instagram.[72] On the other end of the spectrum, in the months before the release of *The Force Awakens*, disappointed fans campaigned via the social media hashtag #wheresrey about the near-complete absence of Rey—the film's protagonist—from prerelease merchandising in favor of the male characters. This, as it turned out, was a deliberate decision by Disney based on what Brown argues is the "longstanding corporate assumption that boys and girls are only interested in, and will only purchase, toys that align with their own gender."[73] However, the grassroots resistance to excluding Rey eventually drew a response, and Disney and its licensees produced several Rey products in a sec-ond, postrelease wave. Importantly, though, according to Brown, "the #wheresRey efforts appear to have shifted industrial thinking about girls' toys and boys' toys."[74] An audience and a fan base, in other words, had been identified and was being listened to. This, as I show, was long overdue.

STAR WARS DISCOVERS ITS AUDIENCE

Any suggestion that women had waited for the arrival of *The Force Awakens* to love *Star Wars* is fantastical at best, and even malicious at worst. Despite Lucas's "boy film" characterization, women *Star Wars* fans have always existed and have always been part of the core *Star Wars* audience. In his book *Using the Force: Creativity, Community, and Star Wars Fans*, Will Brooker spends some time examining the visibility and presence of women *Star Wars* fans. Written and published even before the prequel trilogy had run its course, Brooker describes how female *Star Wars* fans

> have loved the saga since they were young and found ways to explore it in make-believe games and fiction during their childhood, despite pressure to ditch *Star Wars* and conform to more traditional gender roles. . . . young female fans managed to negotiate these gender stereotypes to pursue their investment in a "boys film."[75]

To have been a female *Star Wars* fan during this period is to constantly have been reminded of the gulf between the imagined male fan and yourself (often literalized in advertising featuring boys playing with *Star Wars* merchandise), and to assemble various tactics to bridge that gap. Yet these female fans existed from the day *Star Wars* was released into cinemas: it was the films, their official merchandise, and the broader media culture that surrounded and constituted *Star Wars* fandom that failed to recognize these women.

"There is a curious discrepancy between the number of female Jedis in fan photographs," notes Brooker, "and the number in the official *Star Wars* texts."[76] If Lucas did not provide fans with *Star Wars* role models, however, they frequently took matters into their own hands through cosplay, fan communities, and advocacy. For example, an online campaign from 1999 called for Lucasfilm to cast a female actor as Boba Fett (much in the same way that in *Return of the Jedi*, the presumed-male bounty hunter Boushh removes his mask to reveal Leia in disguise). Tory Hoke, the writer and comic book artist behind the campaign, argued that "the casting of a female actor in the role of Boba Fett would demonstrate that women are not a forgotten or negligible demographic, as well as provide evidence that women can serve a cinematic purpose other than romance and reproduction."[77] Such a sentiment would fit neatly into the Disney era of *Star Wars* fan discourse.

Of course, the most popular method of fan intervention in the *Star Wars* franchise must surely be fan fiction, where fans create and share their own fan-written, unsanctioned narratives—and its salacious variant, slash fiction, which depicts fan-written romance and sex. Beyond the official *Star Wars* texts, it was through these methods that women, people of color, and perhaps most pointedly, queer people, managed to insert and discover their own narratives in the *Star Wars* universe. "Qui-Gon strokes Obi-Wan's face at the end of *Phantom Menace,* and a host of slash writers propose that the two Jedi had a loving relationship," writes Brooker.[78] Before the Disney era, finding a place for women and people of color in *Star Wars* was not so much impossible as it was one of audience-led imagination and creativity. This was about identification and visibility, yes, but it was also about reconfiguration, and to some extent, creative participation in fandom and the franchise.

Henry Jenkins describes slash fiction as "a genre about the limitations of traditional masculinity and about reconfiguring male identity,"[79] and in this sense it is important to reemphasize that *Star Wars* does not yet have an on-screen queer character even in the Disney era. Accordingly, we might see an echo of slash fiction in the widespread "shipping" of Finn and Poe on social media and beyond. What began as a playful subversion of the presumed heterosexuality of two male blockbuster characters gained sustained life as the guarded hope that finally, an on-screen queer relationship in *Star Wars* might catch up with what the franchise's fan base has been doing for decades. It's something that Lucasfilm and the Disney-era cast have publicly toyed with. When asked by Ellen DeGeneres about fan hopes for a queer romance, Oscar Isaac coyly replied, "You have to just look very closely you have to watch it a few times to see the little hints but there was. At least, I was playing romance."[80] Daisy Ridley and *The Last Jedi* actor Kelly Marie Tran also later joined in with this sentiment,[81] and in 2016 Joshua Yehl spoke with Kennedy after a petition to introduce a gay character as a tribute to Drew Leinonen, a friend of his who was murdered in the 2016 Orlando Pulse nightclub shooting, gained twelve thousand signatures. "[Kennedy] said she would consider putting a gay character in *Star Wars* if it was the right story and the right character," Yehl reported.[82]

Lucasfilm's open and continuing courtship of its queer audience through such platitudes reminds us that the battle to recognize *Star Wars*' substantial nonwhite male audience was long and hard-fought. These were battles fought largely by fans, by women, and by people of color, most of whom will go unrecognized by the franchise's official history. "I would say that our attempting to make the female *SW* fans known and recognized could definitely be seen as a political act," Tamela Loos, administrator of the Star Wars Chicks website, told Brooker in 2002.[83]

It would take until 2015 for the political significance of this kind of move to be recognized by Lucasfilm, as well as the move from independence to ownership by Disney and management by Kennedy. Although it would be easy to identify this as Lucasfilm acknowledging that the *Star Wars* audience has shifted, this simplistic interpretation would ignore the fact that women, people of color, and queer audiences have always enjoyed *Star Wars* and been part of its fan communities. Indeed, perhaps the actual audience shift identified by Lucasfilm is instead the more recent appearance of vocally angry young men among the *Star Wars* fan base. A number of critics wondered whether Kylo Ren, the ultimate Darth Vader fanboy, might actually be a kind of analogy for the type of *Star Wars* fan nobody has any love for. "It seems like J.J. Abrams has read the same rants I have, the ones where nerds argue about the presence of fake nerds mucking up their beloved franchises," wrote Hale Goetz.[84] Lucasfilm, of course, won't be drawn too deeply into this analysis. "I will say," tweeted Story Group member Pablo Hidalgo, "Kylo feels like the right type of villain for today."[85]

Ultimately, the strategy of diversifying the *Star Wars* audience appears to have been a financially sensible one for Lucasfilm and Disney. As an opening gambit, *The Force Awakens* was certainly a success. But by the time of *The Last Jedi*, the *Star Wars* film was not only top of the box office but one of three women-led films to be top-grossing of 2017 (along with *Beauty and the Beast* and *Wonder Woman*). Kennedy and her team at Lucasfilm had landed ahead of the curve. More importantly, they'd gone beyond identifying and authorizing the *Star Wars* audience to possibly even taking an active role in shifting the franchise's core demographics. In the wake of *The Force Awakens*, the midnight premiere of *The Last Jedi*—usually the domain of the most dedicated and eager fans—saw a leap of 10 percent in women attendees from the previous film, leaving the gender

breakdown at 43 percent female and 58 percent male. *The Last Jedi,*
reported *Newsweek,* "owed its box office success to women."[86] And
all this against a backdrop of a renewed attack on the franchise by
arch-conservatives (one of whom called it "social justice warrior
crap about income inequality and animal rights"[87]). By May 2018
the wisdom of diversity as a sound financial strategy for the *Star
Wars* franchise was so widely accepted that *Solo*'s relative box office
failure was seen by some as at least partly down to its throwback,
white male lead.[88] The Disney era has irrevocably reset the terms of
the appeal of *Star Wars*: it is now a diverse franchise.

In retrospect, then, both *The Force Awakens*' politics and its fi-
nances are intertwined in a stew of newness and nostalgia, diversity,
and audiences. By renewing the conversation about gender and
race in the *Star Wars* universe, *The Force Awakens* recognized and
expanded its audience, and identified what made it a contemporary
Star Wars film.

5

JUST LIKE OLD TIMES?

Music, Seriality, and the
Fugue of The Force Awakens

Very little is more important to me about *Star Wars* than its music. Its melodies defined my affection for the series and turned me on to the greater history of orchestral music of all kinds—film music, yes, but also symphonies, ballets, and opera. As a nostalgic franchise, John Williams's music has come to serve as a kind of transmedial brand, with video games, animated series, and radio plays not quite being officially *Star Wars* until sufficient reference to the musical sounds of the series has been paid. I'm not alone in my love of the music: the American Film Institute in 2005 voted the first *Star Wars* score as the greatest of all time, and even the four-CD reissued box set of the scores sold over 150,000 copies in 1994, eleven years after the last film and several years before anything new was on the horizon.[1] "Aside from George Lucas, nobody deserves more credit for the success of *Star Wars* than John Williams," said Mark Hamill in 2018.[2] For *The Force Awakens* director J. J. Abrams, Williams was even more an intimate part of his *Star Wars* experience. Williams "was the DVD or Blu-ray of my childhood because we didn't, of course, have VHS tapes of movies to watch when we wanted to. So I would buy John Williams soundtracks, often for movies I had not seen yet, and I would lie on the floor in my room with my head-phones on listening to the soundtracks which would essentially tell me the story of the movie that I didn't know."[3] *Star Wars* is almost unimaginable without John Williams.

This, it must be said, was not the original plan. Lucas, following Stanley Kubrick's lead from *2001: A Space Odyssey*, had thought that the film would work best with some of the classical greats inserted into the film. The original opening crawl was to have been played to Gustav Holst's "Mars, the Bringer of War," for example—a piece of music that, while ultimately influential for the *Star Wars* sound, would have changed the feel of the film immeasurably. Another possible musical world of *Star Wars* can be glimpsed through the *Flash Gordon* remake that followed on the coattails of *Star Wars* in 1980, which features a glam rock soundtrack written and performed by Queen. The pop soundtrack was much more in fashion at the time, and it is easy to imagine a world where studio pressure led to Lucas adopting one, fresh off the pop music success of *American Graf-fiti*. Instead, though, Lucas was keen to rework his *Graffiti* success in *Star Wars* with classical music.

It was Williams, whom Lucas had been introduced to via Ste-ven Spielberg, who convinced him otherwise. "I don't want to hear a piece of Dvorak here, a piece of Tchaikovsky there," said Williams. "What I wanted to hear was something to do with Ben Kenobi more developed here, something to do with his death over there. What we needed were themes of our own, which one could put through all the permutations of a dramatic situation."[4] *Star Wars* needed its own musical personality—one that could adapt to the needs of the film and give each moment its own identity.

The result was a score that reflected not just the romantic, ad-venturous tone of the first film but also followed its lead when it came to looking toward, and updating, the patterns of the past. Wil-liams's music self-consciously borrowed from the great Hollywood composers of the golden age—particularly Erich Wolfgang Korn-gold (whose theme for the 1942 *King's Row* is frequently compared to the main theme for *Star Wars*[5]) and Max Steiner. Williams himself describes his compositional approach to *Star Wars* as one deliberately rooted in evoking a collective sense of memory:

> But maybe the combination of the audio and the visual hitting people in the way that it does must speak to some collective memory. . . . that we don't quite understand. Some memory of Buck Rogers or King Arthur or something earlier in the cultural salts of our brains, memories of lives lived in the past, I don't know. . . . it isn't only notes, it's this reaching back into the past. As creatures we don't know if we have a future, but we certainly share a great past. We remember it, in language and in pre-language, and that's where music lives—it's to this area in our souls that it can speak.[6]

The music of *Star Wars,* and its bold and lush orchestration, was of a kind that Hollywood had not heard for years. For Royal S. Brown, the film music critic, with *Star Wars,* Williams "almost single-filmedly revived the fairy-talish, heroic genre popular in the late 1930s and early 1940s."[7] Even Williams's previous work, which had most notably been focused on the disaster films of the 1970s (such as *The Poseidon Adventure* [dir. Ronald Neame, 1972], *The Towering Inferno* [dir. Irwin Allen, 1974], *Earthquake* [dir. Mark Robson, 1974], and in its own way, his collaboration with Spielberg, *Jaws* [dir. 1975]), his film music was more contemporary and spare. "Directors were interested in super-realism and a kind of proletarian leanness, where the cosmetic effect of a large symphony orchestra was just exactly what was not wanted," remarked Williams later.[8]

Star Wars was by comparison significantly more loaded with themes and motifs for characters and locations (Kenobi, Luke Skywalker, Princess Leia, the Rebels, the Imperials, the Jawas, and the Death Star all get distinct melodic material) that often evoked straightforward musical emotions. The film music historian Mervyn Cooke describes John Williams as the leader of what he calls "the new symphonism,"[9] a revival of older film scores that used a large-scale orchestra to almost saturate a film in melody and rhythm for much of its runtime. This musical style borrowed not just from old Hollywood composers but greats like Pyotr Tchaikovsky, Sergey Prokofiev, Dmitri Shostakovich, Holst, Igor Stravinsky, William

Walton, and even Benny Goodman for the Cantina Bar jazz. "So memorably ahistorical is the result," argues Cooke, "that it has not dated."[10] Williams's music, like the film that accompanies it, is most effectively nostalgic through its broad-based and pluralistic references to the past. "I'm a very lucky man," said Williams much later. "If it weren't for the movies, no one would be able to write this kind of music anymore."[11] This is music that is at once nostalgic and utterly contemporary: composed to ape the aesthetics of a bygone era, but born into a world capable of fetishizing this music's peculiar alliance with commercial, blockbuster cinema.

Yet beyond the more specific elements of the *Star Wars* musical style, Williams himself over the course of the series (he has written music for every film except *Rogue One*) routinely displays a canny understanding of the crucial filmic developments of each installment. The original film needed something "emotionally familiar," as Williams puts it, "music that would put us in touch with very familiar and remembered emotions, which for me as a musician translated into the use of a nineteenth-century operatic idiom."[12] For *The Empire Strikes Back,* when the series was establishing itself as a multifilm franchise, and redeploying the once-outdated concept of a sequel in a serial mode, Williams made his music deeper, denser, and more Wagnerian in tone. For *The Phantom Menace* in 1999, when Lucas's storytelling became more rhetorical and baroque, Williams went with him, providing choral showpieces and demure brass declarations to reflect this ornate turn. Williams's music marks changes in each *Star Wars* entry as films as much as any plot or narrative developments.

So it is with *The Force Awakens.* It was in some ways a surprise that Williams would return for his seventh *Star Wars* film, given his age (Williams was almost eighty-four when *The Force Awakens* was released) and the fact that he had only composed music for two non-Spielberg-directed films since *Revenge of the Sith* in 2005. At the time, I had expected that a new composer would be brought in to help create a new era of *Star Wars* films, such as Michael Giacchino (who went on to score *Rogue One*). Such a change seemed warranted for a new, Disney-led era of *Star Wars*: if the series was to break with Lucas, a more contemporary musical sound might be needed too. Yet

Williams, along with the scriptwriter Lawrence Kasdan and some original cast members, joined an exclusive club of long-term *Star Wars* creatives who would also be part of the post-Lucas era. A new *Star Wars* film could be made without Lucas—but to birth this new era, the Williams touch would again be required. Indeed, Abrams talks about working with Williams with a kind of giddy reverence that he doesn't seem to have for almost any other element of the whole project. Describing showing Williams footage from the film for the first time as "the weirdest moment" of his time working on *Star Wars*, Abrams told *Vanity Fair*: "All I will say is, just to state the facts of it: I am about to show John Williams 30 minutes of a *Star Wars* movie that he has not seen that I directed. . . . that's probably as surreal as it gets in my professional life experience."[13] Tellingly, Rian Johnson made much the same remark when it came time to score *The Last Jedi*.[14]

As with his previous *Star Wars* scores, Williams's music for *The Force Awakens* is perceptive and illuminating. Indeed, it is possible that his music for the first post-Lucas *Star Wars* entry reveals a lot more about the film's own cultural significance than many of the more obvious criticisms of the film featured in the previous chapter. The score for *The Force Awakens* finds Williams in high franchise mode, drawing on some complex concepts of musical repetition and iteration that illuminates how the film itself is more than a by-the-numbers reheating of old material. Indeed, though Williams is often associated with major Hollywood franchises—most notably *Indiana Jones, Superman, Jurassic Park,* and *Harry Potter*—*Star Wars* remains the series he has worked on the most by some margin (*The Last Jedi* and the new theme for *Solo* make it nine *Star Wars* films—four *Indiana Jones* films is next). *The Force Awakens* therefore also presents an unparalleled opportunity to see the development of Williams's music deeper into any mode of seriality than any other film. Williams himself interestingly describes composing for *Star Wars* as an ongoing process rather than any directly linear project: "[We have over twenty years] of adding bits and pieces of material to a musical tapestry that started to pile up off the floors, quite an extensive library of music. . . . And that, I think, is a unique opportunity for a composer, to go back over and perhaps improve some of the things

I'd done."[15] Another film that both added a new set of lead characters and revisited older ones affords an excellent opportunity to
augment the *Star Wars* musical universe yet again.

Thinking about *Star Wars'* seriality through music is immediately more instructional and nuanced than as merely narrative or
images alone. Each new score provides new and imaginative contexts for old themes, as well as adding to the "musical tapestry,"
as Williams phrases it. It would be difficult to argue that the reuse of Williams's "force theme" in a new *Star Wars* film was somehow unimaginative in the same way that some have suggested the
similarities in plot between the films is: it is simply part of the *Star
Wars* landscape. In fact, as Cooke argues, Williams's "adherence to
a leitmotivic manner of construction offered considerable practical
benefits when recycling music for sequels."[16] In other words, the
style of music being used here means that repeating and developing
previously established ideas is not just completely normal but entirely productive for the mode of music making at work. This is true
to the point that a hypothetical new *Star Wars* score constructed out
of entirely new thematic material would struggle to make any sense.
Could it really be so different for the narrative ideas and imagery of
these films?

None of this is to say that the music for *The Force Awakens* was
universally praised on release. Williams's seventh *Star Wars* score
was often mentioned briefly in reviews as being "familiar" or "welcome," or other such synonyms that suggest that the score registered in the minds of reviewers only long enough to note that it
was reliably good. More dedicated reviewers, however, often noted
that *The Force Awakens*, while good, was perhaps not up to the lofty
Williams *Star Wars* standard. "The fact is that this score is not even
close to the classic trilogy and it struggles with the prequel trilogy as
well," wrote a reviewer for *Soundtrack Geek*.[17] *Gizmodo* equally noted
that some of the "lack of awe towards the Force in the movie could
be down to John Williams's music, which is great but never has
any of the 'wonder' moments" of the original trilogy.[18] Alex Ross
in the *New Yorker*, meanwhile, notes that "deft as the new score is, it
mirrors the déjà vu of the entire *Star Wars* experience."[19] *The Force
Awakens* secured Williams his fiftieth Academy Award nomination

(the most of any living person, and second of all time only behind Walt Disney), though he eventually lost to Ennio Morricone for *The Hateful Eight*.

By almost any measure, some of the most successful American film music of the twentieth century was written by Williams for the *Star Wars* films, and so *The Force Awakens* was always going to have a high standard to meet. Certainly, it is also true that the melodic material is probably less immediately memorable than, say, "the Imperial march or "the force theme." The major new melodies— "Rey's theme," "The March of the Resistance," and the motivic material for Kylo Ren—all work well as new entries into the *Star Wars* musical galaxy, but this is a universe already replete with shining, bright stars.

However, what these musical themes might lack for the first-time listener, they make up in complexity. Perhaps this reflects both Williams's ability to reflect the nature of each *Star Wars* film, as well as his multiple decades spent composing for the franchise. Indeed, much of the surprising musical strength of *The Force Awakens* can be summed up by just one theme: "The March of the Resistance." This music, used to represent the film's heroes in general, is a theme that, for a *Star Wars* film, clearly defies expectations. The heroic music from both the original and prequel trilogies was bold, brassy, and designed to be perfectly memorable. The Rebel Alliance fanfare from the original trilogy, for example, is bouncy and joyful, and is used to complete the end credits suite of each of the original trilogy as well as more recently becoming the musical theme for the animated *Rebels* series. It is likely for many the most cheerful and optimistic theme from any of the films: its "dah-dah, dah / dah-dah, dah" trumpet peal is irresistibly triumphant.

"The March of the Resistance," however, as the music for our new generation of heroes, is by contrast ambiguous and opaque. Unlike the Rebel Alliance fanfare, "The March of the Resistance" never quite lets the audience rejoice in the knowledge that this is the call-sign, the brand, of the team we're cheering for. It's dashing, determined music, certainly, but it's hardly a fanfare of any description. Where the Rebel Alliance is jubilant and thrilling, "The March of the Resistance" is resolute and obdurate instead.

Perhaps most surprisingly of all, "The March of the Resistance" is in fact musically speaking not a march at all: it is, instead, a fugue.[20] The fugue is hardly the first choice of musical technique for today's action adventure films: it is something that had its heyday in the baroque era, when composers like J. S. Bach were making music. The different tone that "The March of the Resistance" conveys makes more sense in this light, as the fugue is not quite a joyous style of music but instead considered, thoughtful, and even intellectual. Based on repetition and contrast, the fugue takes a melody and twists it, alters it, and represents it in an impossibly different number of ways over its duration. It does this by playing it against itself through different voices. Maybe they're literal voices, in a choir, or maybe they're oboe, trombone, and cello, all working in counterpoint together. Sometimes the melody is played backward, forward, in adjacent keys, in transpositions. Sometimes new material is introduced against it. You can see why it's not commonly used today: it's the kind of music that needs a puzzler's mind, someone who can write a Möbius strip of a melody.

Williams has in fact used fugues before, and *The Force Awakens* is not his first use of the form. Probably the best-known instance is in his score for *Jaws*, where he uses a fugue in the strings to underscore the gravity of the shark chase at the end ("The Shark Cage Fugue"). It's a clever piece of music in a clever score; Williams uses the complexity of the music to create gut-churning suspense that offsets the simplicity of his famous "duh-duh" two-note shark motif. Cooke talks about how the fugue has been used, particularly by Hollywood composers, to suggest industriousness, productivity, or pursuit, but that "the idea extends back to a wide range of classical music from the baroque to the romantic era, where fugues might be used to suggest conflict, as in a battle sequence from Giuseppe Verdi's *Macbeth* cited by Sergei Eisenstein. Miklós Rósza admitted that he often scored chase scenes in a fugal manner, noting that the Latin word *fuga* means flight."[21]

It's still a little odd to discover a fugue in an action blockbuster in 2015. The technique, while certainly not unprecedented, has more of a grounding in Hollywood golden age film music than in contemporary science fiction. Beyond Williams's own use of the fugue (which had mostly diminished by the 2000s following his use of it in *Jaws, Close Encounters,* and *Home Alone*) and a few stand-alone pieces by other composers,[22] the technique had more or less disappeared from contemporary film music. In other words, while having a fugue turn up in *The Force Awakens* was not groundbreaking, it certainly was a little old-fashioned, even anachronistic.

So why choose a fugue for our heroes in *The Force Awakens?*

SERIALITY AND *STAR WARS*

The answer lies, in part, in how *Star Wars* works as a franchise and the new directions that *The Force Awakens* pushes it in. If *The Force Awakens* is a film that takes delight in re-presenting old material in different contexts and new arrangements, then a fugue is its perfect match. Remember: this is a musical form that is constructed around repetition and surprise. A fugue begins with a statement of a melody and then matches it with its alteration. We hear a new melody in counterpoint, and an old melody return. New, old, new, old, new, old. This is how the fugue works: it is about presenting established material in inventive ways.

As I've shown, the *Star Wars* films have always been films in conversation with other films. The original film was the product of a cataloguer's mind of film history, embracing everything from serials like *Flash Gordon* to war films like *The Dam Busters,* to Kurosawa samurai films like *The Hidden Fortress,* to westerns like *The Searchers.* The prequel trilogy continued many of these obsessions while attempting, in their own way, to respond to the criticisms of the original films' political legacy. In another way, these have always been films made in response to other films.

The Force Awakens also drew much of its strength—and criticism—by performing the same maneuver. This time, however, the cultural touchstones weren't mined from a cinephiliac history but from the *Star Wars* franchise itself. Yet there are a number of complicating factors—primarily in the politics of casting—that make *The Force Awakens* genuinely new, as well. Rey, as a woman protagonist, and a woman who doesn't need to be saved, and who is clearly more capable than anyone else around her, is in many ways a new development for *Star Wars.* Finn, as a deserting Stormtrooper, and a character who begins his character arc by changing allegiances, is also genuinely new for *Star Wars*. The set of fraught parental relationships introduced in *The Force Awakens* also echoes the original series and its core familial drama, but also sets up an entirely new story to tell: one of a fallen, patricidal child taking up arms against his heroic parents. By inverting the question of legacies and generational conflict, *The Force Awakens* takes the dramatic material that fans were familiar with and renders it new again. Novel narrative possibilities are opened up by returning to older patterns.

When discussing the points of similarities and divergence, it is also worth thinking about the more unexpected echoes of the original trilogy, too. Indeed, it is worth mentioning the emotional, tone-based similarities that *The Force Awakens* shares with *A New Hope* in particular. In 1977, the first *Star Wars* film was unusual in its relatively uncomplicated character relationships and general positivity. Leia, Luke, and Han quickly become comrades-in-arms, and despite Han's cynicism and Luke and Leia's misgivings about his loyalty, the three generally seem to enjoy each other's company and come to rely on each other in the first film alone. This was out of keeping with the more generally pessimistic worlds that dominated Hollywood cinema in the 1970s and that were a hallmark of that era of filmmaking. Think here of films like *The Graduate* (dir. Mike Nichols, 1967), which thematizes suburban middle-class ennui, or *Midnight Cowboy*'s (dir. John Schlesinger, 1969) discussion of sex work, drugs, and poverty. Lucas chose to push against that mode of moviemaking: "We also know, as every movie made in the last ten years points out, how terrible we are, how we have ruined the world and what schmucks we are and how rotten everything is. And I said, what we really need is something more positive."[23] Lucas specifically wanted to create a film that reintroduced "fairy tales" to popular media and rejected the trend of cynical, "social realist" filmmaking that was popular at the time. "Once I got into *Star Wars*, it struck me that we had lost all that—a whole generation has grown up without fairy tales."[24] Part of Lucas's agenda, then, manifested itself in the generally happy-go-lucky and friendly characters who drove the narrative of *Star Wars*: such positivity and hope was in many respects old-fashioned in 1977.

In many ways, the same is true of *The Force Awakens*. There is even less cynicism in the fast friendship that Rey, Finn, and Poe strike up than in the original trio's comradery: though Rey and Poe actually never meet over the course of the film (something awkwardly resolved in *The Last Jedi*), the independent relationships that are forged are genuine and uncomplicatedly positive. Poe Dameron, though briefly skeptical of Finn's self-interest in rescuing him, nonetheless happily gives him a name (instead of the FN-2187 designation he receives from the First Order) and befriends him. Later in the film, the pair greet each other so happily at the Resistance Base that it would inspire those widespread fan hopes that they might become a couple ("I was playing romance"). Finn and Rey, meanwhile, despite some initial mistrust surrounding Finn's ruse about being a Resistance member, form a quick bond, and affectionately babble together after their first victory in the Millennium Falcon early in the film. The final battle against Kylo Ren, also, is clearly as much motivated by their need to protect and support each other than the need to avenge Han Solo. Even the aged and sardonic Han himself seems to be genuinely moved by Rey and Finn over the course of *The Force Awakens*.

All this positivity seems somehow even more out of place in the Hollywood landscape of 2015 than it did in 1977. Though the kinds of films and mode of filmmaking that were dominant in 1977 are very different to those of 2015, sincere, naive positivity is similarly absent. This is a filmic landscape whose megahits largely consist of superheroes who "enact painful retribution against evildoers, just as the U.S. military attempted to punish the Taliban and al Qaeda," as Tom Pollard puts it.[25] It is difficult to name many high-profile films or franchises released around the same period as *The Force Awakens* that feature heroic characters who get along and genuinely like each other. The heroes of the Marvel Cinematic Universe, for instance, seem predicated on fractious allegiances that fuel narrative conflict, while the DC Comics universe films seem even more deeply mired in cynicism and masculine posturing. By contrast, *The Force Awakens*' positive tone and genuine friendships are a throwback to another era of filmmaking as much as any other nostalgic strategy.

This is the other way of thinking about *The Force Awakens* as a remix, or remake, or however the critics featured in chapter 3 would prefer to render it. *The Force Awakens* works by balancing the new and the reworked with the old and the referential. This is the pattern for this first post-Lucas *Star Wars* film: new stories, new material, and new characters, all clearly framed by the constant repetition of old ideas, old plot devices, and old characters. New, old, new, old. In the rush to identify the obvious similarities between *The Force Awakens* and the earlier *Star Wars* films, perhaps this was the missed point. It is not just that *The Force Awakens* consciously borrows older, reliably successful material, but that it does so by reworking the material and rearticulating it in new contexts and alongside newer themes. This is the filmic equivalent of a fugue. Williams's otherwise somewhat perplexing inclusion of one in a prominent place on the soundtrack actually provides us with a blueprint for understanding the film.

THE HOMESTEAD BURNS AGAIN

The differences in understanding how seriality works in *The Force Awakens* comes down to one key distinction: restatement is not the same as recapitulation. Reinserting familiar material in a new context is not necessarily the same as regurgitating it without thought or contemplation. Instead, repetition can be a meaningful and even deep strategy.

This also has context in the music of *The Force Awakens*, even beyond the fugue. In perhaps the film's most pivotal moment—where Rey uses the force to draw Luke Skywalker's lightsaber before Kylo Ren does—the music provides us with an instance of direct series memory. Though original music was written by Williams for this scene and left unused, the moment the lightsaber hits Rey's hands provides us with a highly unusual moment of tracked music in *Star Wars*, where a recording from a previous film is directly copied into the soundtrack. This music has not been rerecorded or orchestrated—the performance we hear in *The Force Awakens* is one from several decades ago. Why choose this scene to directly musically recall another moment from the *Star Wars* franchise? The answer tells us a lot about the mode of seriality at work.

Significantly, here, the music in question is a rendition of "the force theme" taken from the first *Star Wars* film's score. It is the track

Rey draws the lightsaber in *The Force Awakens*.

"Burning Homestead," where Luke returns to his family home to discover his aunt and uncle murdered at the hands of the Empire. There is perhaps no bigger moment of foreshadowed destiny in any of the *Star Wars* films. The death of Luke's guardians simultaneously provides him with a personal reason to fight the Empire and also the autonomy to do it with. It is the moment where he outgrows the farmboy persona and opens himself to becoming a future Jedi Knight and savior of the galaxy. This kind of moment is key to the entire appeal of the *Star Wars* films—in the commentary track for *THX 1138* Lucas himself suggests that the thematic basis for all his films is "this issue of leaving a safe environment and going into the unknown."[26] In a similar vein, we could point to the Campbellian monomyth-inspired readings of *Star Wars* (including "The Call to Adventure," where the everyday hero is presented with a quest). Campbell was indeed influential for *Star Wars*, but more so for the sequels, as his writings were discovered by Lucas only late in the making of the first film. Yet the homestead moment is perhaps the clearest narrative beat that fits the Campbellian worldview: although moments earlier, Luke had performed "The Refusal of the Call" (another monomyth stage) by opting to stay on Tatooine out of obligation to his uncle, the burning of the homestead frees him of this debt and allows him to pursue adventure. The boy leaves his hometown and goes into the unknown. The hero accepts his calling.

The theme of fate in this scene is boldly reinforced by the music.

Though the most prominent musical theme at work in the "Burn-ing Homestead" cue is the famous "force theme" played by the strings, another, much older musical idea plays alongside it. These are the eight steady, punctuating brass notes at the end of the scene, sounding a clarion call, like the tolling bells that draw the Templar Knights to the Grail ceremony in Richard Wagner's *Parsifal*. This is what is known as the "Dies Irae" ("Day of Wrath") melody. This is a musical idea dating back to a hymn from the Middle Ages that has been repeatedly quoted by composers from Hector Berlioz to Franz Liszt to Holst, usually to indicate a sense of doom or fate. It is, for the music historian Robin Gregory, "one of the oldest and most frequently borrowed of all melodies,"[27] and it not infrequently turns up in film music. Musical quotation of this kind more broadly is a tradition associated with composers of the Romantic period. For Philip Kepler, a professor of music in the 1950s, it is a technique with "a flavour of intellectual appeal," and a "predilection to associ-ate a musical work with events outside itself."[28] The "Dies Irae" is therefore a musical tradition in its own right: as something passed from composer to composer, it becomes a recombinant gesture to-ward history, multiplying with each invocation.

In the *Star Wars* series, the "Dies Irae" melody is used several times (particularly in the prequels), but never more prominently or precisely than in the "Burning Homestead" scene. Here, this centuries-old melody of doom underscores the turning fates moment of Luke embracing his destiny, as well as the tragedy of the murder of his aunt and uncle. It serves as a musical sign both of death and of providence, set against Williams's major spiritual melody of the series in "the force theme." There is a sense that the world of *Star Wars* shifts on the playing of this music: it is the moment when the story becomes about Skywalker.

The direct reuse of this music in *The Force Awakens* presents an irresistible echo of this idea. In many ways, this music draws at-tention to just how thematically similar these moments in fact are. Although Rey has for most of the film enthusiastically embraced a heroic role, the drawing of the lightsaber clearly marks her out at the film's climax as a kind of fated savior, similarly to Luke in the first film. Earlier in *The Force Awakens*, Rey triggers a traumatic flashback sequence by picking up Luke's blue lightsaber that he lost at the end of *The Empire Strikes Back*. In this, what Abrams describes as the "forceback" sequence, Rey witnesses the slaughter of the Jedi academy at the hands of Kylo Ren and her own abandonment on Jakku, as well as some more incoherent memories that neither she nor the audience comprehends. After this unwanted nightmare, she swears that she's "never touching that thing again," in a clear echo of Campbell's "Refusal of the Call" monomyth stage. In the same way that Luke feels obliged to his uncle on Tatooine, Rey feels that she has a responsibility to wait for her parents to return and find her on Jakku. She cannot be the hero yet.

Accordingly, Rey's climactic drawing of the lightsaber to fight Kylo Ren is decisive. By using the weapon she had earlier vowed to never touch again, she accepts her central role in the narrative and her abilities to use the force. It is a turning fates moment of embraced destinies, just as it is with Luke's aunt and uncle in *A New Hope*. Accordingly, the direct reuse of the "Burning Homestead" cue, including the "Dies Irae" quotation, reveals multiple levels of meaning making through repetition, and a framework for understanding *The Force Awakens* itself as a franchise film. (And indeed, it is worth briefly noting the similarities between one section[29] of Rey's theme and the "Dies Irae.") Here, we can see at least three forms of citation going on: a citation of the "embrace of the call" heroic narrative moment between generations of *Star Wars* heroes, as Luke and Rey accept their place in the larger world; a citation of the Williams composition that is repeated across both scenes; and a citation of this specific "Dies Irae" invocation, and also the centuries-old tradition of the "Dies Irae" along with it.

Indeed, the "Dies Irae" itself provides an alternative logic for what we're talking about when we talk about *The Force Awakens* as a film in conversation with other *Star Wars* films. If the "Dies Irae" as a musical tradition acts as a recombinant gesture toward history, then we might read some of *The Force Awakens*' conscious points of resemblance to previous *Star Wars* films through a similar light. Through this lens, perhaps the points of similarity in *The Force Awakens* aren't simply an easy recycling of successful material as some critics have claimed, but are instead instances of familiarity that develop with each restatement. As with the "Dies Irae," each restatement develops the tradition as a whole, prompting an informed audience to consider each instance in relation to the series.

If the drawing of the lightsabers can be directly compared to the "Burning Homestead," then the use of BB-8 to smuggle information from the First Order can be directly compared to R2-D2 and the Death Star plans, the Starkiller Base can be directly compared to the Death Star, and so on and so on. This is not incidental or by mistake: confronting these resemblances directly is much more interesting than assuming they are the errors of a stagnant homage. Like the musical ideas at the heart of *The Force Awakens*, each point of similarity builds in aggregate. It does not point to simple-minded repetition but instead to the integrity of the whole.

Such an understanding of the *Star Wars* films requires a different framework of seriality than perhaps we are used to. Indeed, even from the first film, the *Star Wars* franchise pushed seriality as a narrative form not just by beginning in media res but by including text that introduces events not depicted on-screen until decades after with *Rogue One*. What started as a nostalgic homage to the B-movie serials of Hollywood's past has become a complex model for contemporary franchise building. In arguing for the differences between what she describes as the oppositional forms of the "classical" and the "baroque," Angela Ndalianis actually draws on *Star Wars* in particular as an ideal example of the latter.[30] The series' obfuscated beginnings and ends (which have subsequently grown even more complex than when Ndalianis was writing in 2004) and ever-expanding narrative time connect with the baroque fascination for testing the boundaries of art. In a similar way that a baroque trompe l'oeil, or a large-scale basilica ceiling painting, deliberately blurs the threshold between our world and that of representation, *Star Wars* suggests a fictional world with dilating narrative events instead of a fixed and linear traditional narrative structure.

For *Star Wars*, serial narrative spills outward instead of in a singular trajectory. Seriality, under this logic, "relates to the copy that seeks to reproduce, multiply, or allude to versions of an 'original,'" says Ndalianis.[31] From this perspective, *The Force Awakens* cannot be understood as a discrete text that has the power to make meaning in a classical model more interested in characterization, continuity, and closure. As a film, *The Force Awakens* was never intended to be seen by an audience as an isolated work, but was instead heavily framed by the legacies of each previous film. In a franchise like *Star Wars*, meaning is dispersed across multiple entries and on multiple levels. That there are similarities across films is not a weakness: it is entirely the point.

Not only is *The Force Awakens* partly constituted by the legacy of all other *Star Wars* films, but even individual scenes, characters, and themes are part of a dialogue with others that are peppered across all eight films. The insertion of the "Burning Homestead" music in *The Force Awakens* directly acknowledges this and underscores the point being made at a deep, series-level plane. To write off moments of citation such as these as simple plagiarism or a lack of originality is to misunderstand *The Force Awakens* entirely and to misjudge the mode of storytelling at work in the *Star Wars* franchise.

This, of course, has implications for how nostalgia works in *Star Wars* as well as for its seriality. As I suggested in chapter 2, *The Force Awakens* in particular clearly attempted to evoke a sense of nostalgia for the original *Star Wars* trilogy in its marketing. It would be obvious to point to a similar process at work in the film itself, where the nostalgia for the B-movie serial and all the myriad of *Star Wars'* influences is replaced by nostalgia for *Star Wars* itself. But as I've shown in this chapter, it is not quite as simple as all that (and indeed, perhaps nostalgia is never as straightforward as its critics would have it). Certainly, nostalgia for the original series is being performed here, but it is complicated by the mode of seriality at work.

As we see with both the fugue and the "Burning Homestead" cue, as *Star Wars* memories are recalled in *The Force Awakens*, they are simultaneously rewritten and revised. When we are dealing with meaning created via the aesthetics of repetition, nostalgia must necessarily function differently. In describing the replicant robots of *Blade Runner*, Omar Calabrese talks about how the copy may eventually appear to be better than the original. *Blade Runner's* villainous replicant Roy Batty is autonomous and in many ways improved from the human original (in terms of strength and stamina, for example). "But their own perfection produces, in a more or

less involuntary way, an aesthetic: specifically, an aesthetic of repetition," Calabrese writes.[32] Such iteration implies steady improvement as well as duplication.

Could *The Force Awakens* be better than *Star Wars*? It "would
be held up as untouchable had it come first," wrote Christopher
Hooten in his review of the film in the *Independent*.[33] Perhaps in many
ways this is true: *The Force Awakens* by today's standards moves more
quickly, has better special effects, more developed and original
characters, and contains significantly better gender and racial representation than the original film. How can we hold up this film as
simple nostalgia for the original when in many respects, like Roy
Batty, it has exceeded it?

This is the aesthetic of repetition at work that precludes simple
understandings of nostalgia. We can think of *The Force Awakens* in
some respects as a serial television show from years past, like *The
Brady Bunch* or *Law & Order* or *Columbo*: the goal is not necessarily to
extend or build on the last episode's narrative (though that may also
happen) but to repeat the thrills it provided to the point where the
viewer forgets last week's episode entirely. "The trick," Calabrese
writes, "consists in the extremely subtle variation—at an iconic, thematic, and narrative level . . . in which Columbo is able to beat his
adversary at his own game."[34] The point is not the beginning or the
end of the overarching series but the arrangement of the familiar
patterns within each episode and their interaction with repetition,
variation, and newness.

Now, of course, *Star Wars* as a series lays some sort of claim to
the significance of an overarching story—that of the Skywalker clan,
from Anakin to Luke and Leia, to Kylo Ren and possibly others.
There are necessarily articulation points and discrete sections that
can be marked off as broadly tracing a more familiar classical narrative where closure is to a certain extent provided. The Death Star
is blown up in *Star Wars*. The Emperor is defeated and Darth Vader
redeemed in *Return of the Jedi*. But, a film like *The Force Awakens*,
whose function in the series is to reopen narrative end points (what
happened to Luke after Darth Vader's death? What happened to
Leia and Han after the fall of the Empire? Did the Jedi in fact return?) cannot be understood in isolation in any real sense. This is

even more clear when thinking about the legacy of the prequels and the unease surrounding the sale of Lucasfilm to Disney that *The Force Awakens* needed to confront. As a commercial product, more than any other film in the *Star Wars* series, *The Force Awakens* is designed to be viewed as a replicant: recalling the originals, yet better than the copies that have gone before it. Nostalgia has an important role here, certainly—but it is not a simple one by any means.

THE RETURN

Let's conclude by making a return of our own to the music of *The Force Awakens*. That this logic of recombining the new with the old was intentional—to say nothing of its illuminating power over the serial mode of the entire film—is made stunningly clear by Williams in his almost final notes for the film. This, a short and quiet musical section toward the dying moments of the end credits suite, is perhaps most breathtaking moment of the whole *Force Awakens* soundtrack. Listening from 7:28 on the official soundtrack, Williams gives us "the force theme" on French horn, the most frequently played theme from all six previous *Star Wars* films, and perhaps the most emblematic of its various musical identities.

This performance of "the force theme" is different: Williams brilliantly merges it, in the style of a fugue, perhaps, with "Rey's theme," the most prominent of *The Force Awakens'* new melodies. The two augment each other in ways that I had previously not imagined—after being played almost simultaneously, they call and answer each other, perform one phrase from "the force theme," and one in turn from "Rey's theme." Williams reveals his greatest trick for *The Force Awakens*: hidden in plain sight, this new musical idea for the post-Lucas era is in fact completely compatible with the old, even when played over the top of each other. He has been using the same musical language in new and interesting ways, even if we never noticed it directly. He has, as he says, been simply adding to his "musical tapestry."

This final musical puzzle is old and new together. This is one of *Star Wars'* most iconic musical ideas being delicately interwoven with its newest. By presenting both in the context of each other, each is somehow lifted beyond its usual significance. This is, of course, also how *The Force Awakens* itself works. It presents us with a thoughtful and complex model of franchise extension: one based in repetition, seriality, and a nuanced understanding of nostalgia. Yet again the film's logic is encapsulated by Williams's music.

If perhaps we thought this subtle musical repetition, along with the Resistance fugue, was a one-off idea for the new generation of *Star Wars* films, it is worth turning our attention briefly to the score for the first non-Williams *Star Wars* film: *Rogue One*. I examine this film in detail in the next few chapters. But for the topic of music, for this film, for the first time, new composer Michael Giacchino was called on to create a modern, Williams-inflected sound for the first of the non-"saga" *Star Wars* installments. In doing so, Giacchino mined the original trilogy's scores relentlessly, inserting reference to "the force theme," "Princess Leia's theme," the Imperial motif, the Death Star motif, and of course, "the Imperial march," along with his own melodies for the new characters and locations.

Yet interestingly, none of this material comes to the fore in the only track named after the film on the official soundtrack album, "Rogue One" (track 12). Instead, we get a fugue, of course. Not just any fugue—this one clearly and deliberately refers to Williams's "Shark Cage Fugue" from *Jaws*, of all things. Perhaps the suggestion was that returning to a mid-1970s Williams sound more broadly would be ideal for this film that leads directly into the opening moments of 1977's *Star Wars*. That, in many respects, makes a lot of sense.

But I like to think that it was more about something else. Giacchino was a composer fresh to the franchise. For him to also resurrect this somewhat underused, out-of-fashion musical idea for yet another *Star Wars* film relying heavily on complicated uses of nostalgia and seriality implies some thought. Perhaps, while taking in Williams's *Star Wars* music, perhaps, while watching *The Force Awakens*—perhaps, Giacchino was listening to the fugue too.[35]

6

YOU HAVE TO START SOMEWHERE

Contrasting Nostalgias in
The Force Awakens *and* Rogue One

We can now fast-forward to December 2016, the moment a second new *Star Wars* film came into view on the horizon. In some ways, *Rogue One: A Star Wars Story* was to be more important to Disney's designs for *Star Wars* than *The Force Awakens*—and it certainly faced an array of different, and in many ways more complex, expectations. Audiences were always going to have curiosity about the future of the Skywalker saga, and selling *The Force Awakens* as the latest adventures of their old friends Luke, Leia, and Han was not going to end up a complete failure. But with *Rogue One,* Disney were showing its hand for a dramatically expanded *Star Wars* franchise that would launch a new film every year for the foreseeable future while also telling new and divergent stories. Though the *Star Wars* franchise had always meandered through its own canon with books, novels, and video games, never before had a major cinematic release so clearly left the Skywalkers—and the "saga"—behind to look elsewhere in the galaxy. *Star Wars,*

133

in Disney's *Rogue One*–tinted vision, was to be a rival for their own Marvel films: an annual, multipronged franchise with intersecting and complex moving parts. *Rogue One* was a new story, with an almost entirely new cast of characters and one stratospheric remit: to open up new narrative space for *Star Wars* to become what *Wired* magazine described as "the forever franchise." "If everything works out for Disney, and if you are (like me) old enough to have been conscious for the first Star Wars film," wrote Adam Rogers, "you will probably not live to see the last one."[1]

Yet for all the fanfare *Rogue One* received for being new and divergent, its heart couldn't be closer to the beginnings of the franchise. In telling the story of the theft of the Death Star plans, *Rogue One* literally took inspiration from the first film's opening crawl, where we learn that "Rebel spies" have "managed to steal secret plans to the Emperor's ultimate weapon, the Death Star." This was an idea not from the Lucasfilm Story Group or Kathleen Kennedy but from John Knoll, ILM visual effects supervisor and a Photoshop co-creator who had previously attached the idea to George Lucas's planned (and never made) live-action television series following the release of *Revenge of the Sith* in 2005.[2] The idea for nonsaga, "standalone" films was always part of Lucas's sale to Disney, too, and was the topic of one of the first conversations Kennedy had when she joined the company. "George talked to me about doing this when I first came aboard," Kennedy said. "He had often thought about doing it and he had actually written down three or four thoughts and ideas, directions you could go."[3] When Knoll heard that Kennedy was looking for new ideas beyond the Skywalker saga, he pitched it for a second time. "If I don't," reflected Knoll, "I'll always wonder what might've happened if I had."[4] The idea was rapidly earmarked as the first candidate for the stand-alone film strategy as a kind of Episode 3.5. *Star Wars* would begin its wandering away from the Skywalkers very close to home.

In some ways, what most clearly sets *Rogue One* apart from the saga films is its tone. It is a desperate and grim war movie focused on the heist of the Death Star plans. Like many of the World War II films that inspired it—*The Dirty Dozen, The Guns of Navarone, The Eagle Has Landed*—it is an ensemble film with characters who are distinguished more by archetype than by detail or development: the criminal (Jyn Erso), the spy (Cassian Andor), the pilot (Bodhi Rook), the monk (Chirrut Îmwe), the mercenary (Baze Malbus), and the soldier (K-2SO). Though there are moments of levity in *Rogue One*—particularly in the guise of K-2SO, the cynical, dry-witted droid—unlike other *Star Wars* films these moments are used to balance out the otherwise dour tone. *Rogue One* is not a happy film, and the way it eventually dispatches its ensemble cast, death after death, is another uncharacteristic element for the *Star Wars* films, which usually contains its major character deaths to just one or two per film. Even the apocalyptic *Revenge of the Sith* only kills off four major characters (Padmé Amidala, Count Dooku, General Grievous, and Mace Windu): the bloodthirsty *Rogue One*, on the other hand, not only features the deaths of all six of its main ensemble listed earlier but also Galen Erso, Saw Gerrera, and Orson Krennic. The idea, evidently, was that *Rogue One* was a test of which directions the tone of *Star Wars* could be effectively pushed. "*Star Wars* is its own genre," Lawrence Kasdan, screenwriter for *The Force Awakens* and *Solo*, told *Wired* in 2015. "For that reason, like all genre it can hold a million different kinds of artists and stories. . . . It can be anything you want it to be."[5] In Disney's eyes, *Rogue One* was the initial statement in a broader declaration that *Star Wars* could be more than just an adventure serial: it could be a heist movie, or a gangster film, perhaps even a romance or a comedy. As a "forever franchise," with an annual release schedule to rival Marvel, *Star Wars* would have to match that franchise's breadth of tone and style. *Rogue One* was the proof of concept.

Nonetheless, and possibly mindful of the "remake" criticism faced by *The Force Awakens*, the marketing tone of *Rogue One* was careful to highlight the newness among the familiar. "We're making a film that's right [next to and] touching my favourite movie of all time," said *Rogue One* director Gareth Edwards in a promotional reel for the film. "But then if you're too respectful of it that you daren't do anything new or different, or take a risk, then what are you bringing to the table?"[6] Certainly, there were a lot of elements—even purely on a stylistic level—from *Rogue One* that were new to the *Star Wars* universe. A significant amount of the film, for example, is shot in handheld Steadicam-style, giving the film an on-the-spot, eyewitness effect in its combat sequences that differs from the Lucas-era films' visual stability and formal composition. Also new to *Star Wars* is the use of title cards to announce each new planet, of which there are a great many, including the research planet Eadu, the religious warzone of Jedha, the hiding spot for the family Erso on Lah'mu, the Imperial data center on Scarif, and the prison colony on Wobani.

Traditional *Star Wars* elements, Kennedy flagged, "may be pretty spare for this first [stand-alone film]."[7] This was compounded by Edwards's unusual filming style. His previous work had been the independent, low-budget sci-fi horror film *Monsters* (2010), where he served as director, writer, cinematographer, and visual effects artist, and the blockbuster *Godzilla* (2014), which was not just a reboot of the Toho *Godzilla* franchise but also the first film in the Legendary Pictures' MonsterVerse. For *Rogue One,* Edwards created his own unusual filmmaking practices for a high-budget blockbuster, including the daily tradition of what Edwards calls "Indie Hour," where unplanned and unscripted shots would be improvised by the cast and crew. This also explains why a number of shots used in the *Rogue One* trailers were infamously not in the feature film: "It would just be things I thought were a beautiful moment or 'This is a great idea,' and a lot of the stuff in the trailer ended up through that process," said Edwards.[8] A number of reshoots were required for *Rogue One* and were supervised by the veteran director Tony Gilroy, an early indication of Kennedy's unshrinking attitude toward taking decisive action to get the quality of *Star Wars* films required (after the firing of the director Josh Trank from another stand-alone *Star Wars* film, and before the midproduction firing of the directors Phil Lord and Christopher Miller from *Solo: A Star Wars Story*).

Similarly, though a small number of familiar characters appear in *Rogue One,* the film's core cast are entirely new. Two of these new characters—Chirrut Îmwe and Baze Malbus, two members of the force-worshipping Guardians of the Whills—illuminate another contemporary conundrum (possibly the biggest, financially and industrially) for *Star Wars*. As a franchise, *Star Wars* has never been popular in China: the original trilogy was never screened in theaters because of the long-standing ban on Western cinema dating from the Cultural Revolution, and so Chinese audiences largely don't possess the same widespread cultural nostalgia for the films. Today, however, the Chinese film market is the second biggest in the world and is fast encroaching on American box office dominance: it is a prime target for film corporations wanting to break international box office records. "Hollywood is increasingly building its products in China and for the Chinese market first," writes the media researcher Aynne Kokas.[9] Without built-in *Star Wars* nostalgia and intergenerational transferral among its Chinese audience, Lucasfilm and Disney embarked on a massive publicity campaign to promote *The Force Awakens*, including staging five hundred Imperial Stormtroopers on the Great Wall and getting Chinese pop megastar Lu Han to release a promotional song ("The Force Inside").[10] Ticket sales for *The Force Awakens* were nonetheless below expectations, with the film performing less successfully than other major Hollywood films in China in 2015, including *Furious 7, Avengers: Age of Ultron,* and *Jurassic World.*[11]

Accordingly, as Churrit and Baze, *Rogue One* featured Chinese megastars Donnie Yen and Jiang Wen and heavily used the two actors in the local promotional campaigns. The inclusion of two Chinese actors whose primary fame was in mainland China (Yen had some international success with Zhang Yimou's *Hero* in 2002 and Wilson Yip's *Ip Man* in 2008) was a point of discussion leading up to the film's release for several reasons. For Edwards, speaking publicly days before *Rogue One*'s release, "It feels right that there'd be Asian characters in *Star Wars*, because it's got such Asian influences. And because it's *Star Wars*, you can kind of go for anyone: 'Who are the best Asian actors in the world?'" Edwards said.

Yet it seems unlikely that the inclusion of two local stars in *Star Wars*' most challenging market was done for purely aesthetic or politically liberal reasons. "This is a longer term play," said the editor of the trade publication *China Film Insider,* Jonathan Landreth, at the time. "[Disney is] hoping to prime the pumps."[12] Making overtures to the Chinese audience was not necessarily groundbreaking for American blockbusters. *X-Men: Days of Future Past* (2014) cast Fan Bingbing, while *Independence Day: Resurgence* (2016) featured the actress Angelababy; even *Last Jedi* director Rian Johnson's *Looper*

(2012) included expanded sequences set in Shanghai used exclusively for the Chinese release. The use of actors like Angelababy in minor, even negligible roles "left many in China feeling awkward," according to the *Chinese Global Times*, and received the cynicism from local audiences that they likely deserved.[13] In contrast, and although hardly protagonists, Churrit and Baze's roles in *Rogue One* are substantial: a fact emphasized by the film's local marketing. "As Chinese actors in *Rogue One,* we're not just there 'to get some soy oil,' " Donnie Yen says in a Chinese trailer, using slang that's roughly equivalent to mean they're not phoning it in.[14] Nonetheless, the whole endeavor was underscored by Jiang Wen's declaration that he had never actually seen a *Star Wars* film in his life: "I know nothing about them," he told *Empire* on the eve of *Rogue One*'s premiere.[15] In the end, *Rogue One* also failed to find a large audience in China—as would *The Last Jedi*, to an even more disastrous degree a year later. *Star Wars* continues to struggle in China.[16]

Yet perhaps the most widely discussed point of divergence for *Rogue One* from the rest of the *Star Wars* franchise was the lack of an opening crawl and John Williams fanfare, iconic elements of every other *Star Wars* film. Instead, *Rogue One* opens with a startling brass musical stab and a shot of space. The camera proceeds to pan up and the action begins. Kennedy and Edwards foregrounded well before the film's release that this was a deliberate stylistic decision intended to set the stand-alone films apart from the *Star Wars* saga. "The idea is this film is supposed to be different than the saga films," said Edwards. Yet Edwards also noted an irony in *Rogue One*'s removal of the key stylistic element that gave rise to it. "This film is born out of a crawl. The thing that inspired this movie was a crawl and what was written in that. There's this feeling that if we did a crawl, then it'll create another movie."[17] As it is, a few minutes into its running time, *Rogue One* uses a title card of the film's name retreating slowly into space to cut over the time lapse between Jyn Erso as a child and as an adult. Instead of the main Williams *Star Wars* fanfare to accompany this, we hear the composer Michael Giacchino's "hope theme"—a melody that shares the same opening interval and very similar phrasing to Williams's famous theme, yet is clearly not the same.

Similar, yet different: this is the prevailing logic of *Rogue One*. So what was *Star Wars* to become in the wake of this first stand-alone film? Reflecting on this question can tell us a lot not just about *Star Wars* and Disney but about the logic of franchise making in the mid-2010s.

Part of this relates to the idea of the shared universe, which was gaining momentum as a commercial model in Hollywood around the time of Disney's purchase of *Star Wars* thanks to the wild success of the Marvel Cinematic Universe. The shared universe is a coherent diegetic world that spans multiple media instances, characters, and settings. In the guise of the Marvel Cinematic Universe it began with *Iron Man* in 2008 and continued across different phases to encompass both crossover films (*The Avengers* in 2012) and television series (such as *Agent Carter* in 2015–16). For Martin Flanagan, Andrew Livingstone, and Mike McKenny, the shared universe is an idea that transferred "from the pages of comics to the big screen [and] must be regarded as a key moment of recent film history."[18] In the wake of Marvel's success, other studios attempted to build on its model, including Legendary Entertainment's MonsterVerse (including King Kong and Godzilla) and Universal Pictures' Dark Universe (which was to include Frankenstein and the Mummy). There was some expectation that *Star Wars* too would follow this model: though all previous *Star Wars* films had taken place within the same ongoing storyline, the prospect of the shared universe could allow films to be removed from a unified narrative progression and allowed to digress. Boba Fett might appear in the Han Solo film; a new character from the Han Solo film might turn up in Boba Fett's stand-alone adventure, maybe a *Rogue One* villain might return, and so on. "The shared universe represents something rare in Hollywood: a new idea," wrote Adam Rogers in *Wired*. "Marvel prototyped the process; Lucasfilm is trying to industrialize it."[19]

Nonetheless, and despite *Wired*'s breathless assessment, the shared universe is perhaps not quite so new after all—nor did Lucasfilm end up industrializing it in quite such a direct fashion. Even putting aside its uses in the comic book world, the shared universe found its feet in cinema as early as the 1930s and 1940s, with Universal Studios' revolving cast of "Universal Monsters." The first direct crossover film that made this shared universe explicit was *Frankenstein Meets the Wolf Man* from 1943, and this would continue with *House of Frankenstein* (1943), *House of Dracula* (1945), before finally entering the realm of crossover parody with *Abbott and Costello Meet Frankenstein* (1948). There is no small irony, then, in considering Universal's recent (and apparently failed) excursion into the shared universe model with the Dark Universe, as well as Legendary's Monster-Verse, as imitators of Marvel, considering that both Universal Monsters and Toho's Godzilla were early pioneers of this very model.

What was genuinely new for Hollywood about the Marvel Cinematic Universe, and what *Star Wars* actually had to contend with, was not the simple sharing of characters across multiple films. Instead, it was the assumption that a branching storyline would be explored via such an integrated, multifilm model. The forces that prompted this kind of assumption are many: *Star Wars* had been revived into an era of technological, economic, and audience complexity. Certainly, the rise of television and the shifts in narrative that accompanied it was one significant factor. Jason Mittel argues that television in recent years moved toward "narrative complexity" as a distinct narrational mode, as something that "redefines episodic forms under the influence of serial narration."[20] This is an aesthetic mode for television defined by unconventionality, a rejection of narrative closure within individual episodes, and a reliance on an engaged audience's ability to keep up. Similarly, Omar Calabrese identifies five key shifts in television storytelling over time, which begins with distinct episodes with common characters but no overall series goal (such as *I Love Lucy*) and culminates in a narrative form characterized by open, dynamic structures, multiple narrative centers, and continuing episodes in series time (found in *The Sopranos* or *The Wire*).[21] As a project built on the foundations of old 1940s adventure serials, and always interested in serial storytelling, *Star Wars* began life by re-empowering the sequel and building a cinematic narrative that spanned three films, a beginning, a middle, and an end. It seems only fitting that it should be revived in an era where compounded serial storytelling has evolved to the point where such a straightforward, forward-facing narrative should seem out-of-date.

Technology also plays a role in the narrative complexity that *Rogue One* was hoped to provide. Mittel argues that complex television was partly shaped by the shifting temporality of "collecting episodes into bound volumes of DVD box sets . . . as screen time becomes far more controllable and variable for viewers," as well as later, the practice of binge-watching on streaming services like Netflix.[22] Just as these technological changes in distribution shaped television narrative, it also resituates Disney's *Star Wars* films in relation to the rest of the saga, which is now never more than a DVD, a download, or a stream away. Even in the era of *The Phantom Menace*, comparing a lightsaber fight across films most likely meant finding the exact spot on a paused VHS tape. Today the same comparison can be achieved through a few seconds spent on Google Image search or YouTube. Ironically, for a series so interested in nostalgia, memory has in the new era of *Star Wars* become increasingly technologically enhanced.

Yet despite redefining *Star Wars* in the era of the cinematic shared universe, *Rogue One* did not open up narrative space for *Star Wars* to follow this model in any obvious way. In fact, leading up to the film's release, Kennedy seemed to suggest that the opposite was the priority. Far from forming overlapping individual films that would lead to an ongoing and ever-expanding series narrative, Kennedy argued that the strength of the *Star Wars* Story model was to make films that stood entirely by themselves. "I think that that's exciting for fans," Kennedy said. "It's certainly exciting as a filmmaker, the notion that we can explore these stories that genuinely have a beginning, middle and an end, and don't necessarily have to tie into something specific."[23] Ostensibly, *Star Wars* had once again gone against the prevailing wisdom of Hollywood franchise-making of the time: series narrative was out, and singular narrative was in. Similar, but different.

BACK TO THE *STAR WARS* FUTURE

Yet *Rogue One* was never going to be a complete departure for the franchise. *The Force Awakens* had signaled that nostalgia was a powerful tool for Disney's rejuvenation of the *Star Wars* franchise; it would hardly be thrown out with just the second film, even if *Rogue*

One was intended to function as a stand-alone endeavor. As a result, and enhanced by its narrative proximity to *A New Hope, Rogue One* contains an interesting approach to nostalgia that is both direct and modulated: it looks to revive the past by looking to the cutting edge; it takes us back in time by looking to the future.

Unlike the sequel trilogy, *Rogue One*'s time setting within the *Star Wars* universe prompts a kind of ambient nostalgic presence within even the production design alone: original Stormtroopers patrol planets, Red Squadron X-wings fly sorties in space, and the cast and extras exude a kind of carefully updated 1970s chic (moustaches abound). As with *The Force Awakens,* Ralph McQuarrie, the original *Star Wars* concept designer, was a significant influence on the look of *Rogue One.* Doug Chiang, Lucasfilm production designer, went so far as to describe McQuarrie as "our safety net" for *Rogue One*'s look, such was the importance of creating a visual tone for the film that would allow it to lead directly into *A New Hope.*[24] Indeed, the legibility and coherency of the visual regime of the *Star Wars* films has always been one of its major strengths. Will Brooker notes that, for *A New Hope,* "The briefest glimpse of a freeze-frame would instantly reveal, from its colour scheme, whose world we are in, whether cold monochrome or warm earth."[25] The rebels, Brooker points out, live in a world of dirt and trash, making do with whatever materials they have to hand, whereas the Imperials value pristine and polish above all, with smooth and full-metal surfaces dominating. Chiang reminds us how this aesthetic, created largely by McQuarrie's concept art, was carefully and deliberately filtered through to *Rogue One*: despite the many new locations and circumstances, the aesthetic stakes remain familiar. In *Rogue One,* as in *A New Hope,* the Empire's aesthetic is one of squares and circles and flat surfaces, in gray and black, with accents of red. The Rebels use compound and complex shapes, with more earthy colors. It is machine against organics, automaton against invention.

Nostalgia is as treacherous as memory, however, and one difficulty faced by *Rogue One* was the rose-tinted glasses imposed by *A New Hope*'s enormous cultural legacy. "When you actually go back and you look at the films, or you look at the designs, they're not quite as good as you remember them," said Gareth Edwards.[26]

Rogue One Stormtrooper, complete with improved grill.

Despite transforming the film industry with its special effects and production design in 1977, *Star Wars* was nonetheless made over four decades ago and on a limited budget. "The nostalgic past is irrecoverable partly because it is idealized," writes Carly Kocurek.[27] Nostalgia makes an appeal to the past being at least partly better than the present, so paradoxically if *Rogue One* were to actually be faithful in its re-creation of the sets and costumes of *A New Hope*, it would be a failure as a nostalgic project. In a "Making Of" feature, Edwards talks about a grill on the side of the Imperial Stormtroopers' helmet that in the original trilogy was simply a flat sticker that could peel off. With *Rogue One*'s contemporary blockbuster budget and production value, of course, the logic of nostalgia rules over re-creating the actual quality of the original: "So on ours," boasts Edwards, "we made them actually a grill, and it's got a proper embossed gap in it."[28] *Rogue One* didn't just re-create the past: it improved on it.

Rogue One is *Star Wars* as the filmmakers remembered it, not as it was. Edwards, like J. J. Abrams and Johnson, is a *Star Wars* fan. Suzanne Scott has discussed the advantages of the "fanboy auteur" director beloved by Hollywood, the kind of creative who possesses "the perceived ability to speak the promotional language of both visionary auteur and faithful fanboy" of which franchise directors like Zack Snyder, Joss Whedon, or Christopher Nolan are ideal examples.[29] These are directors who, when on display at fan events like Comic-Con and promotional tours, can helpfully display a combination of creativity and reverence in a single motion: they are artists, but they are also faithful and respectful of the original text or franchise. Edwards freely spoke of the importance of *Star Wars* to his life while promoting *Rogue One*: in particular, he often leaned on an anecdote about his travels for his thirtieth birthday to Tunisia to visit the original Tatooine set, which remains viable as a tourist attraction to this day. "And I took some blue dye with me, so I could have some blue milk, at the very table where Luke drank blue milk, and then I watched the sunset on the salt flats." Edwards, the fanboy auteur, seemed to like that his status as *Star Wars* director could now authorize this story for both himself and the film. "That's something I would never tell anybody. . . . Now that I've got to do *Star Wars*, it's a really nice story," he told the *Telegraph*.[30]

Perhaps, in part, this can help explain *Rogue One*'s eagerness—in direct, oppositional contrast with its numerous attempts at stylistic newness—to provide moments of direct nostalgia for *Star Wars* trainspotters. Characters play Dejarrik (the space chess seen on the Falcon in the first film), drink blue milk, and are entertained by dancing Twi'leks; idle Stormtroopers discuss the obsolete VT-15 (in *A New Hope* two idle Stormtroopers discuss the new VT-16), a character heals in a Bacta tank, and references are made to the Guardians of the Whills (Lucas's original name for the force).

An array of supporting characters also make a reappearance in the *Star Wars* franchise, bridging the prequel and original trilogies. Jimmy Smits, who in the prequel trilogy played Bail Organa, an early rebellion leader and Leia's adoptive father, returns in the most substantial prequel trilogy connection of the Disney-era films so far. Interestingly, Genevieve O'Reilly also returns as Mon Mothma, the Rebel Alliance leader first played by Caroline Blakiston in *Return of the Jedi*, and then portrayed by O'Reilly in a silent cameo in *Revenge of the Sith* (all her lines were cut in editing). C-3PO and R2-D2 also return in the briefest of cameos, giving Anthony Daniels a line ("Scarif? We're going to Scarif? Why does nobody tell me anything, R2?"), ensuring that he continues to be the only actor to have dialogue in all the canon *Star Wars* films. And Darth Vader, of course, gets one of the most prominent action scenes of all the *Star Wars* films in a moment of pure horror at the film's climax.

For all that *Rogue One* spoke of letting go of the Skywalkers, Vader's (and voice actor James Earl Jones's) sparing presence in the film was often described as one of the film's highlights.

Indeed, there are indications that Disney viewed this level of integrated callback to the other *Star Wars* films in *Rogue One* as somewhat restrained. More classic character cameos were seemingly at one stage planned during production but later cut. "We don't have to be winking at the audience all the time," said Gary Whitta, *Rogue One*'s screenwriter. "We did have some other characters but the reason why they're not in the film is because any time we did something like, where I'm wearing the fanboy hat and not the professional writer's hat, someone would come along and say, let's *not* do that character again."[31] In fact, it seems that there was some disagreement about another fairly pointed original trilogy cameo in *Rogue One*. While on the streets of Jedha, Jyn and Cassian literally bump into Ponda Baba and Dr. Evazan, the two characters who threaten Luke and Obi-Wan in the Mos Eisley cantina in *A New Hope*. The aggressive Dr. Evazan threatens Jyn while Ponda Baba (sometimes known as "Walrus Man") restrains him. "I thought having Evazan and Walrus Man was a little too much," Whitta told *EW*. "You have to reign [*sic*] in that instinct to go back and put things in just because you loved them when you were a kid."[32]

Nostalgic memory for *A New Hope* was even further inscribed in film in some sequences of *Rogue One*. Unused, archival footage from *A New Hope* was manipulated by ILM in order to insert Red Leader Garven Dreis (Drewe Henley) and Gold Leader Dutch Vander (Angus MacInnes), the Rebel pilot leaders from *A New Hope*'s climax, into *Rogue One*'s space battle above Scarif. This came from Edwards's tour of the Skywalker Ranch archives, where he discovered discarded, undigitized reels from the original film. "We got the neg documents and found the clips from *A New Hope* that hadn't been used," Edwards told *RadioTimes*. Conflicted, Edwards apparently wondered whether such an homage would be noticed by audience members, but "at the world premiere in LA, there was this massive cheer [when the archival Red Leader reports in]," Edwards said. "It was the only time during the premiere where I actually punched the air."[33] Again, we can see the broader "similar, but different" logic to

Drewe Henley posthumously reprises his role as
Red Leader in *Rogue One* via archival footage.

nostalgia being stretched in *Rogue One*. The film literally transplants footage and characters from the original film and digitally updates it to create a moment of nostalgia. The past is recovered, remembered, idealized, and updated, in one motion.

THE FACE OF NOSTALGIA

Of course, by far the most widely discussed element of *Star Wars* nostalgia in *Rogue One* was its digital faces. Two major characters from *A New Hope* return in *Rogue One* via digitally created faces: Grand Moff Tarkin and a youthful Princess Leia. Although Leia has only one line (a significant one, but one line nonetheless), Tarkin's role is prominent and spans many scenes and lines of dialogue. Peter Cushing, the cult English actor known primarily for his many roles in Hammer Horror films as well as for Tarkin in *A New Hope,* died in 1994. However, Lucasfilm felt that Tarkin's absence would be felt too keenly, given *Rogue One*'s setting and interest in the Death Star, the station he commands in *A New Hope*. "If he's not in the movie, we're going to have to explain why he's not in the movie," said Kiri Hart, Lucasfilm Story Group Development Lead and *Rogue One*'s producer.[34]

Accordingly, Tarkin's role was performed on-set by the British actor Guy Henry, who wore motion capture materials (including passive markers on his face) while acting. In postproduction,

Henry's face was replaced by ILM with a meticulous, state-of-the-art digital reconstruction of Cushing's. John Knoll described it as "a super high-tech and labor-intensive version of doing makeup,"[35] and indeed, tiny details seem to have taken months to perfect. Differences between the way Henry and Cushing delivered their "ahh" sounds were manipulated to be as close as possible: for example, with Cushing's delivery, according to Knoll, "he doesn't move his upper lip. He only opens his jaw about halfway, and makes this square shape with his lower lip, that exposes his lower teeth."[36] Fine details like this were massaged until a workable likeness was achieved, but for the filmmakers, a sense of overall realism overrode any exact likeness. When the lighting on the digital Tarkin was adjusted to match that of *A New Hope*, for example, he looked more like the original but stood out as a digital re-creation because of the different on-set lighting Henry had been filmed with (*Rogue One*'s scenes are noticeably darker and more dour compared to Lucas's flat Death Star lighting).[37] Princess Leia's single scene was created in much the same way, with the Norwegian actress Ingvild Deila used as a stand-in and archival recordings of Fisher's voice used for her sole line ("Hope").

The strategy for Tarkin proved effective. Although this digital resurrection was done with the approval of and in consultation with

Peter Cushing's face was meticulously re-created via CGI for *Rogue One*.

Cushing's estate, Joyce Broughton, Cushing's former secretary and the overseer of his estate, was emotionally taken aback when she saw the finished product. "When you're with somebody for thirty-five years, what do you expect?" Broughton told *Variety*. "I can't say any more because I get very upset about it. He was the most beautiful man. He had his own private way of living."[38] This kind of digital nostalgia is a sensitive issue, and the right to the postmortem control of a person's image is something that has legally been contested in the United States. In the United Kingdom, where Cushing's estate has legal power, there is no legal recognition of the right to control one's image after death—yet Lucasfilm was nonetheless careful to get the estate's permission anyway. "We wouldn't do this if the estate had objected," said Knoll.[39] Not that this averted criticism of the use of Cushing's likeness: the *Huffington Post* described it as "a giant breach of respect for the dead,"[40] while *Collider* called it "a terrible miscalculation."[41] On the other hand, others did praise the process (*Popular Mechanics* described it as "a wonder, moving straight past the uncanny valley into a place where what's on screen feels like the real thing"[42]), and *Rogue One* went on to be nominated for an Academy Award for Best Visual Effects.

Why digital actors should cause such a range of reactions is an illuminating question. After all, Fisher was hardly the first living actor to be digitally re-created in her youth, and Cushing was hardly the first actor to be digitally revived from the dead. This practice has been tentatively attempted in different moving-image formats and contexts for decades, from advertising (Fred Astaire died in 1987 and was used in a commercial for Dirt Devil vacuum cleaners in 1997; Audrey Hepburn, who died in 1993, was used in an advertisement for Galaxy Chocolates in 2013), to musical performances (Tupac Shakur, who died in 1996, was turned into a performance hologram on stage with Snoop Dogg at Coachella in 2012), and, of course, acting roles because of untimely death (when Oliver Reed died partway through filming *Gladiator* in 1999, Ridley Scott had one last scene digitally performed; and when Paul Walker died while filming *Furious 7* in 2015, some 350 shots with Walker were digitally created to write him out of the franchise).

Rogue One faced no such necessities: Leia could perhaps have been filmed from behind via a stand-in, and Lucasfilm already had backup plans to feature Tarkin with a reduced screen presence if the CGI version hadn't been satisfactory: "We did talk about Tarkin participating in conversations via hologram, or transferring that dialogue to other characters," said Knoll.[43] Perhaps it was the fact that the use of Tarkin and Leia was so clearly a creative choice that underscored such strong reactions. Carrie Fisher, unlike Cushing, was very much alive during the filming of *Rogue One* and could have reprised her role as with the other Disney-era *Star Wars* films (Fisher apparently enjoyed the final product, thinking it was created via archival footage rather than an entirely digital version).[44]

Instead, what these faces represent in *Rogue One* is, quite literally, the face of nostalgia. Here we have two performances so deeply digitally manipulated to their core that it could hardly be an overstatement to imagine that Fisher's one-shot digital performance in *Rogue One* was worked and reflected on to a significant degree more than her entire performance in *A New Hope*. It is labor, reviving the past. In this instance, memory and nostalgia are meticulous exercises involving thousands of work hours of highly skilled creatives and cutting-edge digital technology. They are creative, technical, and financial decisions. Indeed, technology was pushed forward via these creative, nostalgic strategies: in the wake of *Rogue One*, many wondered whether such new technology might be used to replace entire performances, such were the new possibilities opened up by the film (this was something that Knoll dismissed at the time given that "it is extremely labor-intensive and expensive to do"[45]).

The face serves as a link to the past in *Rogue One*. In this sense, it is very much in line with the kind of legacy film described in chapter 4, and contemporary serial storytelling in general. Digital faces have been used for overtly nostalgic purposes in the legacy films *Tron: Legacy, Terminator Genisys*, and *Blade Runner 2049*. In each, a key character from the original is made young again: in *Tron: Legacy*, Jeff Bridges plays both his current age and a younger version of himself in the guise of the villainous CLU, which was painstakingly re-created using footage of Bridges as a younger actor around the time of the first *Tron* film, which he starred in. In *Terminator Genisys*, Arnold Schwarzenegger performs a similar role, as both a contemporary,

aged T-800 Terminator ("Pops") and a digitally re-created original Terminator with Schwarzenegger's younger 1984 appearance.
Finally, in *Blade Runner 2048,* a young Sean Young was digitally inserted into the film to represent a clone of her replicant character
from the original, Rachael. Similar digital de-aging techniques have
also been used in nonlegacy franchise films, such as *Ant-Man* (2015)
and *Captain America: Civil War* (2016), which both use the technology
to de-age key actors in order to substantiate scenes set many years
before the main events of each film, highlighting the intertwining of
this technology with memory and serial storytelling.

The digital face, then, is seemingly fundamentally linked with
not only memory and nostalgia but also seriality. It is no coincidence
that all these films are part of franchises that take place over many
years and multiple (in some cases, many) films. The underlying logic
for the use of a digital Tarkin, Leia, CLU, T-800, and the replicant
Rachael is one of telling the stories of characters over many decades, both in fiction and in reality as actors age and grow older and
franchises ebb and flow in popularity. Discussing Bridges's digital
face in *Tron: Legacy,* Angela Ndalianis points toward a conceptual
doubling of the facade and the face, taking both to be instances
of "a porous barrier that connects the exterior to the interior, and
the interior to the exterior."[46] They are both midpoints, surfaces
that are concerned with both the insides of buildings and souls, and
the exterior of architecture and bodies. But they are also objects of
scrutiny in and of themselves, as the vehement reaction to the digital Tarkin and Leia in *Rogue One* suggests. These faces are virtuosic
performances of technology designed to both disappear and be visible simultaneously.[47] *Rogue One*'s effectiveness relies at least partly
on the audience's awareness of the materiality of each face and of
the assumed technology at work. Though each scene functions ad-
equately for the unaware, naive viewer, those who know that Cushing was long dead and that Fisher had aged encounter these illusions
on an altogether different level. These viewers—hardly a minority,
given the original film's legacy and popularity—will be aware of
how Cushing and Fisher looked in their original *Star Wars* appearances, and scrutinize their digital stand-ins for flaws accordingly. It
becomes a game of sorts for the filmmakers and the audience, with

Cushing presented in overwhelming close-up partway through the film, as though the creators and digital artists were daring the audience to find fault in their work.

"Bridges's face is a performance—a theatre—about the iconic impact of the cult film *Tron*; about *Tron: Legacy*'s virtuosic updating of that history and an even grander staged event; and about the role performed by Jeff Bridges—and his face—as façade that opens up a time-travel passageway between past and present," writes Ndalianis.[48] In a similar sense, we could say that Tarkin's and Leia's faces are performances about *Star Wars*, on many levels. They are certainly about the impact of the original film, and about the virtuosity of *Rogue One* in its re-creation of them. Yet they are not simple and straightforward facsimiles; as the question of Tarkin's lighting goes to show, they have in some ways been altered and updated to suit the filmmaking aesthetic of the current day. Tarkin's face is also paradoxically about reaching into history by going into the future with technology. Nostalgia has always been a contradictory force, and here we see this written into the film's obsession with achieving the old via the new. Media has long been the animating force of nostalgia, which came of age, according to Svetlana Boym, "with the birth of mass culture."[49] Memory is revisited and even improved on by cutting-edge technology. This is fitting for *Rogue One*, a film whose concept was devised by Knoll, a special effects creative.

ENDING WITH A BEGINNING

To say that *Rogue One*'s nostalgia is therefore quite complicated is to understate things. On the one hand, it was clearly Lucasfilm's aim to move away from the original trilogy's legacy via a number of stylistic decisions and to set up the "*Star Wars* Story" films as venues for newness, aesthetic exploration, and difference for the franchise. "We can go through a period of nostalgia," said Kathleen Kennedy at the time of the film's release, "but what are we going to do with future generations who want to step into their own era of this vast mythology and universe called *Star Wars*? And that's what I think these original *Star Wars* Stories are going to give us an opportunity to explore."[50]

In attempting to move away from the past, though, *Rogue One* seems somehow to have ended up conjoined with it. This is true in a literal sense, given the way *Rogue One* ends with *A New Hope*'s beginning, but it is also true in the sense of the broader essence of the film. *Rogue One* is a film that can never escape the foundations of the *Star Wars* franchise, and the longer it unfolds, the closer it gets to the original nostalgic trappings the franchise was trying to shift away from. From the slavishly mimed production design and costuming, to the numerous callbacks to original trilogy characters and situations, to the legacy film–like use of digital faces for memory and nostalgia, *Rogue One* is a film that inextricably ties progression with regression, and memory with the present. As a film intended to represent the way that the *Star Wars* franchise could break out of the familiar and redesign itself, *Rogue One* is curiously captive to seriality and film history and what has already been assembled (and reassembled). This is a compellingly strange turn for the future of nostalgia. Perhaps, then, far from exploring new directions, *Rogue One* shows us a *Star Wars* franchise that is always already remade.

7

YOU THINK ANYBODY'S LISTENING?

Fighting Fascism in Rogue One *and* Rebels

One month before *Rogue One* was released, Donald Trump was elected president of the United States in a result few had anticipated. This was a landmark event in American history: Trump, with no experience in government or the military (a first for the presidency), had won a campaign marked for its unprecedented animosity and hate. During the campaign, Trump had called Mexican migrants "criminals, drug dealers, rapists,"[1] threatened to put his opponent, Hillary Clinton in jail,[2] and was endorsed by only two of the United States' one hundred largest newspapers by paid circulation. The *Atlantic*, which had until 2016 made only two presidential endorsements in its 159-year history, called Trump "a demagogue, a xenophobe, a sexist, a know-nothing and a liar," and "the most ostentatiously unqualified major-party candidate in the 227-year history of the American presidency."[3] At the election, more than a third of American voters said that they would be frightened of a Trump presidency.[4] Even the right-wing *Fox News*, momentarily taken aback on the evening of the vote, called Trump's win "the most unreal, surreal election we have ever seen."[5]

Five months earlier the United Kingdom voted to withdraw from the European Union, in another shock victory for what would have otherwise been considered fringe right-wing groups. The Brexit decision claimed the resignation of the British prime minister, the conservative David Cameron, who in the view of the *Guardian* had "gambled the country's future as a way out of a party difficulty. . . . A prime minister is gone, but that is of nothing compared to the fallout for the economy, our union and Europe."[6] This was a result that renewed questions of Scottish independence only two years after a referendum on the topic was defeated, raised concerns around the Good Friday agreement on the Northern Irish border, and saw hate crimes in Britain escalate by 42 percent in a matter of months.[7]

Globally, in 2016, right-wing politics of a kind not seen for generations was on the rise. This was hardly a phenomenon limited only to English-speaking countries. In Poland, tens of thousands of right-wing nationalists marched in Warsaw under the slogan "Poland, the Bastion of Europe," with some even carrying banners of the falanga, a 1930s fascist symbol.[8] In Denmark, parliament passed a highly contested "jewellery law" that allowed the government to confiscate valuables from arriving asylum seekers to ostensibly offset the cost of their accommodation in the country.[9] In the Philippines, Rodrigo Duterte was voted in as president after promising to kill criminals if elected, and being accused of running vigilante death squads as mayor of the southern Philippine city of Davao.[10] *Time* magazine described the global rise of such popular right-wing politicians as seeming to share the same slogans in different languages: "On immigration: Send them back! On Muslims: Keep them out! On the media: Full of lies! On the Establishment: Crooked! On the elections: Rigged!"[11]

Star Wars has always been political. But with *Rogue One,* subtext became context. In light of the prodigious political shifts of 2016, and in particular Trump's election and the fallout that followed it, the appearance of a film featuring a diverse band of freedom fighters taking on a very white and male Imperial army was too obvious a parallel for audiences, critics, politicians, and even the filmmakers themselves. If *A New Hope* had been a parable, the prequels an extended analogy, and *The Force Awakens* a response to its time, then *Rogue One* was now a statement. Yet again we see the tension between *Star Wars* as political allegory and its political reception in context.

It was only a matter of days before the links were drawn. Trump was elected on a Tuesday, November 8. By Friday, Chris Weitz, one of the screenwriters for *Rogue One*, tweeted, "Please note that the Empire is a white supremacist (human organization)." *Rogue One* co-writer Gary Whitta replied, "Opposed by a multi-cultural group led by brave women." Both changed their Twitter avatars to a Rebel Alliance insignia adorned with a safety pin, a reference to a short-lived symbol of resistance and solidarity widely popular after the election.[12] For their defiance, both were widely lambasted by Trump supporters online: both writers took down their tweets within twenty-four hours, and Weitz issued an apology. Disney's CEO, Bob Iger, emerged to try and dull the flames, albeit unconvincingly. "I have no reaction to [this] story at all," Iger told *EW*. "Frankly, this is a film that the world should enjoy. It is not a film that is, in any way, a political film. There are no political statements in it, at all."[13]

Iger's downplaying of the politics of *Rogue One* might have been the diplomatic and rote business response (and indeed, Iger sat on Trump's Strategic and Policy Forum with other business leaders until June 1, 2017), but it doesn't hold much weight when compared with the film itself. As a film that leads directly into George Lucas's *A New Hope*, *Rogue One* is as contracted to the original film's political terrain as it is to its nostalgia. As is well established by now, *A New Hope* is at the very least undeniably an anti-Nazi and anti-imperialist allegory in even the broadest of strokes. To even include the same forces and settings as *A New Hope* is, in 2016, to take on a different complexion, especially combined with the added diversity in casting that Disney instituted with *The Force Awakens*. "It's one thing to watch blue-eyed Luke Skywalker blow up a weapon of mass destruction populated by guys in Nazi uniforms in the 1970s," wrote Dan Hassler-Forest. "But it is something else entirely to see a young woman leading a crack squad of minorities on a suicide mission against an arrogant gang of white supremacists in the age of Trump, the 'alt-right,' and neo-fascist populism."[14] Despite Iger's protests, and Weitz's and Whitta's deleted tweets, the crux of the matter remains ineluctable: the Empire *is* a white supremacist organization, resisted by a multicultural group led by women. These are the basic terms of *Star Wars*.

Somehow, all of this seemed strangely appropriate. After all, Trump was, before entering politics, not just a businessman but a particularly entertainment-minded one. He had had cameos in *Home Alone 2: Lost in New York* (1992), *Zoolander* (2001), and television shows *The Fresh Prince of Bel-Air* (in 1994), *The Nanny* (in 1996), and two in *Sex and the City* (in 1998 and 1999), before his long-running stint as host of the reality television show *The Apprentice* between 2004 and 2015. Like Ronald Reagan before him, a Hollywood president seemed to beg for a Hollywood response. The poignancy of the moment was apparently not lost on even those closest to Trump. In Michael Wolff's controversial best seller, *Fire and Fury: Inside the Trump White House*, he quotes Katie Walsh, a former deputy chief of staff for Trump, describing the relationship between then White House chief strategist Steve Bannon and his president: "Steve believes he is Darth Vader and that Trump is called to the dark side."[15] Bannon had previously positively likened himself to Vader during the 2016 election campaign.[16]

This was a political moment deeply imbued with popular culture. Trump, the reality television president, had campaigned with unsanctioned support from an online army of "shitposters" who used memes on social media to attack and discredit Hillary Clinton. One of these groups was financially supported by Palmer Luckey, founder of the virtual reality company Oculus.[17] Bannon, of course, had also previously tapped into a potent blend of conservative outrage at popular culture and associated harassment of women and minorities via his website, Breitbart, and its uses of Gamergate.[18] Gamergate was a semi-organized, rolling harassment campaign in the video games industry that Breitbart personality Milo Yiannopoulos used, in his own description, "to give the left a bloody nose."[19] A harassment campaign about popular culture, waged largely in the public sphere, was accordingly deliberately used as a recruiting ground for far-right politics. For a time, it looked within the realm of possibility that Yiannopoulos might also be considered for a position in the White House for his troubles (the *Washington Post* suggested him, not entirely seriously, for press secretary[20]), before Bannon eventually publicly distanced himself from Yiannopoulos after the latter made remarks that appeared to excuse pedophilia.[21]

In an era where political conflict is at least partly waged via the internet and popular culture, it is not surprising that Weitz and Whitta would make *Star Wars'* political allegiances plain and obvious. It is also unsurprising that so-called alt-right online warriors would take the bait and run (yet another) patently unsuccessful boycott under the tagline #DumpStarWars. "They are brainwashing kids into hating white men," read one anonymous online post about *Rogue One.* "All the villains are white and all the 'good guys' are minorities and women."[22]

But what is the political heart of *Rogue One,* anyway? And how did *Star Wars* find itself fighting fascism all over again in 2016?

WHAT IS SO FASCIST ABOUT SPACE FASCISTS?

What actually is fascist about the Imperials of *Star Wars* has long been a source of fan debate. Certainly, there is a visual tenor to the Galactic Empire that reflects the rigid aesthetic authority of the German and Italian fascists of the twentieth century. John Mollo, costume designer for *A New Hope,* said that Lucas "wanted the Imperial people to look efficient, totalitarian, fascist; and the Rebels, the goodies, to look like something out of a Western or the US Marines."[23] The visual topography of World War II inflected the original trilogy in many respects, from dogfights and spaceships to uniforms and even names (the Imperial Stormtroopers are named after the Sturmabteilung (Storm Detachment), Nazi paramilitary troops[24]). Yet much of their evildoing is connoted rather than actually depicted: we get little sense of what life under the Imperial yoke is like or why a band of freedom fighters would want to sacrifice so much to rid the galaxy of their rule. With the one considerable exception of the galactic war crime of the destruction of Alderaan, all we are left with is the slaughter of the Jawas and Luke's aunt and uncle as evidence that the Imperials are actually evil. Ideological difference is suggested rather than articulated: the Empire seems to value order and control and the Rebels seem to respect difference and independence, but this is communicated through visual design as much as by dialogue or acts.

Rogue One, on the other hand, makes these divisions manifest. Though some effort is expended on showing a more unpleasant Rebel Alliance willing to put the ends above the means ("we've all done terrible things on behalf of the Rebellion," Cassian Andor tells Jyn Erso), *Rogue One*'s Imperial ideology is perhaps the clearest of the series. Director Orson Krennic is shown to be a self-interested careerist who has correctly identified fear, power, and order as desired Imperial ends for his own advancement. In the film's opening scene, Krennic tells the scientist Galen Erso that the Death Star can provide peace and security for the galaxy. "You're confusing peace with terror," Erso replies. "Well, you have to start somewhere," says Krennic.

Similarly, Grand Moff Tarkin is shown to be skeptical of Krennic's Death Star project but quick to identify its potential once it is tested—as well as its liabilities. Tarkin confronts Krennic about the defector Imperial pilot smuggling out information about the Death Star: "If the Senate gets wind of our project, countless systems will flock to the Rebellion." Not only does Tarkin understand the oppressive power of the Death Star, but he also recognizes its potential as a galvanizing focus for his otherwise disorganized and disintegrated opposition.

In *Rogue One*, the Imperials are shown to be absorbed with maintaining power and control for its own sake, and it is this that most clearly makes them fascist. Hannah Arendt argued that totalitarianism was tied to racism and imperialism (and in *Rogue One* we can identify the Empire both by its white human-centeredness and by its exploitation of Jedha in an imperialist manner) but was fundamentally about the accumulation of power and the removal of all restraints on power. "Violence has always been the *ultima ratio* in political action and power has always been the visible expression of rule and government," Arendt writes. "But neither had ever before been the conscious aim of the body politic or the ultimate goal of any definite policy."[25] Though this is perhaps articulated most clearly in *Rogue One*, it is not out of keeping with previous *Star Wars* films: Vader and the Emperor both talk about control of the galaxy in the original trilogy. What sets *Rogue One* apart, however, is the clarity of this position, as well as the depiction of what the everyday imposition of that control looks like. Even from its early scenes we see Stormtroopers patroling the mining colony of the Ring of Kafrene and requesting people's identity documents. We also see prisoner labor camps and witness Erso the scientist being conscripted into the service of the Empire at gunpoint, and the casual murder of his wife.

Nowhere is this sense of everyday galactic oppression more palpable than on the planet of Jedha. Here for the first time in the *Star Wars* saga we see an insurgent city under Imperial occupation. Imperial troops patrol the streets in large groups, accompanied by armored vehicles and the watchful eye of a lingering Star Destroyer. Here the *Star Wars* aesthetic is less World War II than the twentieth-century wars of decolonization, such as those in Indonesia, Vietnam, and Algeria. We are witness to a foreign power—the Galactic Empire—forcefully colonizing a city in order to strip it of its natural resources (the kyber crystals). Finally the Empire lives up to its name, and fulfills Vladimir Lenin's claim that politically, imperialism is interested in the annexation of territories for financial reasons.[26]

Life under Imperial occupation has, in the case of Jedha, inspired guerrilla resistance. We are shown an attack by the partisan leader Saw Gerrera (whose surname surely acts as a play on the Spanish and Italian word for war, *guerra*), which operates much like the kind of guerrilla street battle that characterized colonialist wars. Idle citizens become unidentifiable combatants in a single moment; the patrolling occupying forces are met with violence and death in a matter of seconds. This shift in the aesthetics of warfare for *Star Wars* from World War II to the later wars of colonial independence is accompanied by a matching shift in cinematic inspiration. While Lucas was heavily inspired by World War II action films (such as *The Dam Busters* and *The Guns of Navarone*) in *A New Hope* combat sequences, Gareth Edwards, director of *Rogue One*, acknowledged that the Jedha sequence was partly inspired by Gillo Pontecorvo's

landmark work of postcolonial cinema, *The Battle of Algiers* (1965).[27]
A striking, neorealist-inspired representation of the Algerian war of
independence against the occupying French, this film reset the cinematic representation of war through the use of "documentarian"
aesthetics: handheld camerawork, on-location shooting, nonprofes-
sional actors (many of whom had lived through the actual events
depicted), and an episodic, discontinuous narrative.

Saw Gerrera's guerrilla attack on the Imperial patrol in Jedha
matches this aesthetic closely. Handheld camerawork and chaotic
editing ensure that the scene plays out in disarray. Jyn's and Cassian's role as, initially, observers caught in the middle of the conflict
amplifies this: it is uncertain who is attacking whom, where they
have come from, and what they are trying to achieve. According
to Edwards, the rough edit of *Rogue One* even included "pieces of
war footage and photography just to see what the rhythm and feel
of that would be like."[28] This is very much in keeping with the *Star
Wars* tradition, as Lucas used World War II dogfight footage to illustrate what he wanted his space dogfights to look like; however, in
this case, the source material and overall effect are quite different.
We are on the ground and in the thick of it.

It was not just *The Battle of Algiers'* aesthetics of filmmaking that
carried across into *Rogue One*. Yacef Saadi, an actor and co-producer
of *The Battle of Algiers* and a former Front de Libération Nationale
(FLN) leader, described the film's ideological strategy in blunt terms:
"I have substituted the camera for the machine gun."[29] The French
are depicted in *The Battle of Algiers* as technologically, organization-
ally, and financially superior to the local Algerians in every way,
yet ultimately undone by their own dominance. The Algerians, in
the words of Michel de Certeau, "make do" with what is to hand[30]
and fight with surprise and resourcefulness, intercepting French
weapons and using them against the French, and hiding improvised
bombs in bins and baskets. Bombs and arms are smuggled under
the veils of Muslim women; in *Rogue One*, blasters are concealed under the kaftans of Gerrera's insurgents. In a famous scene from *The
Battle of Algiers,* FLN leader Ben M'Hidi confronts the French military leadership at a press conference and is challenged on his "cowardly" tactics: "Isn't it even more cowardly to attack defenseless

Pontecorvo's *The Battle of Algiers* (1965).

Rogue One's Jedha scenes.

villages with napalm bombs that kill many thousands of times more?" he responds. "Obviously, planes would make things easier for us. Give us your bombers, sir, and you can have our baskets."

The power imbalance of *The Battle of Algiers* is replicated by *Rogue One*'s allusions to colonial conflict, recalling and amplifying Lucas's bee and hammer motif from *A New Hope*. The might and resources of the Imperial army have come to Jedha and cannot be effectively resisted with any similar attempt at strength. The rebels cannot openly contend either with a protective Star Destroyer or the armored combat vehicles on the ground. The scales in this conflict are not equal. Instead, the locals and Gerrera's guerrillas must respond, like the Algerians, by "making do" and emphasizing surprise, strategy, and creativity. The rebels use the urban environment to blend in and take shelter, as well as to take the initiative and shape the terms of combat to suit themselves. The architect Eyal Weizman describes a similar setting for combat between the Israeli Defense Forces and Palestinian guerrilla fighters in the West Bank in 2002: "Since Palestinian guerrilla fighters were sometimes manoeuvring . . . through pre-planned openings, most fighting took place in private homes. Some buildings became like layer cakes, with Israeli soldiers both above and below a floor where Palestinians were trapped."[31] The street fighting in Jedha is enabled and conditioned by the city itself, which serves as protector and facilitator. This is a fact keenly identified by the Imperial occupiers, who opt to use the Death Star to destroy the city entirely when they have exhausted their use for it, rather than leave it for the Rebels to reclaim. Such an act recalls the United States' decision to drop napalm bombs in Vietnam as an alternative to fighting the North Vietnamese guerrillas in their own territory. Might and technology are used against ingenuity and surprise. This has, to some extent, always been the message of *Star Wars*. But with *Rogue One*, it is explicitly built on twentieth-century, colonial settings.

AND NOW I AM BECOME DEATH STAR, DESTROYER OF WORLDS

Another major thematic preoccupation of *Rogue One* surrounds political conscience and making active decisions to fight for a just cause. Certainly, the most obvious example of this is Galen Erso, whom the filmmakers consciously painted as a Robert Oppenheimer–type figure in the lead-up to the film's release. Oppenheimer, a theoretical physicist, played a key role in the Manhattan Project and the American development of the atomic bomb. Oppenheimer came to deeply regret his involvement in developing the bomb and felt that he had "blood on his hands," and went on to advocate for the international control of atomic weaponry.[32] Edwards described this kind of conflict between conscience and action as a grayness that "I find incredibly interesting. Someone is trying to do the right thing, trying to be good, genuinely trying to end a war, and then it turns out they might have done something terrible and then trying to put something right again."[33] Galen Erso's subsequent betrayal of the Empire and his sabotage of the Death Star project therefore has similarities to Oppenheimer's antinuclear advocacy. We could also liken Erso to the German scientists like Albert Einstein and Leó Szilárd, who wrote to President Franklin D. Roosevelt to warn the United States of Nazi Germany's plans to develop an atomic bomb, urging him to develop a US atomic program in response.[34]

Erso is a forced conscript to the Empire's cause. He funnels his ethical dissent into disruption and sabotage, taking a needlessly slow pace and inserting the fatal flaw in his designs that will go on to allow the Rebels to destroy the Death Star in *A New Hope*. "I played the part of a beaten man resigned to the sanctuary of his work," Erso tells his daughter. "I made myself indispensable, and all the while I laid the groundwork of my revenge." He continually chooses to fight in the pragmatic and, ultimately, most effective avenues open to him. This is a major theme of *Rogue One*. The Imperial pilot defector, Bodhi Rook, has similar issues of conscience and was counseled by Erso. "He said I could get right by myself," Rook tells Jyn. "He said I could make it right, if I was brave enough and listened to what was in my heart. Do something about it." Accordingly, he repudiates the Empire and takes Galen Erso's message to Gerrera, who unfortunately misidentifies it as an Imperial trap. Yet the inference in *Rogue One* is clear: Rook is yet another character who has knowledge of impending disaster and has chosen to combat that threat by doing what is difficult and morally right. That this act results in his own death—but also in collective victory— underscores this point. Rook does not die climactically, but instead rather mundanely as part of battle. He does not even live to see the information he so desperately fought for in the hands of the Rebels. Rook's death ultimately means very little. His courageous decision to defect, on the other hand, means everything. When and how individuals join the political struggle is a continuing question that *Rogue One* grapples with.

Along similar lines, Gerrera and Cassian are used in *Rogue One* as contrasts for Jyn's character arc. She begins *Rogue One* as an outsider to the galactic conflict, willing to get by and survive by herself, but uninterested in joining a wider political battle. "I've never had the luxury of political opinions," she tells the Rebel commanders, as a way to suggest that her own focus on individual survival has precluded any possibility of investing in collective change. This, of course, is revealed to be not quite true—as a trusted soldier in Gerrera's band of rebels, Jyn would have been exposed to high-level political discussions with ramifications for the entire galaxy. Gerrera, on the other hand, is painted as a political extremist who has caused significant difficulties not just for the Empire but for the Rebel Alliance too. "He's someone that's gone so far to be good that he's gone right to the edge of what's acceptable to achieve good that he's nearly become the enemy himself," said Edwards.[35] Yet despite his paranoia and his wounds, Gerrera still believes in the need to defeat the Empire. He is no Captain Kurtz or Lieutenant Colonel Nicholson, who in Francis Ford Coppola's *Apocalypse Now* (1979) and David Lean's *Bridge on the River Kwai* (1957), respectively, become so compromised by war that they end up harming their own sides. Despite everything, and in spite of his supposedly extreme actions, Gerrera still challenges Jyn to join the fight against the Empire. "You can stand to see the Imperial flag reign across the galaxy?" he asks. "It's not a problem if you don't look up," replies a cynical Jyn.

Cassian is similarly used as a foil for Jyn's reluctance. Despite also having performed morally dubious acts for the Rebellion, Cassian is ideologically committed to the fight against the Empire and reproves Jyn for her detachment. "We don't all have the luxury of deciding when and where we want to care about something," he tells her. "You're not the only one who lost everything. Some of us just decided to do something about it." In contrast to Rook, to her father, to Cassian, and to Gerrera, Jyn is therefore positioned by *Rogue One* as struggling to choose to be part of a conflict, rather than passively have it affect her. As a result of the examples of those around her, however, she elects also to act—and to lead when others will not.

Jyn's affirmative decision to join the Rebellion despite losing her father—her decision to embrace a cause other than her own and fight the Empire—is the key point of *Rogue One*. "You give way to an enemy this evil, with this much power, and you condemn the galaxy to an eternity of submission. The time to fight is now," a changed Jyn tells a gathered Rebel Alliance assembly. She has made an active decision to challenge a seemingly unstoppable enemy and is now imploring others to join her. Avoiding political struggle and conflict for self-preservation's sake is shown to be a self-defeating act. Danger and conflict will come for you anyway—*Rogue One* asks its characters to make the decision to approach it head-on, and on its characters' own terms.

"If there's a story, if there's a moral at the heart of *Star Wars*," says Edwards, "it's that we have to come together and work together to something good. When you work on your own, when you write off a particular culture, you're never going to stop anything."[36] This might seem obvious for a group of heroes that forms something called the Alliance, but in 2016, such discourse took on a decidedly different complexion.

ALLEGIANCES AND COALITIONS IN *STAR WARS REBELS*

At this point, I need to pause this discussion of *Rogue One* and look closely at another Lucasfilm project so far undiscussed: *Star Wars Rebels*. This animated television series, screened in twenty-two-minute-long episodes on the child-friendly DisneyXD channel, has not always received the same notice as its big-screen relatives. This is a mistake: for Kathleen Kennedy, "*Rebels* is really what kicked off the new generation of *Star Wars* for [Lucasfilm],"[37] and over its four seasons from 2014 to 2018, Disney-era *Star Wars* ideas have been tested and refined within the confines of this animated series. In some ways, *Rebels* is the bellwether for Disney-era *Star Wars*: where it went over its four-year run, the films generally followed.

Rebels, a spiritual successor to the beloved but poorly rated *Star Wars: The Clone Wars* (2008–14), is set across the five years leading up to *A New Hope* and tells the story of the formation of the Rebel Alliance. It does this by focusing on a small group of proto-Alliance fighters based on the outer rim planet of Lothal. These are "the Spectres": Kanan Jarrus, a Jedi survivor of the purge; his orphaned apprentice, Ezra Bridger; Hera Syndulla, a Twi'lek pilot; a Mandalorian explosives expert, Sabine Wren; one of the few survivors of the Lasat alien race, Garazeb Orrelios; and a droid, C1-10P, "Chopper." Although the Spectres are an important early instance of resistance against the Empire, over the course of *Rebels'* four seasons, they gradually discover that they are part of a larger, currently disconnected network of smaller groups fighting for freedom, and help recruit others and gather resources for their cause.

Despite being an episodic, serial adventure sometimes concerned with character arcs and villain-of-the-week-type scenarios, in *Rebels* we see more of the quotidian, under-the-yoke-of-the-Empire-type stories that would eventually give substance to *Rogue One*. These stories of resistance often seem broadly familiar, as though inspired by real-world history. The Spectres disrupt propagandistic "Empire Day" celebrations, intercept and steal Imperial shipments, and communicate via pirate radio broadcasts as part of their basic, day-to-day activities as insurgents. Several plotlines stand out, however. In the season 3 premiere, "Steps into Shadow," the Rebels discover a squadron of decrepit Y-wing starfighters due for demolition at an Imperial shipyard, which is manned by indentured Ugnaught alien laborers who agree to help steal the ships in exchange for their liberation. The addition of these ramshackle and aged Y-wings to the Rebel fleet comes at great cost, yet it is still a victory for the Rebels to be able to use the Empire's machinery of war against it. The Rebels also undertake supply runs to the planet Ryloth, which is under Imperial blockade (season 3, episode 5, "Hera's Heroes"), recalling the German blockade of Leningrad during World War II, or the Soviet blockade of Berlin during the Cold War.

Actions that boil down to what would in the present day be considered war crimes by the Imperials form a reoccurring backbone of *Rebels*. In season 3, episode 10 ("An Inside Man"), the Rebels discover that Rebel sympathizers have been working inside weapons factories to sabotage Imperial supplies. In response, one of the Imperial leaders has factory workers personally test the equipment that they personally make, which kills one worker in the process. Equally, in the season 2 premiere ("The Siege of Lothal"), a refugee town formed by displaced farmers is razed by the Empire in retaliation for its inhabitants accepting Rebel help. This brings to mind shocking examples of German troops executing civilians in response to partisan attacks during World War II, such as the Kragujevac massacre in 1941, which followed a personal decree from Adolf Hitler that 100 hostages be shot for every German soldier killed and 50 for every wounded (more than 2,700 men and boys were killed in this instance).[38]

Perhaps most shocking of all is *Rebels*' Geonosis plotline (season 3, episodes 12 and 13, "Ghosts of Geonosis: Part One and Part Two"), where it is discovered that the entire planet, once densely populated, has been abandoned. Geonosis was key to the Lucas-era prequel *Attack of the Clones*, and is identified in that film not only as a weapon-manufacturing capital but as the originators of the Death Star plan. In these two *Rebels* episodes, the Spectres journey to Geonosis with Gererra (played again by Forest Whitaker, in the character's *Rebels* debut) and discover that the Imperials have used poisonous gas canisters in the planet's underground chambers to exterminate the entire Geonosian race. That this was done by the Imperials to ostensibly leave no trace of the Death Star plan does little to attenuate the obvious twentieth-century analogy for such barefaced genocide. It is quite horrifying. "You're seeing the impact of the Empire, of Stormtroopers around the galaxy, abusing and oppressing people," said the executive producer Simon Kinberg before *Rebels* premiered. "Thematically and politically, it goes to some dark places."[39] "Dark" does not quite do *Rebels* justice, for an animated television series aimed at children and dealing in genocide. Perhaps more than any other *Star Wars* installment, *Rebels* makes the case for the overthrow of a fascist, war criminal Galactic Empire.

As with *Rogue One*, themes of political conscience and joining together to fight for just causes are also particularly resonant. One of the main Spectre characters, Sabine Wren, sees her major character arc unfold along similar lines to Galen Erso. In season 3, episode 15 ("Trials of the Darksaber"), it is revealed that as a young woman at the Imperial Academy, she had enthusiastically helped design and build a weapon of mass destruction that was later used against her people (the Mandalorians) by the Empire. Filled with regret, and shunned by her family, Wren fled the academy and her planet,

Mandalore, and joined the Rebellion. Like Jyn Erso, she chose the collective good over her own safety. "I left to save everyone," she tells Kanan Jarrus. "My mother, my father, my brother. Everything I did was for family—for Mandalore."

Rebels also frequently reinforces the point made in *Rogue One* (and in other *Star Wars* films) that centrality or neutrality is in fact not a viable option. This is most powerfully made through the character of the Bendu, a force-using mystical creature that Jarrus encounters while the Rebels are based on the planet Atollon (this is also another example of Disney-era *Star Wars* returning to disused Lucas-era material, as the name for the Jedi in the original *Star Wars* script was "the Jedi-Bendu"). The Bendu proclaims that he is "the one in the middle" of the light and the dark, expressing preference for neither. This extends to the point where, upon becoming friendly, Jarrus asks the Bendu for assistance (in season 3's finale, "Zero Hour") to defeat the rapidly approaching Empire, which he refuses. The Bendu attempts here, like Uncle Owen and Han Solo in *A New Hope*, and Jyn Erso in *Rogue One*, to not get involved—which only makes getting involved more likely, and on worse terms. The Bendu is eventually provoked into a rage upon seeing the Empire's desecration of his planet and transforms himself into a storm, destroying the Empire's forces on Atollon and himself in the process. For *Star Wars*, neutrality is a position that harms the neutralist the most: if you will not come to the fight, the fight will come to you, and more powerfully. (Incidentally, this was why fan rumors that *The Last Jedi* would see the emergence of a new, "gray Jedi" position that was neither light nor dark were always off the mark.)

"If you can't do anything about the Empire, the Empire will eventually crush you," said Lucas in a draft of *Star Wars* from 1975. "To not make a decision is a decision." In states witnessing the rise of an unpalatable force, Lucas wrote, "what usually happens is a small minority stands up against it, and the major portion are a lot of indifferent people who aren't doing anything one way or the other. And by not accepting the responsibility, those people eventually have to confront the issue in a more painful way."[40] This is surely one of *Star Wars*' most central and consistent themes: to be a bystander is to embrace inevitable defeat. Perhaps, then, the criticism of *Star Wars*' moral stakes as a Reaganite black-and-white binary is misplaced. *Rogue One* and *Rebels* show us a galaxy far, far away where "good guys" and "bad guys" certainly contain nuances and contradictions. The most important point is not about good or evil, however. It is that neutrality is a hopeless, even vain position. The middle is no place to be.

Indeed, the need to form alliances for the collective good is the entire thematic point of *Rebels*. From the first episode to the last, the series tells a story of disparate and disconnected groups of individuals linking up and continually growing as a substantial threat to their shared enemy: the Empire. Sometimes, those who aid the Rebels are self-aggrandizing, morally dubious hucksters (like the smuggler Hondo Ohnaka). Sometimes they are former enemies who find a greater purpose with the Rebellion (such as the clone trooper Rex or the Imperial droid AP-5). Sometimes, they are even defecting Imperial leaders who formally served as antagonists for the Spectre group (such as Agent Kallus, or Minister Tua, though her defection attempt was unsuccessful). These allies, though often treated with skepticism, are always eventually accepted by the Rebels despite their genuine differences. This has interesting correspondence for real-world antifascist alliances. In late 2016 the theorist Judith Butler discussed the precarious nature of leftist alliances in a timely interview with the *Cairo Review of Global Affairs*:

> How is it that groups which identify with very different kinds of issues—sexual rights, or questions of poverty, or issues of literacy, or perhaps non-violence, or anti-militarism—how do they articulate with one another? How do they come together? Not just physically in the square or on the street, but how do they begin to articulate their political demands in a coalition that demands that they identify what they wish to achieve and who they wish to defeat, having that kind of clear sense of the primary antagonism. And how then do those groups work together even when they do not fully identify with each other, or they do not fully agree with one another? That interests me on the left. We have to assume that harmonious ideas of left unity are not plausible. . . . My sense is rather that

we have to think more about how to live with those we don't particularly like, and never chose to be in solidarity with, but with whom we are obligated to cohabit the world and enter into solidaristic alliances despite what might be some pretty heartfelt hostilities.[41]

Indeed, as *Rebels* progresses, it takes up—in simplified form—a lot of the concerns shared by Butler here. As it is fundamentally the story of the formation of the Rebellion, *Rebels* tells the story of hard-fought alliances that are able to contain their inherent fractious-ness only because of the external and shared threat of the Empire. "We've kind of made clear that they were on their own at the be-ginning, and in the second season they link up with more groups," says Dave Filoni, *Rebels* supervising director. "Once [Rebel leader] Mon Mothma gets involved I guess that's more of an alliance be-cause she's declaring them pretty openly."[42] This open declaration occurs in season 3, episode 18 ("Secret Cargo") as the Spectres take Mon Mothma to the Rebel base on Dantooine, where she delivers a galvanizing speech broadcast across the galaxy. "I have no fear as I take new action," she tells the galaxy, "for I am not alone. Begin-ning today, we stand together as allies."

Yet despite their open intentions to defeat the Empire, the

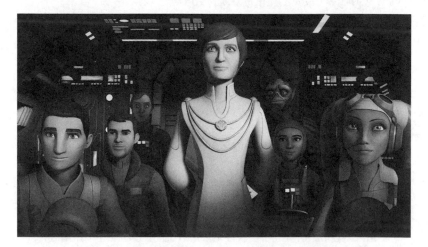

Mon Mothma openly declares the Rebellion against the Empire in *Rebels*.

Rebel Alliance over the course of *Rebels* remains unsteady and faces internal disagreements. When the Rebels discover the Empire's genocide on Geonosis, they also grasp the significance that proof of such a horrific crime would have for their cause. Although they eventually lose the gas canisters themselves while trying to escape the planet, they nonetheless leave with photographic evidence: not enough to convince the Senate but sufficient to continue recruiting for their cause, Bail Organa tells the Spectres. As an uneven alliance, the Rebels on some level realize that they need an externally galvanizing force to unite powerfully enough to take on the Empire. This is, of course, eventually provided in *Rogue One* by the Death Star. As Pablo Hidalgo of the Lucasfilm Story Group says of the Alliance during *Rebels,* "We know from *Rogue One* that there is still disagreements about how they're going to operate. . . . What it takes is a threat like the Death Star to congeal these disparate groups into a Rebel Alliance."[43] *Rebels,* like *Rogue One,* repeatedly illustrates that being in the middle is no way to be, and that people with genuine disagreements can still work together—in fact, *must* work together—to defeat a greater threat.

CASTING THE REBELLION

In *Rogue One,* like *The Force Awakens*—and pointedly unlike the original trilogy—the strength of our heroes' alliance is embodied through diversity in casting. *Rogue One*'s cast, like *The Force Awakens,* does not contain any new white Anglo heroes, instead giving us a white woman (Felicity Jones), a Mexican man (Diego Luna), a British man of Pakistani descent (Riz Ahmed), an action star from Hong Kong (Donnie Yen), a Chinese man (Jiang Wen), and a robot, performed and voiced by Alan Tudyk (a white man who is not seen in the film). This, of course, has form for *Star Wars*: as David S. Meyer wrote about the original trilogy, "The heroic rebels succeeded by virtue not of technological advantages, but through greater commitment, diversity and justness of cause."[44] Given the whiteness of the original trilogy, *Rogue One* finally illustrates that diversity through more than just the use of background aliens. By the film's climax, our *Rogue One* heroes are certainly more committed to their cause than their Imperial counterparts (who even have to be reminded by

Krennic to counterattack on Scarif), and the film certainly suggests that their difference makes them stronger as a unit. This point was politicized enough that Bob Iger felt it necessary to address it in his public hosing down of Weitz's and Whitta's anti-Trump tweets: "[*Rogue One*] has one of the greatest and most diverse casts of any film we have ever made, and we are very proud of that," Iger said. "And that is not a political statement at all."[45]

Loathe as they might be to contradict their boss, others involved in *Rogue One* disagreed about the political statement that diversity makes. For Luna, the diverse cast of *Rogue One* "gives me hope" because "it's making a comment on the world we live in today."[46] This sentiment seems to be shared by Lucasfilm's creative management, as well. "I will always have a particular soft spot for having someone of his particular heritage on screen," says Hidalgo in the official *Rogue One* DVD special features. "I mean my name's Pablo Hidalgo—having someone like Luna embody a *Star Wars* character, we haven't really had that before."[47] Edwards confirmed that this approach was hardly accidental. "It was definitely a deliberate thing to have diverse characters," he told *Empire* in advance of the film's release.[48]

In context, *Rogue One* was imagined by many to be as fully charged of the moment as possible. "It may be an accident," wrote Owen Gleiberman for *Variety*, "but *Rogue One* is the most politically relevant movie of the year."[49] This was helped by *Rogue One*'s political agenda being both malleable and highly specific. Our crack team of Rebels could have been undertaking their brave, last-ditch suicide mission to defeat Trump, or the forces advocating for Brexit, or against the Polish neofascists, or against Rodrigo Duterte and his alleged vigilante death squads. "When I look at the *Rogue One* trailers," wrote Brett White for CBR.com, "I see what I want from America. I see a multicultural group standing strong *together* led by a rebellious and courageous woman."[50] Against the backdrop of the global rise of the populist Right, *Rogue One* seemed to stand for individuality, for difference, for community, and for the oppressed.

Whatever *Rogue One*'s political motives might be, however, they are also dramatically undercut by some fairly decisive factors. One of these is the total lack of women in the film. The Rebel group that Jyn leads is nothing if not male, a point underscored by the establishing shot of Cassian's motley crew on Yavin IV as they volunteer for the Scarif suicide mission. "Jyn Erso is the lone woman surrounded by many, many men," wrote Carolyn Petit and Anita Sarkeesian for *The Mary Sue*.[51] Not only is this particular group exclusively male, but there is a conspicuous lack of women extras in almost all Rebel Alliance scenes. For *Rogue One*, Rebel women are, by and large, strategists, leaders, and support, and are kept far from perilous on-the-ground activity.

Perhaps the only way that Jyn escaped a similar fate was through a somewhat perverse strategy. Although the lead in *Rogue One* was always a woman in John Knoll's original pitch ("I just thought: *Star Wars* could use more good strong female leads"[52]), Edwards had the *Rogue One* team develop the script as though Jyn were a man. "We were very keen to not view this character as a woman, and have her do things because she's a woman, and just view her as a really cool character that we like and we just happened to cast a female," said Edwards. "We tried to write Jyn as a guy, just to get it off the group, and then tried not to do anything to pander to the fact that she's a female."[53] Edwards refers to *Alien* as the gold standard for this approach. In effect, though, this strategy meant that the scriptwriters were developing six central male protagonists, plus three male villains (Krennic, Tarkin, and Vader). Presumably, at the scripting stage, this meant that the only women characters who were written as women were Mon Mothma (four scenes), Lyra Erso (two scenes), and Leia (one word of dialogue). This is, charitably, a very male galaxy.

Also undercutting any political progressiveness on *Rogue One*'s part were material decisions affecting the filmmaking. *Rogue One*'s climactic Scarif scenes were filmed in the Maldives, a small island nation in the Indian Ocean. "Scarif is based on a paradise world, so we had to go to paradise to film it," said Edwards.[54] The Maldives is not commonly used as a shooting location for major Hollywood productions, and *Rogue One* was supported by the Maldivian government—which allegedly included personal help from the Maldivian president, Abdulla Yameen.[55] Certainly, the *Rogue One* filmmakers, including Edwards, seemed more than happy to promote the tourist-friendly image of the Maldives as an Indian Ocean island paradise during *Rogue One*'s marketing campaign. However, the Maldives was going through a time of acute political distress during *Rogue One*'s production: "It was the toughest time in the country's history while the movie was shooting," said Mohamed Ibrahim, who runs a production coordination service that was engaged by Disney in the Maldives.[56] In 2015 the nation's first democratically elected president, and respected human rights and environment campaigner, Mohamed Nasheed—who had previously been forced to resign at gunpoint[57]—was convicted of terrorism offenses and sentenced to thirteen years in prison. The United Nations, the United States, and several human rights groups called for his release, warning that due process had not been followed in the court case and that Nasheed's jailing was politically motivated.[58] Nasheed was eventually freed and allowed to travel internationally, but the Maldives crises seemed to only intensify: in late November 2015 President Yameen declared a state of emergency that suspended all basic rights ahead of an opposition party protest,[59] and in August 2017, in a move that would befit the Galactic Empire, the Maldives army occupied parliament in order to stop a no-confidence vote against Yameen going ahead.[60] Journalists in the Maldives face the prospect of routine arrest as part of their work, and to date there has been no progress in the case of Ahmed Rilwan Abdulla, a journalist who was abducted in 2014 and has not been seen since.[61] In the view of Amnesty International, in 2016 and 2017, the Maldives government has intensified a "crackdown on the rights to freedom of expression and of peaceful assembly," and "authorities used new laws and criminal cases to silence political opponents, as well as human rights defenders, journalists and civil society."[62] The *Star Wars* brand may advocate for freedom, individuality, and democracy in its films, but in practice by making *Rogue One*, Disney gave and received material aid from an increasingly authoritarian regime in the Maldives.

At the conclusion of *Rogue One*'s mission to transmit the stolen Death Star plans to the Rebel Alliance, Cassian wonders aloud to Jyn: "You think anybody's listening?" For Dan Hassler-Forest, writing in the *Los Angeles Review of Books* at the time of *Rogue One*'s release, this line ensures that "even through all the techno-hubris and nostalgiaphilia, the backward-glancing *Rogue One* somehow makes important steps forward, as its anti-fascist payload thankfully manages to come through loud and clear."[63] Given *Rogue One*'s male-centeredness and its support of the Maldives regime, I am not so sure. For all its interest in how coalitions of diverse and fractious groups can overcome a fascist-style threat, *Rogue One* has, at its heart, more political contradictions than clarity.

One audience member, however, was certainly not listening. In April 2017, after *Rogue One* was released on home media and online, Donald Trump took an impromptu press conference on board Air Force One. Asked about catastrophic events in Syria, Trump decried them as a "disgrace to humanity" and suggested that Syrian president Bashar al-Assad should leave. But there was, as there usually is with Trump, a distraction. Behind the president throughout his press conference was, of course, *Rogue One,* playing on one of Air Force One's in-flight entertainment screens. The image of Trump standing directly in front of an image of Darth Vader was too much for some, and illustrated the pliability of popular culture and politics. "*Rogue One?*" tweeted Mark Hamill. "I thought they were just screening Steve Bannon's home movies."[64]

8

I'VE ALWAYS HATED WATCHING YOU LEAVE

Death, Han Solo, and Carrie Fisher

April 13, 2017, was a day of celebration. Forty years of *Star Wars* was being commemorated officially by Lucasfilm and Disney at the annual *Star Wars* Celebration convention, held that year in Orlando, Florida. In a panel streamed live around the world, Kathleen Kennedy, George Lucas, Mark Hamill, Harrison Ford, Billy Dee Williams, and many more reminisced about their experiences of four decades of *Star Wars*. Hayden Christiansen returned for his first convention appearance in fifteen years (possibly indicating a thawing of the deep-seated fan dislike of the prequels), and John Williams made a surprise appearance with the Orlando Symphony.

Carrie Fisher's absence was palpable. She had died unexpectedly just four months earlier, on December 27, 2016, after a heart attack on a flight. Her death had provided a particularly shocking end to a year where celebrity death had become routinely saddening, where space was regularly opened in public and on social media for "sincere mourning, for real feeling, and for shared memory."[1] Her mother, the great actress Debbie Reynolds, suffered a stroke

A still of Billie Lourd at Star Wars Celebration 2016 from the YouTube livestream.

the day after Fisher died, and also passed away. "I want to be with Carrie," she told her son, Todd (Fisher's brother), just moments before the stroke.[2]

It was therefore deeply moving to see Fisher's daughter, Billie Lourd, onstage by herself at Orlando after being gifted the stage by Kennedy and Lucas. Dressed in a white dress reminiscent of Leia in *A New Hope*, three enormous photos of Fisher in costume were projected above and behind Lourd as she spoke uninterrupted for five minutes, this young woman literally dwarfed by the memory of her mother. "[Carrie] loved these movies, she loved the people she got to make them with," Lourd concluded, "and she loved this incredible character she got to create, this force called Leia." She paused nervously while those present in the auditorium clapped. "She taught me three important things—one thing all mothers should teach their daughters."

Lourd looked around the auditorium, closed her eyes, and sighed. "General Kenobi. Years ago, you served my father in the Clone Wars," she recited, before the crowd burst out in emotional recognition.

> Now he begs you to help him in his struggle against the
> Empire. I regret that I am unable to present my father's
> request to you in person, but my ship has fallen under attack

and I'm afraid my mission to bring you to Alderaan has failed. I have placed information vital to the survival of the Rebellion into the memory systems of this R2 unit. My father will know how to retrieve it. You must see this droid safely delivered to him on Alderaan. This is our most desperate hour. Help me, Obi-Wan Kenobi. You're my only hope.

"Thank you for loving her and for carrying on what she stood for," Lourd told the crowd before walking off. "I'm beyond grateful."

This speech—Leia's plea for help from Kenobi—means more than the words it contains. Fisher had used it throughout the years in many different guises: interviews, public appearances, chat shows. She would recite it to diffuse fan expectations of her as someone who had moved beyond *Star Wars,* as someone who no longer cared— she would begin it with humor, usually, a biting look toward the camera that dared the audience to laugh with her. Yet the ultimate delivery of this speech—word perfect, always—was sincere. Fisher first invited people to laugh along with her as a public figure trapped by her very first words in the role that made her famous, but then to relinquish themselves to sincerity, for her to show that this speech was a way for her to acknowledge what she—and Leia—meant to millions of fans. By reciting these words, she summed it all up: she saw the humor in it, as well as the desperate causticity of being only Leia to millions, and also, most important, the profound depth of meaning in all of it. In her 2016 memoir, *The Princess Diarist,* she calls it "a speech I'll remember all my life until I get dementia because I had to say it so many times."[3] And here it was, being used to memorialize her—outliving her, even. Carrie Fisher had become fixed as Leia, unable to escape her even in death. She had used Leia's words to mean so much more than they had inside *Star Wars,* to outgrow the character and turn nostalgia for the franchise into dry, witty clear-sightedness. Carrie Fisher had used nostalgia to outrun death.

DEATH COMES FOR NOSTALGIA

It is no surprise that death, both in fiction and in reality, should have provided *Star Wars* with irreversible articulation points after Lucas. Death loomed large over the *Star Wars* franchise even before Fisher's untimely passing. *The Force Awakens* had featured the climactic death of Han Solo at the hands of his son, perhaps the biggest pop culture talking point to emerge out of the film. In many ways, it was no surprise: Harrison Ford was the oldest of the core returning cast, and he had been agitating for Han Solo to be martyred since at least *Return of the Jedi*. Structurally, the death had also reinforced *The Force Awakens* as a film transitioning between eras—a legacy film, with Solo's death marking the decline of the older generation—as well as Solo's place as departing mentor for Rey and Finn. But it also raised death as an ongoing specter for the sequel trilogy. Each film, we were told, would be focused on the story of one of the original three characters: Han in *The Force Awakens*, Luke in *The Last Jedi*, and Leia in *Episode IX*.[4] Now that Solo had completed his arc by dying, would the sequel trilogy be a mournful parade of death, with a new saga film every two years set up to murder a beloved icon of popular culture? As it happened, that seems to have indeed been the case, with Luke passing into the force in *The Last Jedi*, and Fisher's death meaning Leia won't likely live beyond *Episode IX*.

Death haunts the legacy film. Frequently, legacy characters sacrifice themselves for the new era in order to mark the moment of handover between generations of characters. The legacy accordingly becomes a bequeathal. Incidentally, this is why Hamill was wrong about his now well-known suggestion that *The Force Awakens* should have ended with Luke and Leia witnessing Han's death instead of Rey and Finn, "two people who have known Han for 20 minutes."[5] The death of a legacy character like Han does not serve to reanimate other legacy characters—it serves to cede narrative agency to the new, younger protagonists. In *Star Trek Generations*, Kirk dies fighting for the new captain of the Enterprise. In *Terminator Genisys*, the aged Terminator, "Pops," sacrifices himself to destroy the younger Terminator and save the heroes. In *Independence Day: Resurgence*, former president Whitmore blows himself up to destroy the alien Queen's ship and save his daughter. In *Tron: Legacy*, perhaps the most poignant of these moments, the present-day Jeff Bridges (as Kevin Flynn) destroys himself and his digitally de-aged version (as CLU) in order to allow his son to escape. Death even haunts *Creed*, which doesn't kill Rocky Balboa but instead sees him diagnosed with non-Hodgkin's lymphoma.

Interestingly for *Star Wars*, Fisher's death—and presumably, Leia's approaching off-screen passing—also has precedent for the legacy film. Shortly before production began on *Star Trek Beyond* (2016), the second sequel to J. J. Abrams's *Star Trek* legacy film, Leonard Nimoy died as the result of complications from chronic obstructive pulmonary disease. The script was accordingly rewritten to include a brief scene where Spock the younger (Zachary Quinto) learns of Spock Prime's passing and inherits some of his personal effects. "It was so sweet to see dad there, still resonating, still present," Nimoy's son, Adam, said of the inclusion in *Star Trek Beyond*.[6] A similar use of a photograph is made in *Indiana Jones and the Kingdom of the Crystal Skull* to allow the passing of Denholm Elliott (who played Marcus Brody) to be acknowledged.

Death is, of course, an unavoidable end of nostalgia, as well as one of its major thematic preoccupations. Remember, of course, that Johannes Hofer, the Swiss physician who coined the term, referred to nostalgia as a potentially fatal disease. Until even as late as the 1950s, nostalgia was a diagnosis for extreme depression, and even a substitute for what today would be recognized as mental illnesses that resulted in death.[7]

The relationship between nostalgia and death is a complicated one. By looking to the power of the past, nostalgia allows us to downplay mortality and give authority to what has already been lost, expired, or ended. We might even think of nostalgia as the poetics of evading death's grasp. Nostalgia allows us to revisit the past and imbue it with meaning, often in direct relation to the present. "Nostalgia is part of the arsenal of psychological mechanisms that enables people to use the past to fight the future," writes Jacob Juhl and a team of psychology researchers in the *Journal of Research in Personality*. This is not meant poetically. In their research, Juhl and colleagues discovered a curious side effect of strong nostalgic feelings: they help people psychologically fight against what they term "death anxiety" and "mortality reminders."[8] In other words, for the nostalgic, the fear of death is less of a pressing existential threat than it otherwise would be. Nostalgia defangs death.

Images are today an intrinsic part of our relationship to the past and, inherently, death. Photography, in particular, allows us to re-

gard the past both intimately and at a reserve. Susan Sontag wrote
that photographs exercise a dual fascination through reminding
viewers of death and inviting them to sentimentality: "Photographs
turn the past into an object of tender regard, scrambling moral dis-
tinctions and disarming historical judgements by the generalized
pathos of looking at time past."[9] The photograph allows what has
been lost—the moment, the past, even people—to become an object to be regarded at the viewer's leisure. A photograph, as an index
of a moment in time, also marks the passing of time. The more one
returns to a photo, the further one is from the time that it presents.
Bryan Turner sums this up bleakly: "The family album functions
as a portable graveyard."[10] People are never entirely lost so long as
they are memorialized, and the past is never truly dead when it has
been photographed.

Nancy Martha West provides a striking example of the complex relationship between death, nostalgia, and photography in her
book *Kodak and the Lens of Nostalgia*. West narrates how she happened
upon an obscure, unused Kodak advertising campaign from 1932
called the "Death Campaign." These were advertisements created
by the J. Walter Thompson agency for Kodak that featured cap-
tioned photographs of a fairly striking pattern: "That was the last
time Dad was with us," "Thanksgiving 1930—the last time we were
ever to be together," "Your Mother was the loveliest woman that
ever lived, my son," and so on. Perhaps the most extreme of these
advertisements invokes the death of a child: "Here's our boy with
his first dog—I'll never forget how happy he was." These advertisements so mundanely depict a staggeringly confronting use of death
that it is hardly a surprise that they were unused by Kodak, a corporation so deeply otherwise involved in painting an idyllic vision
of daily life. They also recognize the fundamental melancholy of
photography and its relationship to mortality—far too disturbing an
admission for an advertisement to make. As West writes:

> The Death Campaign violated the very foundation on
> which Kodak advertising had been based—indeed, on which
> all advertising is based. In this campaign, Kodak acknowl-
> edged for one brief moment that we take photos to ward

off death and sorrow—and that when death does strike,
photos can have a meaningfulness that outweighs and cuts
through the usual nostalgia when such documents are taken
for granted.[11]

Photographs, as objects, are desirable at least partly because they
can serve as our memories of the dead. This is what the Death Campaign reveals so strikingly. The same is true of all image-based media. Films similarly preserve life through their recording and representation of it. Rudolph Valentino, a man who died sixty-one years
before I was born, is as alive to me when I watch *The Sheik* as he was
to viewers in 1921 when it premiered. This is precisely one of the
reasons that nostalgia is such a powerful filmic device: it is endlessly
renewable through its escape of death. Han Solo will never be dead
as long as he exists in *Star Wars* Episodes IV–VII and beyond, a fact
laid bare by Disney's immediate revival of him in a stand-alone film
the moment he was murdered in *The Force Awakens*. Han Solo is
dead, long live Han Solo. To borrow a line from Obi-Wan Kenobi,
a character whose death in the first *Star Wars* film has not made him
any less central to the series: "If you strike me down, I shall become
more powerful than you can possibly imagine." As memory objects,
media can cheat death in nostalgic ways.

Absences and end points are crucial questions for seriality and
nostalgia, however. The deaths of Han, Luke, and Carrie Fisher
may be moments of finitude, but they mark only one end of a media
cycle that can be endlessly renewed by audiences and even creators.
This is assured by the very nature of serial storytelling, which is always in flux in terms of its reception. A viewer cannot ever behold
the entirety of a serial narrative at once—there are always gaps, if
only in the chasm between the first and the final episodes. This is
why serial narratives are fundamentally nostalgic forms. Katharina
Neimeyer and Daniela Wentz go so far as to argue that television
series can never "*not* evoke a feeling of nostalgia, because they are
based on the imperative to always leave a void." This void, Neimeyer and Wentz argue, can be found in the "temporal gaps between episodes and seasons, the void a long-watched series leaves
when it finally ends, or the never-arriving closure of an unfinished

narrative." Nostalgia is created by the ungraspable nature of the series itself: one can only directly apprehend one segment of the narrative at any given moment, and all else is mediated via memory. I cannot meaningfully watch all episodes of *Star Wars* at once, so the only way to make sense of *A New Hope* while watching *The Force Awakens* is through my memories of it. "Series always create gaps that can never be filled, even by rewatching them," write Neimeyer and Wentz.[12] This is true regardless of whether I am encountering the *Star Wars* films for the first time or the five hundredth. Such voids define the nostalgic quotidian experience of engaging with serial storytelling.

The void and the absence are deathly for serial storytelling. As viewers, we crave for what is not present—this is the logic of nostalgia. Nostalgic longing, writes Svetlana Boym, is "defined by loss of the original object of desire, and by its spatial and temporal displacement."[13] When I am watching the final episode of a series I am nostalgic for the first, and when it is finished, I am nostalgic for the series itself. This is especially true for series that follow a variation on a theme model, like *Law & Order,* where according to Ndalianis, "each additional episode lays itself over prior episodes in an attempt to perfect on predecessors and, partially at least, erase their presence throughout performance."[14] The best James Bond film is always the next one, for example.

Serial storytelling's inherent nostalgia has been taken advantage of by various formats over the years. For the written word, the way that serial stories could be published in magazines and then packaged and released as complete books (as with much of the work of Charles Dickens, for example) allowed readers to experience the story in an enforced, temporal fashion and then once again, if they wished, as a collated work. For television, the rerun is the obvious example, and even underpins the logic of entire networks. It has been possible to watch shows like *I Love Lucy* and *Gunsmoke* in rerun or syndication in the United States (and many other countries) since they were first broadcast in the 1950s, for example. Time may progress in an overall series narrative for these shows, but it is practically speaking always suspended within an endless loop that can be entered at will via the rerun.

As Neimeyer and Wentz note, series can of course become nostalgic for themselves, too. A common trait that plays on inherent nostalgia within the serial is the clip show, where the characters remember the series' own past in the form of montage.[15] "Look back over your time together," Joey implores Chandler in the *Friends* clip show episode from season 7, "The One with the Vows." Part of the appeal is enabled by technology—in an era before DVD box sets or binge streaming services, the clip show enabled access to nostalgic favorite moments only otherwise possible through the laborious (and sometimes chance-based) practice of tracking reruns. Yet the clip show also doubles the audience's inherent nostalgia for the serial with the show's characters': serial nostalgia becomes part of the diegesis. The void is momentarily closed; the wound of nostalgia is temporarily healed. Past becomes present, death is reanimated.

We can see similar examples of this kind of diegetic serial nostalgia in *Star Wars*, too, which highlights the degree to which nostalgia is inherently part of serial storytelling. In *Return of the Jedi*, C-3PO retells the story of our heroes to the Ewoks by the fireside, complete with sound effects from the Death Star dogfight, AT-AT battle, and the Vader and Skywalker duel at Cloud City from *Empire Strikes Back*. Within *Return of the Jedi*'s plot, it is a moment of bonding between the Ewoks and our heroes (one goes so far as to hug Han Solo's leg upon hearing about the carbonite). Within the film, however, it functions as a moment of nostalgic respite for the audience before the renewed tension of the original trilogy's final climax. In *Return of the Jedi*, our nostalgia for the adventures of the first two films is authorized and enhanced, even as we watch the (then) final installment. Another audacious example of this comes from *The Last Jedi*, where in the final scene we are shown a child retelling the climactic events of the very same film—essentially legitimizing and playing on nostalgia for events that have occurred on-screen in this serial narrative only minutes previously.

The most reflexive example of this kind of diegetic serial nostalgia is from earlier in *The Last Jedi*, as R2-D2 replays—of course—the hologram of Leia's "Help me Obi-Wan Kenobi, you're my only hope" speech from *A New Hope* in order to convince him to rejoin the fight. "A cheap move," Luke tells us, but the use of this material

"You're my only hope."

is illustrative, and not just for its nostalgic links to the way the speech was used to memorialize Fisher (and presumably this scene was written and shot well before she died). "Nostalgia obviously has links to the inevitably mediatised past," write Neimeyer and Wentz. "It is based on the indivisible connection between one's own past and the media that accompanied that past."[16] R2's Leia hologram is the only on-screen example of diegetic media being used as a nostalgic device in *Star Wars* so far. It is as though the clip show could somehow be inserted within the world of *Friends*, and not just be used as a stand-in for the characters' memories. Luke is actually watching the media of his youth, and he accordingly feels a nostalgic pang. Interestingly, it is not quite so straightforward to invoke nostalgia via media today, as the hologram had to be painstakingly reconstructed by *The Last Jedi*'s special effects team, who found the original dailies and re-created the distorted video effect.[17]

Again, this is not an isolated strategy: in *Star Trek Beyond*, Spock the younger—and the audience—are allowed to memorialize Spock Prime via a photograph of the original cast (in actuality a promotional photo for *Star Trek V: The Final Frontier*) found among the older Spock's possessions. Audience memory and series nostalgia come together in the guise of the mediated past. It is tempting to read these instances as commentary on the way that nostalgia is inherently tied to media, up to and including films like *The Last Jedi* and *Star Trek Beyond*. Like the photos of Fisher projected in the convention center hall in Orlando as her daughter recited her famous speech, Leia has been immortalized through media within the *Star Wars* universe itself. The nostalgia inherent in media serves as our memories of the past and of the dead.

FROM FATHERS TO SONS

It is worth asking where Leia has been in the Disney era. As much as Leia is a presence in the post-Lucas *Star Wars* era, in marketing and fan discourse, we have to admit that she has hardly been in the films at all. Though there is little reason not to believe Kennedy's assertion that *Episode IX* would have been Leia's film—after Han's (*The Force Awakens*) and Luke's (*The Last Jedi*)—the fact of the matter is that we have been left with two films that foreground other characters (even new ones) at her expense. This was set up by *The Force Awakens*: Han Solo, the fan favorite and with Ford the most active actor, has the major emotional arc of the first film, while Luke is positioned as the MacGuffin mystery that must be unveiled in the second. Our now General Leia simply gets on with the job, setting the events of the film in motion by sending Poe to Jakku, taking the threat presented by the First Order seriously, and trying to persuade the New Republic to do likewise. For her efforts, she receives only a handful of scenes (and at least one, with Maisie Richardson-Sellers, that was cut). In *The Last Jedi*, she fares little better—despite having more screen time than in *The Force Awakens*, Leia is in a coma for a large portion of the film.

This is in line with the broader patterns of the legacy film. Whether because the original franchises that the legacy films revive were male dominated, or whether because of lingering misogyny in a film industry that has little place for aging women actors, legacy characters are predominantly men. Consider the field: in *Tron: Legacy*, *Terminator Genisys*, and *Jurassic World*, there are no women legacy characters/actors whatsoever. The *Jurassic Park* series, more broadly, only ever brought back Laura Dern's original character for a few minutes in *Jurassic Park III* (in a cameo that suggests she has given up paleontology to become a mother), despite extended return appearances for Sam Neill, Jeff Goldblum, and even B.D. Wong. In *Independence Day Resurgence*, Vivica Fox does make a brief reappearance as Jasmine Hiller—though not only is she killed off, but this must be placed against the legacy-like extended returns of Goldblum, Bill Pullman, Judd Hirsch, and Brent Spiner. In *Vacation*, Beverly D'Angelo makes about as much of an appearance as Ellen Griswold as Chevy Chase does as Clarke, but the transferal of the legacy still clearly takes place between father and son.

Also notable is the absence of mothers in these films, as compared with the ubiquity of fathers and father figures. *Creed* is about Adonis Creed's need to come to terms with the legacy of his dead father, and his search for a substitute father figure (which he finds in Rocky). His adoptive mother, Mary Anne Creed (Phylicia Rashad), is mostly used in the film to warn him about the dangers of boxing and to object to his pursuit of a career like his father's. In *Star Trek*, we spend a small amount of time with Spock's human mother, Amanda Grayson (Winona Ryder) before she dies dramatically, serving as a moment of crisis for Spock. We also see both of Kirk's parents in the film's dramatic opening sequence: his mother is in childbirth with Kirk, while his father bravely sacrifices himself to save her (and many others) during a surprise attack. For the rest of the film, Kirk's father's heroism drives him, while his mother is unseen, leaving *Star Trek* interested only in Kirk's father's actions and choices, and his mother's reproductive abilities. Even in the legacy-like Abrams project *Super 8*, mothers are notable only through their absence. The film, of course, begins with the death of Joe Courtney's mother in a workplace accident. Joe becomes close to a young girl, Alice Dainard, whose mother left her and her father when she was young. Joe's father blames Alice's father for the death of Joe's mother: thus, the film is about the conflict between fathers and the absence of mothers, as seen through the eyes of children.

Of all the legacy films identified in this book, *Indiana Jones and the Kingdom of the Crystal Skull* is alone in featuring a meaningful woman legacy character. Marion Ravenwood (Karen Allen) may be surrounded by men—Indiana Jones, Mutt Williams, George "Mac" McHale, Harold "Ox" Oxley—but she has a good amount of screen time and is a reoccurring character from a previous franchise entry. She is also a mother, and the fact that *Crystal Skull* allows her to at least tag along for the main adventure (much less her agency or characterization in the film) places it at odds with the general patterns of the legacy film. *Crystal Skull* aside, the legacy film as a body of work treats mothers and women legacy characters as absent, nonexistent, sacrificial homebodies unable to join men, young and old, on their adventures.

Moreover, men can embrace their age in the legacy film. They frequently look weathered and aged, in part to highlight the weariness or maturity of their characters, but also to simply mark the passing of time. Hamill even expressed surprise that *The Force Awakens* should emphasize his gray hair and beard: "Chronologically, if this follows *Return of the Jedi*, I'm only in my early fifties," he said. "What's this Methuselah look you have planned for me?"[18] In *Tron: Legacy*, Bridges has flowing, white hair, and in *Crystal Skull*, Spielberg enjoyed showing Indiana Jones being more out of breath in his older age: "Let's have some fun with that. Let's not hide that," he said.[19]

In contrast, in *Blade Runner 2049*, Sean Young does not reappear, but a digital re-creation of her twenty-three-year-old face from the time of the original film does. This version was painstakingly re-created by a VFX company over the course of a year, and then mapped onto the performance of a look-alike actor, who was coached by Young. Young herself was not even able to voice the character, as the director Denis Villeneuve "worked with several actresses in order to find the closest thing that sounds like Sean Young."[20] This is, of course, quite similar to the processes used to digitally re-create Leia for her single shot in *Rogue One*: a digital face was mapped onto a real actor (Ingvild Deila), and in this case, archival recordings were used for her single line ("hope"), despite the then eighty-five-year-old James Earl Jones being asked to record new dialogue for Darth Vader. Fisher was not involved in *Rogue One*, though she was personally shown the end result by Kennedy.[21]

The quest for photorealism is particularly striking here. It is technology in the service of nostalgia, an attempt to use the cutting edge to create a freeze frame of the past. "While nostalgia mourns distances and disjunctures between times and spaces, never bridging them, technology offers solutions and builds bridges, saving the time that the nostalgic loves to waste," writes Svetlana Boym.[22] For the film theorist André Bazin, images (especially realistic ones) help preserve their subjects from death. This "mummy complex," as Bazin terms it after the Egyptian practice of embalming the dead so that they might continue to survive, is a defense against death and the passage of time.[23] For many, especially those who saw *Rogue One* after Fisher's hospitalization and death, this bit of CGI realism (along with Peter Cushing's digital resurrection) seemed ghoulish and zombie-like, a digitally animated corpse forced to perform for the purposes of serial nostalgia.

After Fisher's death, Gareth Edwards (who didn't meet Fisher) said that "the whole thing was, to be honest, one big love letter to Carrie. What we're doing with the entire movie is all building to that one moment [of the Death Star plans being handed to Princess Leia] where we hand the baton to her, to go off and make that film that inspired us all as kids."[24] The "handing the baton" imagery invoked by Edwards is illuminating, as is his use of the present tense. Where leading men are allowed to age in the era of the legacy film, women in *Blade Runner 2049* and *Rogue One* are maintained as ageless through the power of computer imagery. Leia has, in one timeline, become General Leia, an aged leader, strategist, and mother; in another, she has returned as Princess Leia to the beginning of her serial narrative loop, before she was a mother, unable to age, unable to grow old, and unable to escape nostalgia's deathly grasp.

DEAD MEDIA

The dead subjects of nostalgia can, of course, also be media forms. In his original identification of *Star Wars* as a nostalgia film, Fredric Jameson talks of the way that it satisfies the longing to experience what he calls "dead forms" again. For Jameson, "the adult public is able to gratify a deeper and more properly nostalgic desire to return to that older period and to live its strange old aesthetic artefacts through once again."[25] By imitating the old adventure serial, *Star Wars* offers audiences a kind of access to their memories of the past. Nostalgia as a contemporary phenomenon is once again clearly linked to media objects as markers of time and passing. Their resurrection is a kind of illusory necromancy. Dead media forms can no more be truly revived than people can. We can think here of the original *Star Wars*, or of a film like *The Artist*, both of which seemed to revive dormant media practices (the adventure serial and the silent film, respectively) but in fact altered and tweaked them for their new eras. *The Artist* makes extensive use of synchronized sound, for instance, and we have seen time and again how *Star Wars* reacts to changing eras and time. As Boym reminds us, nostalgia is "fantasies of the past determined by needs of the present."[26] Dead media are never really resurrected.

Nor can we ever really return to the media or the culture of our youth, however strong our nostalgic urges may be. If we could actually enact the return, then nostalgia could not function, as it is the act of being in the present and looking back. As a nostalgic franchise, then, it is no surprise that all new *Star Wars* films from *Return of the Jedi* onward have been held to the impossible standard of the past and, in the eyes of many, failed. The prequels were not as good as the originals: *The Force Awakens* was too nostalgic, *Rogue One* too tied to *A New Hope*, *The Last Jedi* not as fun as *The Force Awakens*, and the less said about *Solo* the better. If only George Lucas "weren't hooked on the crap of his childhood," protested Pauline Kael in 1981.[27] We cannot re-create the past or reenter it through media. We cannot hold the past in place, even temporarily, by rewatching the films of one's youth. Once seen for the first time, *Star Wars* can never be reencountered, only revisited and replayed. Those who are nostalgic search for an ineffable essence that is only possible through the lens of the present.

The nostalgic essence is in fact a void, a null, a lack. It is manifested partly through its relationship with death. Nostalgia is fundamentally a poetic strategy for avoiding loss or attempting to recover the unrecoverable. "Nostalgia too easily mates with banality," writes Boym, "by covering up the pain of loss in order to give a specific form to homesickness and to make homecoming available on request."[28] The search for a return to the original essence of time past is one such example of banality, where it is hoped that media will serve our nostalgic yearnings at the press of a DVD remote.

Nostalgia is also fragile, and the solution to its ends with death lies in transferal. This is why the legacy model is so important to this contemporary reworking of the nostalgia film: the past is returned to and sent forward in a single motion. Death is overcome, nostalgia is preserved. Göran Bolin argues that nostalgia is at the root of generational gaps, often appearing between parents and children through insurmountable differences in their respective media landscapes. Nostalgia is an essential part of what Bolin calls the "process of generationing," that is, the delineation of generations as distinct identities, because "it actualises the relation between the present and the past."[29] This is why it is so crucial for the logic of the legacy film to avoid the finality of death and make the transferal between generations.

Fisher, in *The Princess Diarist*, keenly observes this point through her years of interacting with *Star Wars* fans. She notes how *Star Wars* fans have a "common language that runs from five to eighty-five," that is deliberately and almost ritualistically cultivated by parents in their children.

> In a way, it's as if they know they have this great gift to bestow, and they want to bestow it as perfectly as possible—the perfect time, the perfect place, the perfect situation for passing on this life-defining experience. And the kids will always remember for their entire lives how they first felt when they first saw their now favorite movie. And they were given this gift from their parents, and can now share it together. Truly a family affair.[30]

Is it worth wondering, then, why it was Fisher's own daughter, Billie Lourd, who memorialized her at Lucasfilm's *Star Wars* anniversary? Why Lourd herself now has a small role in the sequel trilogy (Lieutenant Connix)? Why Fisher seems, with both humor and sincerity, to have taught her hologram speech from *A New Hope* so carefully to her daughter? Why this speech has, it seems, formed a crucial part of her own response to nostalgia and even the process of generationing—of passing on, of legacy—with her own daughter?

Fisher, for her own part, ends her 2008 memoir *Wishful Drinking* with an enigmatic and reliably witty clue. Fisher notes that for all the important things in her life that she's forgotten through illness, drugs, and the voluntary electroconvulsive therapy (ECT) she undertook for her bipolar disorder, one thing remains.

"I can't forget that stupid, fucking hologram speech! That's why I did dope!"[31]

9

I WILL FINISH
WHAT YOU STARTED

Star Wars *from* The Last Jedi *and Beyond*

"We are what they grow beyond," Yoda tells Luke Skywalker in *The Last Jedi,* in perhaps the film's best contribution to the nearly endless library of *Star Wars* quotable quotes. The optimistic Luke Skywalker of the original trilogy is gone, and in his place is a regretful, old, isolated man. Luke failed to teach Ben Solo, and at this stage in *The Last Jedi,* he has failed to impart much of use to Rey, who has just left him alone on his island again. In a moment of temper, Luke has decided to burn down the Jedi library and destroy the wisdom contained within. Yoda, in a surprise appearance (and one of the film's most closely held production secrets), has returned in ghost form to prod Luke in the right direction, yet again. "Skywalker, still looking to the horizon," Yoda chides Luke in an echo of his training from *The Empire Strikes Back.* "Never here, now, hmm?" To look to the future, we must first be visited by our past. This is the heart of *Star Wars.*

In contrast to the enormous expectations faced by *The Force Awakens* and *Rogue One,* Rian Johnson's *The Last Jedi* might have felt a bit like a victory lap. By 2017 Star Wars had been successfully revived and renewed for a new generation of fans and films, and the Disney model of development had been proved a success. The specter of the previous decade's prequel trilogy was long gone, and the world of popular culture had been recentered on *Star Wars*, Rey, Finn, and Poe. Questions of inheritance and legacy were far less desperate than they had seemed back in 2015: *The Last Jedi* only had to maintain and extend the franchise, and perhaps for some fans, tweak things a little and offer up a few surprises. There were also, of course, always some elements predestined to be marketing and filmmaking coups. Luke Skywalker would speak. Rey's parentage would likely be revealed. Audiences would see Carrie Fisher's final performance in the role that made her an icon.

Yet despite excellent critical reviews and a predictably strong box office, *The Last Jedi* was not quite the straightforward triumph that it might have been. What audiences found instead in December 2017 was a *Star Wars* film concerned more so than ever with history.

Perhaps it should not be surprising that the *Star Wars* franchise, one that began with the words "A long time ago," should continue to converge on the past. Certainly this point has been a consistent one throughout this book and throughout broader analyses of *Star Wars* in general—we need only to point for the umpteenth time to Fredric Jameson and the critique of nostalgia to make this abundantly clear. Nostalgia was one of the key forces at work in the Disney revival era, too. *The Force Awakens* put nostalgia squarely in the service of the legacy film model, reinstating the power of the past while setting up the future of a franchise. In J. J. Abrams's hands, the burden of *Star Wars* was transferred from one generation to another, reviving the myth and the mystery of the franchise in the process.

Yet here was a rueful Luke Skywalker in *The Last Jedi*, sitting downcast with Yoda after the latter had destroyed the Jedi library—Luke having lost his nerve. "Heeded my words not, did you? Pass on what you have learned," the ghost of Yoda tells Luke, invoking his dying words from *Return of the Jedi*. "Luke, we are what they grow beyond. That is the true burden of all masters."

If *The Force Awakens* was about reviving and empowering a legacy, then *The Last Jedi* is about transcending it, of growing beyond

"We are what they grow beyond."

it. It was accordingly not *The Last Jedi*'s concern with history that
made it different for a *Star Wars* film: it was its entire approach to it.
In fact, *The Last Jedi* dramatically reversed a lot of what had come
to be expected from the pattern of the legacy film in its questioning of history. If *The Force Awakens* was about the importance of the
past, then *The Last Jedi* is about upending it. If *The Force Awakens*
was about reinvigorating *Star Wars* as a franchise by looking to its
past successes, then *The Last Jedi* is about pushing beyond that past
success. For *The Force Awakens*, the past is "true, all of it." Kylo Ren
in *The Last Jedi* instead presents history as an ultimatum: you have
to "let the past die," he tells Rey. "Kill it, if you have to." This is a
far cry from the boy who once sat before Darth Vader's mangled
helmet and begged it to tell him what to do.

If we might start to wonder if the rejection of the past is simply
the villain's domain, then *The Last Jedi* shows us both sides of the
galactic conflict taking this attitude. In exile, Luke Skywalker has
concluded that—in a line that was used hungrily by Disney marketing teams—"it's time for the Jedi to end." Having studied Jedi
history—and in effect, Jedi actions during the events of the *Star
Wars* prequel trilogy—Luke has come to view the Jedi as an unhelp-
ful legend that deceives and blinds in equal measure. Here, *The Last
Jedi* rearticulates the critique of the order mounted in the prequels
but perhaps never quite delivered clearly by George Lucas. "The

Jedi are romanticized, deified," Luke tells Rey. "If you strip away the myth and look at their deeds, the legacy of the Jedi is failure." In effect, Luke's belief has followed a mirror trajectory to Han Solo's, who doubted the Force and the Jedi in *A New Hope* but by *The Force Awakens* had embraced their mythos. The two films also follow their characters' leads.

We learn about trauma and loss and failure from Luke Skywalker in *The Last Jedi*. Not only is he scared of Rey's abilities, but he proclaims that he wasn't scared enough of the young Ben Solo's. Luke is scared of his own past and the galaxy's. Like the original trilogy's Obi-Wan Kenobi, Luke bends the truth about his past to Rey, but unlike Obi-Wan he does this out of remorse rather than the need to protect his student. This is a Luke Skywalker who once considered murdering a sleeping boy: "I was left with shame, and with consequence," he confesses to Rey. *The Last Jedi*, as well as Skywalker himself, wishes to begin by diminishing his legacy.

More broadly, *The Last Jedi* draws a picture of a galaxy where people are no longer fascinated by a mythological past but instead going to great lengths to push away from it. Perhaps not coincidentally, this also allows the filmmakers to respond to the "remake" criticism that was leveled at *The Force Awakens* and provides Disney with a clearer agenda for its sequel trilogy. If *The Last Jedi* had been another *Star Wars* film that faced strident criticism for being too similar to previous successes, the franchise's future might have even been in jeopardy. Even the appearance of *Empire Strikes Back*–style walkers in early marketing material necessitated public reassurances from Johnson about the film's originality.[1] Anything too similar to the existing *Star Wars* pattern would have had its own substantial creative risks of a magnitude much larger than the first few Disney films.

The end result was a *Last Jedi* that to some extent turned the legacy film model back in on itself. Far from simply tapping into the power of the existing franchise mythology, *The Last Jedi* actively questioned it. This is a film that draws power from unsettling the status quo, from highlighting the mistakes of the past, and from the need to identify and reject the failures of this history at all costs. Let the past come at us and we will kill it, *The Last Jedi* begins by saying.

We will draw power from its memory before crushing it and pointing to the future.

Even Supreme Leader Snoke, who gleefully agrees with Luke's death wish once he uncovers it from Rey's mind, is discarded in *The Last Jedi*'s desire to push away the past. In the years between the release of *The Force Awakens* and *The Last Jedi*, Snoke had become something of an enigma to be conjectured over by fans, and in perhaps *The Last Jedi*'s biggest surprise, Snoke is discarded without much flourish. Kylo Ren stands before Snoke's murdered body, asking Rey to join him, and do away with such old things: the Jedi, the Sith, the Empire, the Rebellion. In the process, an infinitely more interesting—and less predictable—dynamic between antagonist and protagonist is clearly established, rather than rehearsing the same Vader-Emperor-Luke relationship from *Return of the Jedi*. Such a genuine claim on succession—and perhaps *secession*—has rarely been offered by the *Star Wars* franchise. The questions of legacy so attentively set up by *The Force Awakens* are, one by one, dismissed by *The Last Jedi*. Rey's parents? They do not matter to this story. Snoke's origins? Also insignificant. What will Luke do when he is faced with his past and presented with his old lightsaber? Literally and figuratively, he will throw it all away.

Yet Johnson, the film's writer and director, is neither as dismissive of history as Kylo Ren nor as keen to fumble around in it as Luke. *The Last Jedi* eventually offers an interesting negotiation between history and future. "I always think that if you're cutting off the past you're fooling yourself, you're just burying it somewhere where it's going to come back," said Johnson after the film's release. "The only way forward is where Rey actually lands, which is to build on the past—not necessarily to wallow in it, the way that Luke is doing . . . but to take what's best from it, build on it and appreciate it and move forward, which is what Rey's path is in the movie."[2] Rey meets her hero in Luke Skywalker and quickly learns that he has little interest in either helping her or living up to her expectations. Though she gives him opportunity enough to change his mind and tries to convince him of his remaining importance ("the galaxy may need a legend"), Rey leaves Luke on his island and pursues Kylo. She has sentimentality and appreciation of the past, but not enough to get in the way of what needs to be done in the present. Nevertheless, when confronted by Kylo's revelation about her parents and his invitation to create a new path together, she declines. At the beginning of *The Force Awakens*, we encountered a girl who hoped for nothing more than her parents to return, for a home, and for people to care about her. Earlier in *The Last Jedi*, Rey still begs Luke to "show me my place in all of this." Yet when confronted by Kylo Ren, a man she shares an intimate connection with, who tells her that "you come from nothing. You're nothing. But not to me," she nonetheless refuses. Rey admires the past—but she is not blind to it.

Luke Skywalker, in turn, has one of the most interesting relationships to the past out of all the characters in *The Last Jedi*. In some ways, his character arc recapitulates some of the legacy's journey model discussed earlier in this book. It is Rey who serves as a catalyst for character growth in Luke Skywalker more than the other way around, like Adonis in *Creed* or K in *Blade Runner 2049*. Luke is a reluctant mentor and, unlike many other legacy characters, never fully embraces the role after his failure with Ben. Nonetheless, it is still through Rey that he rediscovers his purpose in this story. Throughout much of *The Last Jedi* Luke dismisses the power of myth as misplaced, and even harmful. Not only was the old Jedi order blinded by their own legend, but Luke feels that he failed as a teacher because of his own: "I failed because I was Luke Skywalker, Jedi master. A legend," he tells Rey.

Yet it is through Rey that Luke realizes that his rejection of the past has gone too far: there is, in fact, power in myth, and he comes to actively wield it as a weapon. Earlier in *The Last Jedi*, he chides Rey for imagining that "I'm going to walk out with a laser sword and face down the entire First Order," yet this is precisely what he ends up doing at the film's climax. Luke sacrifices himself to intensify his myth and gift it to the Resistance. This whole sequence shows us another Luke Skywalker we haven't seen before in *Star Wars*—confident, in control, even brash. He emerges from in front of an almost celestial halo—a callback to his first silhouetted appearance in *Return of the Jedi*—speaks with and reassures his estranged sister, and throws a wink at C-3Po. When an incensed Kylo

Ren commands all of the First Order might to rain down on Luke, he theatrically brushes it off before outmatching Kylo in a duel and quoting his dead father at him ("See you 'round, kid"). Every act in this sequence is a dramatic reversal for Luke, the man who earlier believed symbolic gestures and myths to be hollow burdens.

"What do you think one guy walking out there with a lightsaber [can do]?" asked Johnson after *The Last Jedi*'s release. "The answer is: Create a legend that will spread hope . . . there's nothing more powerful that he could accomplish."[3] Luke Skywalker chooses to become an invincible symbol of hope for the failing Resistance. This is in many respects in keeping with the *Star Wars* ethos that if belief is all that you have, then it can still save the galaxy. The Empire had the resources and the technology, but the Rebels had the devotion to their cause. As *The Last Jedi*'s final sequence of awestruck children reenacting Luke's sacrifice demonstrates, this principle still holds true in today's galaxy far, far away.

This is a challenging piece of filmmaking in the context of the *Star Wars* franchise and its renewal under Disney. Taken to its logical endpoint, Johnson is asking us to believe in the power of *Star Wars* and also in Lucasfilm's ability to exceed what already exists in that universe. To have faith that Kathleen Kennedy and Disney can acknowledge the power of all that Lucas built and still build more. The original trilogy was a trap. As long as the nostalgic fondly cradled their too-perfect memories of *Star Wars*, nothing new would ever be good enough. Luke, Han, Leia, Darth Vader, the Empire, the Rebels—they are what *Star Wars* grows beyond.

THE TRANSFORMATION OF *STAR WARS*

Yoda's aphorism doesn't just encapsulate *The Last Jedi*. A more appropriate epitaph for the transition of *Star Wars* and Lucasfilm from an independent, Lucas-owned company to Disney-owned pop culture behemoth could not be imagined. In a relatively short space of time, Kennedy had gone from inheriting a company whose biggest assets were some spec scripts and an animated television show to managing arguably the biggest media franchise on the planet. The change in prospects for Story Group member Pablo Hidalgo is particularly illustrative: in 2012 he'd just finished work on a big retrospective publishing project, *Star Wars: The Essential Reader's Guide*, a kind of trainspotting book for fans of the Expanded Universe books. Then, in a secretive meeting, his boss revealed that they'd be making Episodes VII, VIII, and IX. In the moment, Hidalgo, for his part, needed to sit down and happily said "something that's unprintable."[4] Five years later, and Hidalgo regularly works on *Rebels*, works closely with every big name *Star Wars* director to ensure *Star Wars* lore is being observed, and serves as the Lucasfilm creative team's public face, routinely answering questions via Twitter from fans desperate for any morsel of information. *Star Wars* is now a major pillar in Disney's entire corporate strategy. Lucasfilm has not just kept up: it has transformed itself accordingly.

How much, though, did *The Last Jedi* actually transform *Star Wars* going forward? To many, it looked like one of the most radical entries in the franchise yet: a film calculated to provide change and direction for a new era that would move beyond *The Force Awakens* and *Rogue One*. The transmedia expert Jeff Gomez described *The Last Jedi* as the "self-disruption" of the *Star Wars* brand, a challenging move designed to "jolt a company out of stasis and jumpstart progress."[5] Yet there are many reasons to think that *The Last Jedi* did not stray as much from the old *Star Wars* model as we might think.

Johnson was presumed by many to be the "radical" force at the heart of *The Last Jedi*'s departures for the series. Nonetheless, he actually shares quite a lot in common with even Abrams and Gareth Edwards. Johnson is another one of Lucasfilm's favored "fanboy auteurs," a director able to claim artistic clout from his well-reviewed filmic oeuvre (which includes the neo-noir *Brick* from 2005 and the sci-fi *Looper* from 2012) as well as a nerd very much at home at Comic-Con talking the language of franchise cinema. We need look no further than his most recent non–*Star Wars* film, *Looper*, to find a scene surprisingly similar to the legacy film model. In *Looper*, of course, we see two versions of the same character—Joe, played by Joseph Gordon-Levitt as a young man and Bruce Willis later in life—within the same timeline. Young Joe has been tasked with killing old Joe, who has time-traveled backward to stop future events from happening. This, in a way, is surprisingly similar to the brief glimpses of the young Spock / Spock Prime sequences in Abrams's *Star Trek* and *Star Trek into Darkness*. Early in *Looper*, we are set up to believe that the film may resolve with old Joe bestowing his legacy to young Joe, as in the legacy model, but this is averted. The central theme of *Looper* is defeating the future and the past simultaneously: "Why don't you do what old men do and die?" young Joe asks old Joe early in the film. We can see already Johnson playing with similar motifs and character structures that he would need to use in his *Star Wars* work.

Equally, far from dismissing the past entirely, *The Last Jedi* is a film deeply engaged with the history of the *Star Wars* franchise. For a film that would supposedly "self-disrupt" the *Star Wars* brand, there are once again a surprising number of allusions to the original films in *The Last Jedi*. Our heroes infiltrate an enemy base in disguise, just like in *A New Hope*. We meet an eccentric rogue-ish type who is revealed to have sold out our heroes to the enemy, just like in *Empire* (though unlike Lando, this character is not redeemed). Also like *Empire* is the appearance of small rebel ships flying out to take on walkers to protect an evacuating base. And, there's a dreamlike sequence where the hero enters a cave in search of answers, only to be presented with their own face in the guise of a parent. Finally, of course, we also have a throne room sequence where an evil apprentice brings his master a Jedi-to-be. The master reveals that the young Jedi's secretive victory plan was in fact the expected result of his own machinations, and shows the Jedi his allies being defeated in a far-off space battle. Instead of converting the Jedi, however, the evil apprentice is coaxed into betraying and killing his master. In this context, it's worth wondering not just whether the film is quite as different as has been claimed, but why *The Last Jedi* was not as widely critiqued for the "remake" or "remix" approach so frequently applied to *The Force Awakens*. Even many of the film's "twists" make sense in retrospect and seem like continuities rather than changes: Kylo Ren's "You're nothing" taunt to Rey actually recalls, if nothing else, the first line anyone ever heard from the character. This is found in the first full *Force Awakens* trailer, where Rey responds to Maz Kanata ("Who are you?") with a simple statement: "I'm no-one." Abrams and Johnson also say that the decision for Rey's parents to be nobodies was decided before *The Force Awakens* was made, and was not some last-minute *Last Jedi* twist.[6]

Equally, just as Lucas drew on a wide variety of filmic references for *Star Wars*, Johnson also created his own—almost official— touchstones for *The Last Jedi*'s production. This selection manifested itself in a film "boot camp," where a number of classics were screened for Lucasfilm staff. Like Lucas's inspirations for *Star Wars*, these included World War II genre films (*Twelve O'Clock High*, *The Bridge on the River Kwai*, *Sahara*), Japanese samurai films (*Three Outlaw Samurai*), and an adventure film (*Gunga Din*).[7] Perhaps all that is missing from the Lucas playbook is a western.

Nonetheless, it is true that *The Last Jedi* contains many departures in terms of *Star Wars* filmic style. Although the traditional wipe transitions and visual spectacle remain, *The Last Jedi* makes a number of tweaks and outright stylistic inventions as far as the franchise has thus far been formally assembled. Even the opening shot suggests this deviation from the norm: while, following the opening crawl, the camera does pan down, it quickly moves from a pan into a kind of hyper dolly, with the camera traveling thousands of kilometers an hour through space, past the evacuating Resistance ships to the planet below. *The Last Jedi* continues this move with stylistic variations. Slow motion is used in almost every fight sequence, for example. Although slow motion has appeared in *Star Wars* before, it was used sparingly: a fleeting shot of Ben Kenobi's death in *A New Hope*, the shot of the Wampa's dismembered arm in *Empire*, and the cave sequence on Dagobah in the same film. In contrast, slow motion is used in *The Last Jedi* during the throne room battle with Rey and Kylo, during the battle between Luke and Kylo on Crait, and extensively during the opening sequence's bombing run. This final instance is also largely without diegetic sound—another new formal decision for *Star Wars*. In the most stylistically dramatic scene of *The Last Jedi*, Holdo's lightspeed sacrifice contains a full ten seconds of silence with no music or sound effects to speak of. We also hear narration for the first time in a *Star Wars* film, as Rey's cave vision is cut to her dialogue from the following scene, creating voice-over in the form of a J cut or audio lead. Cutaways are also featured as part of conversation: while Rey tells Luke and the audience what she sees of the force, we literally see it too in a tour around the island, featuring worms and dirt, wash from the sea, and baby Porgs. Finally, although *The Force Awakens* included a flashback for the first time in a *Star Wars* film, this was mitigated, as it was still from Rey's point of view as she was presented with a vision while touching Luke's old lightsabre. In *The Last Jedi*, on the other hand, we see the same scene from Ben Solo's childhood presented via flashback in three different subjective tellings (in all likelihood this is also an homage to Kurosawa's *Rashomon*).

Nonetheless, what *The Last Jedi* does decisively is set the scene for the conclusion to the Skywalker sequel trilogy in *Episode IX*. Having questioned history, legacy, allegiances, and concluded by reempowering all, *The Last Jedi* ends one of its key relationships with a scene where the force connects Rey and Kylo across time and space (another small stylistic innovation that is heavily used in the film). This time, they are not quite the equals Johnson has painted them as in the rest of the film: Rey looks down on Kylo from the Millennium Falcon as Kylo crouches, holding his father's golden dice, presented by Luke to Leia only minutes earlier. A resolute Rey literally and figuratively closes the door on Kylo (and the audience), and we see her closed off as the Falcon's ramp shuts. She suspends the relationship with Kylo and refuses to grant him the connection with her that he so obviously seeks.

Johnson's use of the closing ramp is a film reference in a long line of film references. In cinematic terms, it is the same door that closes Ethan (John Wayne) out from civilization at the end of *The Searchers* (dir. John Ford, 1956), and that Michael Corleone (Al Pacino) uses to exclude his wife, Kay Adams-Corleone (Diane Keaton), from his "business" affairs at the end of *The Godfather*. This is just to name the most famous two examples of this homage-built-on-homage: it also features in Quentin Tarantino's *Kill Bill* and is parodied in *The Simpsons,* among others. This cinematic shorthand is Johnson's most effective technique for *The Last Jedi*'s climax. We could say much the same about this shot in *The Last Jedi* as David Thomson does about *The Searchers*: "The ending is magnificent, lovely, definitive yet mysterious. And he is not coming in—the door that closes is as final as the one that excludes Kay at the end of *The Godfather*."[8] The con-

nection between Rey and Kylo is, at least for now, voluntarily sev-
ered by Rey in the symbolic closure of the Falcon's door. She might
once have admitted the man she optimistically saw as Ben Solo, but
Rey will no longer welcome a man like Kylo Ren. There were once
alternatives for Kylo, a chance for redemption and salvation, for
leading a life back within the shelter of civilization—but no more.
In one move, Johnson borrows from cinematic history, stylistically
amends it for a galaxy far, far away, and sets the scene for *Episode
IX*. After a film of unsettlement and uncertainty, the battle lines for
the possible conclusion of the Skywalker saga are finally drawn.

A COMPLICATED HOMECOMING

Interestingly, the fan response to *The Last Jedi* was decidedly mixed.
While some had demurred on *The Force Awakens* for being too close
to the original films, *The Last Jedi*'s departures were too radical for
others. The list of complaints against the film from some *Star Wars*
fans was long. *The Last Jedi*, these complaints ran, was too dismissive
of fan theories: almost every response to long-debated fan points
(Snoke's identity, Rey's parentage) was that the answer didn't matter. Alternatively, another criticism was that the film's plot often
hinges on small moments, such as Benicio Del Toro's character
overhearing the Resistance's plan (which allows him to sell them out
to the First Order), a key point that is illustrated in a single ambiguous reaction shot on the stolen freighter. Perhaps the film sometimes
asks the viewer to care about too much simultaneously, as in the
way Rose's heroic and ultimately romantic decision to stop Finn's
sacrifice is played against the near-death of the Resistance, Poe's
maturing character, and Kylo Ren's and General Hux's jostling for
power nearly simultaneously. The character arcs are also largely not
what fans expected, with the once-heroic Poe's arrogance border-
ing on sexist condescension to Admiral Holdo. For my own part, I
found it difficult to embrace the way that *The Last Jedi* pauses for its
humor to land and instrumentalizes BB-8 as a deus ex machina one
too many times.

Regardless of the source of each complaint, however, they
all remind us that *Star Wars*, emotionally if not financially, seems
sometimes to belong to its audience as much as it does to its official

custodians at Lucasfilm. "Its characters and stories have escaped the original text and grown up with the fans, who have developed their own very firm ideas of what *Star Wars* is and is not about," Will Brooker wrote in 2002.[9] The fan response to the prequels was personal, almost intimate. The response to the sequels, now that *The Force Awakens* successfully reestablished legitimacy for the Disney era, is just as marked. Each *Star Wars* film always responds to the last, and also to the response to the last. This is a franchise pervaded by context.

Perhaps predictably, there were also more pernicious responses to *The Last Jedi*. After the improvements in representation made in *The Force Awakens* and *Rogue One*, perhaps this was inevitable. *The Last Jedi* added two more major women characters: Rose Tico, played by Kelly Marie Tran, the franchise's first actor of Asian heritage, and Admiral Holdo, heroic leader of the Resistance, played by Laura Dern. More women and people of color in *Star Wars* was evidently too much for some. Despite critics and audiences giving widely positive assessments of *The Last Jedi*, evidence suggests that an alt-right group algorithmically bombed the Rotten Tomatoes user score, which remains at just below 50 percent.[10] A forty-six-minute "De-Feminized Fanedit" of the film was assembled and distributed via torrenting websites, removing most scenes of powerful women. In response, Johnson tweeted news of the edit with the comment "haha" repeated forty-five times.[11] On a less humorous note, in June 2018 Tran deleted all her Instagram posts because of appalling sustained (and seemingly semi-organized) sexist and racist harassment on the platform, ostensibly from fans who did not like her character.[12] Such behavior seems more in line with the organized trolling associated with Gamergate and other far-right movements of the late 2010s whose modus operandi is to pick and manufacture battles staged online via popular culture. Recall here Milo Yiannopoulos's admission that he entered the video gaming world "to give the left a bloody nose."[13] This is the lamentable context that *Star Wars* finds itself in at the end of its first stage under Disney.

Nonetheless, stepping beyond such bad-faith actors, a segment of fan disturbance can be seen as a response to *The Last Jedi*'s quite political deconstruction of the *Star Wars* mythos. The uncomfortable reaction to Poe's shift in character from heroic derring-do to sexist know-it-all is in this case quite illuminating, and for a committed *Star Wars* fan, troubling. Here, *The Last Jedi* asks the *Star Wars* audience to reflect on how make-it-up-as-you-go heroism might from a different point of view appear like macho bluster, and has us follow Poe's journey to becoming a strategic, collaborative leader instead. In effect, the film questions one of the core pleasures of the *Star Wars* franchise. The ultimate outcome of all this is that *The Last Jedi* asks us to imagine what meaningful diversity for *Star Wars* might look like beyond casting and creatives. Considered to its logical conclusion, this leads to some uneasy propositions. Is the flashy heroism of Poe, in which we can trace a lineage all the way back to Han Solo in 1977, inflected by gender? How deeply are the *Star Wars* mythos, archetypes, and generic pleasures built on troubling gender and racial dynamics? What would a *Star Wars* film look like without those core elements? Would it even still be *Star Wars*?

Each *Star Wars* film is in some way in conversation with the last, and *The Last Jedi* is certainly no different. Perhaps in the end it is most straightforward to observe, as I have with *The Force Awakens* and *Rogue One* in this book, the way that *The Last Jedi* fits into the broader progression of *Star Wars* films. If *The Force Awakens* responded to the widely condemned prequels and gave audiences a nostalgic reason to return to *Star Wars*, and *Rogue One* took that same hit of nostalgia and sufficiently modernized it for the present, then *The Last Jedi* responds to them both by questioning some of the fundamental questions about *Star Wars* that these films took for granted. Each film moved forward in some way, even if that meant returning to the past.

For his part, Johnson tactfully noted that while his filmmaking goal was never to polarize the audience or upset fans, "I do think the conversations that are happening were going to have to happen at some point if [*Star Wars*] is going to grow, move forward and stay vital."[14] We can see this in terms of not just the themes of *The Last Jedi* but also its film style and its narrative trajectory. Accordingly, *The Last Jedi* also closes the first period of *Star Wars* under Disney—a period of renewal and revival, of returning *Star Wars* to popularity, reassuring fans, and restoring the franchise's once-dominating power. *The Last Jedi* therefore marks the beginning of something else. Maybe this is even the beginning of a second stage of *Star Wars* after Lucas: revision. What, *The Last Jedi* asks, can we change about this franchise? What needs to be corrected for today's mythmaking? What assumptions need rethinking, and what remains that needs amplification? After rebirth and rearticulation comes growth and, eventually, maturity. "The movie belongs to you guys now," Johnson tweeted delicately to a fan who had challenged *The Last Jedi*'s interpretation of *Star Wars*.[15]

This was a kind response by Johnson. And while it may be true that *Star Wars* belongs spiritually to the fans, in a literal sense, *Star Wars* actually now belongs to Disney. And in its first five years of ownership, Disney has released two Skywalker films, two spin-off films, an animated television series, and announced plans for a theme park, a whole new trilogy from Johnson, a different series produced by David Benioff and D. B. Weiss, and "not just one, but a few"[16] *Star Wars* television series for Disney's streaming service, including the animated *Star Wars Resistance,* and two new live-action series: *The Mandalorian,* and another focused on *Rogue One*'s Cassian Andor.

Star Wars in the Disney era has so far maintained a difficult balancing act between past and present. These new films have given a warm, nostalgic return "home" for fans of the older *Star Wars* multiple times—the kind of homecoming that Lucas's own prequels had failed to provide. By 2012 *Star Wars* under Lucas had gone somewhere far away, but Disney's *The Force Awakens* represented a return to cure this pain of absence. Yet both *The Force Awakens* and *Rogue One* also played with complex models of seriality and franchise storytelling to provide a new *Star Wars* that felt nostalgic while never really returning to the past. The politics of these films are utterly of their times—there is a lot more in operation than simplistic repetition. The Disney era of Lucasfilm is nothing if not layered.

The Force Awakens, Rogue One, The Last Jedi—this is the starting place, the opening salvo in Disney's plans for its "forever franchise." After four decades and ten films, after calling an end to the franchise, after the prequels and the original trilogy—after Lucas—it turned out that *Star Wars* was only just beginning.

ACKNOWLEDGMENTS

When I was around eight years old, my older brother Tim brought home a VHS copy of the first *Star Wars* film, and that moment set me on a path that has ultimately led to the publication of this book. I'd like to thank Tim and his husband Nick, my parents Liz and Frank, and the rest of my family (Lindy, Michael, Eleanor, Peter, Alex, James, Sam) for indulging me all these years, and my other brother Tim Stewart for coming to all those midnight premieres. I'd very much like to thank Emily van der Nagel and her family of Lea, Andrew, Nicole, Jo, and Jasper for welcoming and supporting me for much of this book's writing process.

My PhD supervisor, Angela Ndalianis, taught me not only how to research but that *Star Wars* could be talked about in a meaningful and scholarly way, despite its having nothing to do with my thesis topic. I'm grateful for my community of friends, as well as my colleagues at Swinburne who encouraged me throughout the writing process: Brendan Keogh, Ben Abraham, Terry Burdak, Natasha Story, César Albarran Torres, Liam Burke, Jessica Balanzategui, Steven Conway, Darshana Jayemanne, Marcus Carter, Ramon Lobato, Jane Stadler, Jason Bainbridge, and all the members of the Swinburne Screen Studies seminar series, particularly Tara Lomax, Naja Later, and Andy Lynch. With my previous coauthor, Leena van Deventer, I learned how to write a book. I'd like to thank Jess West for being equally coy about telling people we met by being moderators on a *Star Wars* message board as teenagers. Mark Serrels encouraged me on multiple occasions to write about *Star*

Wars while he ran *Kotaku Australia*; without his encouragement this book would not exist.

I especially thank University of Minnesota Press editor Jason Weidemann, who has been incredibly supportive at every stage of the development of this book. Without his guidance this book would not exist in any form. I also thank my readers, whose thoughtful and generous feedback helped improved the book immensely.

Finally, I thank my *Art of the Score* compatriots, Andrew Pogson and Nicholas Buc, for sharing my love of film music and sneaking me into rehearsals for John Williams concerts.

NOTES

INTRODUCTION

1 Richard Roeper, "'Star Wars: The Force Awakens': Thrills Are Strong with This One," *Chicago Sun-Times*, December 14, 2015, https://chicago.suntimes.com/entertainment/star-wars-the-force-awakens-review-the-thrills-are-strong-with-this-one/.

2 Peter Sciretta, "Spoiler Free Early Buzz: 'Star Wars: The Force Awakens,'" *Slashfilm*, December 15, 2015, http://www.slashfilm.com/star-wars-the-force-awakens-reviews-early-buzz/.

3 Devin Leonard, "How Disney Bought Lucasfilm—and Its Plans for 'Star Wars,'" *Bloomberg*, March 8, 2013, https://www.bloomberg.com/news/articles/2013-03-07/how-disney-bought-lucasfilm-and-its-plans-for-star-wars.

4 Ryan Parker, "George Lucas Sorry for 'White Slavers' Remark about Disney," *Hollywood Reporter*, December 31, 2015, https://www.hollywoodreporter.com/news/george-lucas-sorry-white-slavers-851661.

5 Daniel Ricwulf, "George Lucas Saw Rogue One: A Star Wars Story and Liked It," *Screenrant*, December 4, 2016, https://screenrant.com/george-lucas-rogue-one-a-star-wars-story-impressions/.

6 The *New York Times* notes that the stock exchange was closed at the time due to Hurricane Sandy, and that Disney had to convene a conference call for investors "hastily" in response. See Michael Cieply, "Disney Buying Lucasfilm for $4 Billion," *New York Times*, October 30, 2012, https://mediadecoder.blogs.nytimes.com/2012/10/30/disney-buying-lucas-films-for-4-billion/.

7 Josh Rottenberg, "Mark Hamill on Star Wars: Episode VII," *Entertainment Weekly*, October 31, 2012, http://ew.com/article/2012/10/31/mark-hamill-star-wars-episode-vii-disney/.

8 "George Lucas Says Hollywood Won't Support Black Films," *BBC News*, January 12, 2012, http://www.bbc.com/news/entertainment-arts-16525977.

9 Lucas and Jonathon Hales won the "Worst Screenplay" award in 2002 for *Attack of the Clones,* and several bad acting awards were given to *Star Wars* prequel stars over the three films, but no *Star Wars* film ever won a "Worst Sequel" or "Worst Picture" award.

10 Helen O'hara, "Spielberg: More Indy & Jurassic Park," *Empire,* October 26, 2011, https://www.empireonline.com/movies/news/spielberg-indy-jurassic-park/.

11 Steven Zeitchik, "Cannes 2010: Shia LaBeouf: We Botched the Last Indiana Jones," *Los Angeles Times,* May 15, 2010, http://latimesblogs.latimes.com/movies/2010/05/shia-labeouf-wall-street-2-indiana-jones-steven-spielberg.html.

12 Chris Taylor, *How Star Wars Conquered the Universe: The Past, Present, and Future of a Multibillion Dollar Franchise* (New York: Basic Books, 2014), 159.

13 Taylor, *How Star Wars Conquered the Universe.*

14 Taylor.

15 Taylor.

16 Simon Pegg, *Nerd Do Well: A Small Boy's Journey to Becoming a Big Kid* (New York: Avery, 2012), 330.

17 Taylor, *How Star Wars Conquered the Universe.*

18 Sally Kline, *George Lucas: Interviews* (Jackson: University Press of Mississippi, 1999), 48.

19 Matthew Leyland, "George Lucas," *Total Film,* May 2008, 74.

20 Leonard, "How Disney Bought Lucasfilm—and Its Plans for 'Star Wars.'"

21 Sarah Ellison, "Meet the Most Powerful Woman in Hollywood," *Vanity Fair,* February 8, 2016, https://www.vanityfair.com/hollywood/2016/02/kathleen-kennedy-hollywood-producer.

22 Leonard, "How Disney Bought Lucasfilm—and Its Plans for 'Star Wars.'"

23 Leonard.

24 Williams Proctor, "'Holy Crap, More *Star Wars*! More *Star Wars*? What If They're Crap?': Disney, Lucasfilm, and *Star Wars* Online Fandom in the Twenty-First Century," *Participations* 10, no. 1 (2013): 213.

25 Adam Rogers, "*Star Wars: The Force Awakens*—the *Wired* Review," *Wired,* December 16, 2015, https://www.wired.com/2015/12/star-wars-force-awakens-movie-review/.

26 Hannah Shaw-Williams, "'Star Wars 7': Why George Lucas Is Happy to Not Be Involved," *Screenrant,* January 16, 2015, https://screenrant.com/star-wars-7-force-awakens-george-lucas-role/.

27 Parker, "George Lucas Sorry for "White Slavers" Remark about Disney."

28 Taylor, *How Star Wars Conquered the Universe,* 365.

29 Tasha Robinson, "Star Wars: The Force Awakens Shows the Joys—and Limits—of Fulfilled Nostalgia," *Verge,* December 18, 2015, https://www.theverge.com/2015/12/18/10543196/star-wars-the-force-awakens-a-new-hope-nostalgia.

30 Gerardo Valero, "Plagiarising 'Star Wars': The Problems with 'The
    Force Awakens,'" RogerEbert.com, January 5, 2016, http://www
    .rogerebert.com/far-flung-correspondents/plagiarizing-star-wars-the
    -problems-with-the-force-awakens.

31 Fredric Jameson, "Postmodernism and Consumer Society," in *Studies in
    Culture: An Introductory Reader*, ed. Ann Gray and Jim McGuigan (London:
    Arnold, 1988), 197.

32 Dale Pollock, *Skywalking: The Life and Films of George Lucas* (New York:
    Da Capo, 1999), 142.

33 Brian Jay Jones, *George Lucas: A Life* (New York: Little, Brown, 2016), 147.

34 Jameson, "Postmodernism and Consumer Society," 197.

35 Noël Carrol, "The Future of Allusion: Hollywood in the Seventies
    (And Beyond)," *October* 20 (Spring 1982): 51–81.

36 Pollock, *Skywalking*, 186.

37 Nadia Atia and Jeremy Davies, "Nostalgia and the Shapes of History,"
    Memory Studies 3, no. 3 (2010): 181.

38 Michael Kammen, *Mystic Chords of Memory: The Transformation of Tradition
    in American Culture* (New York: Knopf, 1991), 688.

39 Janice L. Doane and Devon L. Hodges, *Nostalgia and Sexual Difference:
    The Resistance to Contemporary Feminism* (New York: Methuen, 1987), 3.

40 Samuel Earle, "The Politics of Nostalgia," *Jacobin*, January 20, 2017,
    https://www.jacobinmag.com/2017/01/donald-trump-inauguration
    -nationalism/.

41 Robert C. Tucker, ed., *The Marx-Engels Reader*, 2nd ed. (New York:
    W. W. Norton, 1978), 597.

42 Marcos P. Natali, "History and the Politics of Nostalgia," *Iowa Journal
    of Cultural Studies*, no. 5 (2004): 13.

43 Julie Beck, "When Nostalgia Was a Disease," *Atlantic*, August 14, 2013,
    https://www.theatlantic.com/health/archive/2013/08/when-nostalgia
    -was-a-disease/278648/.

44 Svetlana Boym, *The Future of Nostalgia* (New York: Basic Books, 2001),
    xvii.

45 Pauline Kael, "Whipped," *New Yorker*, June 15, 1981, https://www.new
    yorker.com/magazine/1981/06/15/whipped.

46 Jennifer Fickley-Baker, "Plans Unveiled for *Star Wars*–Inspired Themed
    Resort at Walt Disney World," *Disney Parks Blog*, July 15, 2017, https://
    disneyparks.disney.go.com/blog/2017/07/plans-unveiled-for-star-wars
    -inspired-themed-resort-at-walt-disney-world/.

47 Yohana Desta, "Disney Is Making More *Star Wars* TV Shows, In Case
    You Thought There Wasn't Enough *Star Wars*," *Vanity Fair*, February 7,
    2018, https://www.vanityfair.com/hollywood/2018/02/disney-star
    -wars-tv-shows.

48 Dave McNary, "Josh Trank Explains His Decision to Leave 'Star Wars'
    Spinoff," *Variety*, June 4, 2015, http://variety.com/2015/film/news/josh
    -trank-star-wars-spinoff-exit-1201512969/.

49 Borys Kit and Mia Galuppo, "Colin Trevorrow Out as 'Star Wars:

Episode IX' Director," *Hollywood Reporter,* September 5, 2017, https://
www.hollywoodreporter.com/heat-vision/colin-trevorrow-as-director
-star-wars-episode-ix-1035463.

50 Kim Masters, "'Star Wars' Firing Reveals a Disturbance in the Franchise," *Hollywood Reporter,* June 26, 2017, https://www.hollywoodreporter
.com/heat-vision/star-wars-han-solo-movie-firing-new-details-behind
-phil-lord-chris-miller-exit-1016619.

51 Adam Rogers, "The Force Will Be with Us, Always," *Wired,* December
2015, https://www.wired.com/2015/11/building-the-star-wars-universe/.

1. BEFORE THE EMPIRE

1   David Ames, "'Twins You Say? During Uncertain, Tyrannical Times?
With a Powerful Dark Lord and His Senators Corrupting the Planet?
Hmm . . . ,'" Twitter, February 2, 2017, 11:32 a.m., https://twitter.com
/semadivad/status/826875776008126464?lang=en.

2   Stephanie Marcus, "'Star Wars' Is Pretty Much Happening in Real Life
Because Beyoncé Is Pregnant with Twins," *Huffington Post,* February 5,
2017, http://www.huffingtonpost.com.au/2017/02/04/star-wars-is
-pretty-much-happening-in-real-life-because-beyonc_a_21707179/.

3   Fred Kaplan, "The Force Was with Them: Army's Jedi Knights Forged
Gulf War Strategy," *Boston Globe,* March 17, 1991.

4   Associated Press, "Cheney: Being Darth Vader Not So Bad," *NBC News,*
January 11, 2007, http://www.nbcnews.com/id/21575478/ns/politics
-white_house/t/cheney-being-darth-vader-not-so-bad/#.WoVwmL
ZjK35.

5   John Bonazzo, "Bill Kristol Tried to Defend the Galactic Empire on
Twitter," *Observer,* October 20, 2015, http://observer.com/2015/10/bill
-kristol-tried-to-defend-the-galactic-empire-on-twitter/.

6   Su-Lin Tan, "Darth Vader Has Chris "The Fixer" Pyne's Back," *Sydney
Morning Herald,* March 22, 2015, http://www.smh.com.au/federal-poli
tics/political-news/darth-vader-has-chris-the-fixer-pynes-back-20150322
-1m51q8.html.

7   "It is not surprising, then, that military and political figures have tried to
use imagery from the films to build support for their policies," argues
David S. Meyer, "Star Wars, *Star Wars,* and American Political Culture,"
Journal of Popular Culture 26, no. 2 (1992): 99, https://doi.org/10.1111
/j.0022–3840.1992.260299.x.

8   Heather Urbanski, *Plagues, Apocalypses, and Bug-Eyed Monsters: How
Speculative Fiction Shows Us Our Nightmares* (Jefferson, N.C.: McFarland,
2007), 134.

9   Kline, *George Lucas,* 83.

10 Eric Molinsky, *Empire vs Rebels,* Imaginary Worlds, accessed February 15,
2018, https://www.imaginaryworldspodcast.org/empire-vs-rebels.html.

11 Taylor, *How Star Wars Conquered the Universe,* 281–82.

12 Taylor, 282.

13 Francis X. Clines, "Reagan Plays the Issues in More Than a Single Key," *New York Times,* March 13, 1983.

14 Vincent Canby, "'Star Wars'—a Trip to a Far Galaxy That's Fun and Funny," *New York Times,* May 26, 1977.

15 Vincent Canby, "Not Since 'Flash Gordon Conquers The Universe' . . . ," *New York Times,* June 5, 1977.

16 Derek Malcolm, "Lucas in the Sky with Diamonds," *Guardian,* December 28, 1977.

17 Pauline Kael, "Contrasts," *New Yorker,* September 26, 1977.

18 Will Brooker, *Star Wars* (Houndmills, U.K.: Palgrave Macmillan on behalf of the British Film Institute, 2009), 8.

19 Dan Rubey, "*Star Wars*: Not So Long Ago, Not So Far Away," *Jump Cut: A Review of Contemporary Media,* no. 18 (August 1978): 10.

20 Andrew Britton, "Blissing Out: The Politics of Reaganite Entertainment," in *Britton on Film: The Complete Film Criticism of Andrew Britton,* ed. Barry Keith Grant (Detroit: Wayne State University Press, 2009), 97.

21 Britton, 102.

22 Britton, 106.

23 Britton, 112.

24 John Hellman, *American Myth and the Legacy of Vietnam* (New York: Columbia University Press, 1986), 212.

25 Robin Wood, *Hollywood from Vietnam to Reagan* (New York: Columbia University Press, 1986), 147.

26 Wood.

27 Wood.

28 Rubey, "*Star Wars,*" 12.

29 Rubey, 13.

30 Karina Longworth, *George Lucas* (Paris: Cahiers du cinema Sarl, 2012), 54.

31 Peter Biskind, *Easy Riders, Raging Bulls: How the Sex-Drugs-and Rock 'n Roll Generation Saved Hollywood* (New York: Simon & Schuster, 1998), 316.

32 Thomas Elsaesser, "American Auteur Cinema: The Last—or First—Great Picture Show," in *The Last Great American Picture Show: New Hollywood Cinema in the 1970s,* ed. Thomas Elsaesser, Alexander Horwath, and Noel King (Amsterdam: Amsterdam University Press, 2004), 42.

33 David Thompson, "Who Killed the Movies?," *Esquire,* December 1996, 56.

34 Wheeler Winston Dixon, "Twenty-Five Reasons Why It's All Over," in *The End of Cinema as We Know It: American Film in the Nineties,* ed. Jon Lewis (London: Pluto, 2002), 56–66.

35 Biskind, *Easy Riders, Raging Bulls.*

36 J.W. Rinzler, *The Making of Star Wars: The Definitive Story behind the Original Film* (London: Aurum, 2007), 12.

37 Pollock, *Skywalking,* 94.

38 Pollock, 105.

39 Kline, *George Lucas,* 22.

40 Pollock, *Skywalking,* 104.

41 Kline, *George Lucas,* 14.

42 Pollock, *Skywalking*, 107.

43 Pollock, 121.

44 Pollock, 137.

45 Jones, *George Lucas*, 65.

46 Kline, *George Lucas*, 139.

47 Jones, *George Lucas*, 452.

48 Biskind, *Easy Riders, Raging Bulls*.

49 Taylor, *How Star Wars Conquered the Universe*, 87.

50 Pollock, *Skywalking*, 129.

51 Pollock, 128–29.

52 Longworth, *George Lucas*, 30.

53 Biskind, *Easy Riders, Raging Bulls*.

54 Rinzler, *Making of* Star Wars, 8.

55 Jessica Langer, *Postcolonialism and Science Fiction* (New York: Palgrave Macmillan, 2011), 3.

56 John Rieder, *Colonialism and the Emergence of Science Fiction* (Connecticut: Wesleyan University Press, 2008), 2.

57 Longworth, *George Lucas*, 36.

58 Rinzler, *Making of* Star Wars, 16.

59 Rinzler, 16–17.

60 Taylor, *How Star Wars Conquered the Universe*, 281.

61 Biskind, *Easy Riders, Raging Bulls*.

62 Kline, *George Lucas*, 120.

63 Robert Stam and Ella Shohat, *Flagging Patriotism: Crises of Narcissism and Anti-Americanism* (New York: Routledge, 2007), 179.

64 James F. Clarity and Warren Weaver Jr., "Defending 'Star Wars,'" *New York Times*, November 25, 1985.

65 BBC Staff, "George Lucas Says Hollywood Won't Support Black Films."

66 Anne Lancashire, "'The Phantom Menace': Repetition, Variation, Integration," *Film Criticism* 24, no. 3 (2000): 23–44.

67 Stephen P. McVeigh, "The Galactic Way of Warfare," in *Finding the Force of the Star Wars Franchise: Fans, Merchandise, and Critics*, ed. Matthew Kapell and John Shelton Lawrence, Popular Culture and Everyday Life, vol. 14 (New York: P. Lang, 2006), 49.

68 Douglas M. Kellner, *Cinema Wars: Hollywood Film and Politics in the Bush-Cheney Era* (Hoboken, N.J.: John Wiley & Sons, 2011), 177.

69 Lancashire, "'Phantom Menace.'"

70 Kellner, *Cinema Wars*, 117.

71 Richard Corliss and Jess Cagle, "Dark Victory," *Time*, April 29, 2002.

72 A. O. Scott, "Some Surprises in That Galaxy Far, Far Away," *New York Times*, May 16, 2005, http://www.nytimes.com/2005/05/16/movies/some-surprises-in-that-galaxy-far-far-away.html.

73 Kellner, *Cinema Wars*, 183.

74 Roger Ebert, "Star Wars—Episode I: The Phantom Menace," *Chicago Sun-Times*, May 17, 1999.

75 Joanna Robinson, "George Lucas Explains Why He's Done Directing *Star Wars* Movies," *Vanity Fair,* November 18, 2015, https://www.vanity -fair.com/hollywood/2015/11/george-lucas-star-wars-jar-jar-binks.

76 Thomas Schatz, "Conglomerate Hollywood and American Independent Film," in *American Independent Cinema: Indie, Indiewood, and Beyond,* ed. Geoff King, Claire Molloy, and Yannis Tzioumakis (New York: Rout- ledge, 2013), 127.

2. IT CALLS TO YOU

1 Julia Kennedy and Clarissa Smith, "His Soul Shatters at about 0:23: Spankwire, Self-Scaring, and Hyberbolic Shock," in *Controversial Images: Media Representations on the Edge* (London: Palgrave Macmillan, 2012), 244.

2 Jason Middleton, *Documentary's Awkward Turn: Cringe Comedy and Media Spectatorship* (New York: Routledge, 2014), 110.

3 Sam Anderson, "Watching People Watching People Watching," *New York Times Magazine,* November 27, 2011.

4 John Hudson, "Disney Buys LucasFilm for $4 Billion and Will Make New 'Star Wars' Movies," *Atlantic,* October 30, 2012.

5 "Jar Jar Poppins? Star Wars Fans Go Nuts over #DisneyBuysLucas- Film," news.com.au, October 31, 2012.

6 Mike Krantz, "Disney Buys Lucasfilm for $4 Billion," *USA Today,* October 30, 2012.

7 Henry Jenkins, *Convergence Culture: Where Old and New Media Collide* (New York: New York University Press, 2006), 94.

8 Tony Bennett and Janet Woollacott, *Bond and Beyond: The Political Career of a Popular Hero* (Houndmills, U.K.: Macmillan Education, 1987), 274.

9 Jim Collins, "Genericity in the Nineties: Eclectic Irony and the New Sin- cerity," in *Film Theory Goes to the Movies,* ed. Jim Collins, Hilary Radner, and Ava Collins (New York: Routledge, 1993), 245.

10 Heather Urbanski, *The Science Fiction Reboot: Canon, Innovation, and Fandom in Refashioned Franchises* (Jefferson, N.C.: McFarland, 2013), 7.

11 Grant Morrison, *Supergods: Our World in the Age of the Superhero* (London: Jonathan Cape, 2012), 342.

12 Urbanski, *Science Fiction Reboot,* 10.

13 Robin P. Arnett, "Casino Royale and Franchise Remix: James Bond as Superhero," *SOURCEFilm Criticism* 33, no. 3 (2009): 3.

14 Boym, *Future of Nostalgia,* 355.

15 Fredric Jameson, "Nostalgia for the Present," *South Atlantic Quarterly* 88, no. 2 (1989): 517–37.

16 Carly A. Kocurek, *Coin-Operated Americans: Rebooting Boyhood at the Video Game Arcade* (Minneapolis: University of Minnesota Press, 2015), 160.

17 Angela Ndalianis, *Neo-Baroque Aesthetics and Contemporary Entertainment* (Cambridge, Mass.: MIT Press, 2005), 191.

18 Carroll, "The Future of Allusion: Hollywood in the Seventies (And Beyond)," 52.

19 Brooker, *Star Wars*, 80–82.

20 Bruce Handy, "J.J. Abrams on the Secret Movie References He Snuck into *Star Wars: The Force Awakens*," *Vanity Fair*, May 6, 2015, http://www.vanityfair.com/hollywood/2015/05/jj-abrams-star-wars-extended-interview.

21 Evan Narcisse, "Twenty Thousand per Cell: Why Midi-Chlorians Suck," *Time*, August 10, 2010, http://techland.time.com/2010/08/10/20000-per-cell-why-midi-chlorians-suck/.

22 Taylor, *How Star Wars Conquered the Universe*, 197.

23 Jameson, "Postmodernism and Consumer Society," 197.

24 Atia and Davies, "Nostalgia and the Shapes of History," 184.

25 Kocurek, *Coin-Operated Americans*, 177.

26 Germain Lussier, "So Many Australians Are Claiming 'Jedi' as Their Religion That It's Becoming a Problem," *Gizmodo*, August 2, 2016.

27 Louis Althusser, *Lenin and Philosophy and Other Essays* (London: Verso, 1970), 11.

3. LOOK HOW OLD YOU'VE BECOME

1 Mark Hughes, "'Star Wars: The Force Awakens' to Hit $1 Billion in Record Time," *Forbes*, December 23, 2015, https://www.forbes.com/sites/markhughes/2015/12/23/star-wars-the-force-awakens-to-hit-1-billion-in-record-time/#5a545e664fea.

2 Ann Hornaday, "'Star Wars: The Force Awakens' Gets the Nostalgia-Novelty Mix Just Right," *Washington Post*, December 16, 2015, https://www.washingtonpost.com/lifestyle/star-wars-the-force-awakens-gets-the-nostalgia-novelty-mix-just-right/2015/12/15/c2e8a38e-a365-11e5-b53d-972e2751f433_story.html?utm_term=.6a952cb81a2a.

3 Peter Suderman, "Star Wars: The Force Awakens Is a Prime Example of Hollywood's Nostalgia Problem," *Vox*, December 21, 2015, https://www.vox.com/2015/12/21/10445616/star-wars-hollywood-nostalgia-problem; Eric Kohn, "Review: 'Star Wars: The Force Awakens' Is the Biggest Fan Film Ever Made," *IndieWire*, December 16, 2015, http://www.indiewire.com/2015/12/review-star-wars-the-force-awakens-is-the-biggest-fan-film-ever-made-45115/; Sonny Bunch, "'Star Wars: The Force Awakens' Succumbs to the Worst Parts of Remix Culture," *Washington Post*, December 22, 2015, https://www.washingtonpost.com/news/act-four/wp/2015/12/22/star-wars-the-force-awakens-succumbs-to-the-worst-parts-of-remix-culture/?utm_term=.e76d4d39766a.

4 James Whitbrook, "Rian Johnson Is Fully Aware *The Last Jedi* Might Sound Like *Empire Strikes Back*, and He Doesn't Care," *Gizmodo*, August 10, 2017, https://www.gizmodo.com.au/2017/08/rian-johnson-is-fully-aware-the-last-jedi-might-sound-like-empire-strikes-back-and-he-doesnt-care/.

5 Kevin P. Sullivan, "Star Wars: The Force Awakens, A New Hope Similarities," *Entertainment Weekly*, December 19, 2015, http://www

.ew.com/article/2015/12/19/star-wars-force-awakens-new-hope
-similarities/.

6   Graeme McMillan, "J.J. Abrams Responds to 'Rip-Off' Criticism about
    'Star Wars: The Force Awakens,'" *Hollywood Reporter,* January 8, 2016,
    https://www.hollywoodreporter.com/heat-vision/jj-abrams-responds
    -rip-criticism-853352.

7   Andrew O'Hehir, "'Star Wars: The Force Awakens': You Know All
    the Spoilers in J.J. Abrams' Obsessive Reboot—Because You've Seen
    This Movie Before," *Salon,* December 17, 2015, https://www.salon
    .com/2015/12/16/star_wars_the_force_awakens_you_know_all_the
    _spoilers_in_j_j_abrams_obsessive_reboot_because_youve_seen_this
    _movie_before/.

8   Valero, "Plagiarising Star Wars."

9   Jason Mittell, *Complex TV: The Poetics of Contemporary Television Storytelling,*
    (New York: New York University Press, 2015), 53.

10 Glen Donnar, "Narratives of Cultural and Professional Redundancy:
    Ageing Action Stardom and the "Geri-Action" Film," *Communication,
    Politics & Culture* 49, no. 1 (2016): 1–18.

11 Matt Singer, "Welcome to the Age of the Legacyquel," *ScreenCrush,*
    November 23, 2015, http://screencrush.com/the-age-of-legacyquels/.

12 Heather Urbanski, *The Science Fiction Reboot: Canon, Innovation, and Fandom
    in Refashioned Franchises* (Jefferson, N.C.: London: McFarland, 2013), 7.

13 Singer, "Welcome to the Age of the Legacyquel."

14 Alex Fitzpatrick, "This Is Still the Best Way to Watch the Star Wars
    Movies," *Time,* May 22, 2017, http://time.com/4784685/star-wars-
    machete-order-rogue-one-force-awakens/.

15 The Star Wars Show, "Lucasfilm President Kathleen Kennedy on All
    Things Star Wars, Kylo Ren in Battlefront II, and More!," *Star Wars
    YouTube Channel,* November 1, 2017, https://www.youtube.com/watch
    ?v=tm32FFFbAOk.

16 Robbie Collin, "Han Solo, Indiana Jones, Rick Deckard: Harrison Ford
    Revisits His Biggest Roles," *Sydney Morning Herald,* October 8, 2017,
    http://www.smh.com.au/entertainment/movies/han-solo-indiana
    -jones-rick-deckard-harrison-ford-revisits-his-biggest-roles-20171004
    -gyunzn.html.

17 Although Joseph Campbell, the author of *The Hero with a Thousand
    Faces,* does not explicitly include a "death of the mentor" stage in his
    monomyth model, it is a common element of narratives associated with
    this type, such as *A New Hope* (Obi-Wan Kenobi), *The Phantom Menace*
    (Qui-Gon Jinn), *Lord of the Rings* (Gandalf, and although he returns,
    he does so in a leader role rather than the mentor role he previously
    occupied), the *Harry Potter* series (which repeats the maneuver several
    times with Sirius, Lupin, Snape, and of course, Dumbledore), *The Hunger
    Games* (Cinna), and a host of Marvel and comic book films: *Iron Man* (Ho
    Yinsen), *Captain America: The First Avenger* (Abraham Erskine), and *Spider-
    Man* (Uncle Ben), to list just a few.

18 Will Wright, *Six Guns and Society: A Structural Study of the Western* (Berkeley: University of California Press, 1977), 183.

19 Taylor, *How Star Wars Conquered the Universe.*

20 Christopher Vogler, *The Writer's Journey: Mythic Structure for Writers,* 3rd ed. (Studio City, Calif.: Michael Wiese Productions, 2007).

21 Sam McBride, "Coming of Age in Narnia," in *Revisiting Narnia: Fantasy, Myth, and Religion in C. S. Lewis' Chronicles,* ed. Shanna Caughey (Dallas, Tex.: Benbella Books, 2005), 59–72.

22 McBride, "Coming of Age in Narnia," 60.

23 Stratford Caldecott, "Over the Chasm of Fire: Christian Heroism in *The Silmarillion* and *The Lord of the Rings,*" in *Tolkien—a Celebration: Collected Writings on a Literary Legacy,* ed. Joseph Pearce (San Francisco: Ignatius Press, 2001), 19.

24 "Mission Impossible II," Rotten Tomatoes, 2017, https://www.rotten tomatoes.com/m/mission_impossible_2.

25 Claudia Puig, "Director Energizes Familiar 'Mission,'" *USA Today,* April 5, 2006, https://usatoday30.usatoday.com/life/movies/reviews /2006-05-03-mi3_x.htm.

26 Ty Burr, "Movie Review: 'Star Trek,'" *Boston Globe,* May 5, 2009, http://archive.boston.com/ae/movies/articles/2009/05/05/a_fresh _frontier/?page=2.

27 Roger Ebert, "Super 8," RogerEbert.com, June 8, 2011, 8, https:// www.rogerebert.com/reviews/super-8-2011.

28 Nigel Morris, *The Cinema of Steven Spielberg: Empire of Light* (London: Wallflower, 2007), 7.

29 Richard Corliss, "'What the Hell Would Spielberg Do Here?': J.J. Abrams Talks Super 8," *Time,* June 6, 2011, http://entertainment.time .com/2011/06/06/super-8-director-jj-abrams-interview/.

4. AN AWAKENING

1 David G. Brown, "Why *Star Wars: The Force Awakens* Is a Social Justice Propaganda Film," Return of Kings, December 20, 2015, http:// www.returnofkings.com/75991/why-star-wars-the-force-awakens-is-a -social-justice-propaganda-film.

2 "National Tracking Poll #171116," Crosstabulation Results, Morning Consult, December 4, 2017, https://morningconsult.com/wp-content /uploads/2017/12/171116_crosstabs_BRANDS_v1_DK-2.pdf.

3 Dan Hassler-Forest, *Science Fiction, Fantasy, and Politics: Transmedia World-Building beyond Capitalism* (London: Rowman & Littlefield, 2016), 5.

4 Molly Fischer, "The Great Awokening: What Happens to Culture in an Era of Identity Politics?," The Cut, January 10, 2018, https://www .thecut.com/2018/01/pop-cultures-great-awokening.html.

5 Sara Ahmed, *Living a Feminist Life* (Durham, N.C.: Duke University Press, 2017), 3.

6 bell hooks, *Reel to Real: Race, Class, and Sex at the Movies* (New York: Routledge, 2009), 2–3.

7 Ahmed, *Living a Feminist Life*, 3.

8 Sarah Banet-Weiser and Laura Portwood-Stacer, "The Traffic in Feminism: An Introduction to the Commentary and Criticism on Popular Feminism," *Feminist Media Studies* 17, no. 5 (2017): 884.

9 Brooks Landon, *Science Fiction after 1900: From the Steam Man to the Stars* (New York: Routledge, 2002), 6–7.

10 Istvan Csicsery-Ronay, *The Seven Beauties of Science Fiction* (Middletown, Conn.: Wesleyan University Press, 2011), 2.

11 Angela Ndalianis, "Baroque Facades, Jeff Bridges' Face and Tron: Legacy," in *Special Effects*, ed. Bob Rehak and Dan North (London: Palgrave/BFI, 2014), 154.

12 Jordan Zakarin, "How the Alt-Right and Nostalgic Trolls Hijacked Geek Pop Culture," Syfy Wire, January 17, 2018, http://www.syfy.com/syfywire/how-the-alt-right-and-nostalgic-trolls-hijacked-geek-pop-culture.

13 James Delingpole, "'The Force Awakens' Is the Worst Thing Ever," Breitbart, December 31, 2015, http://www.breitbart.com/london/2015/12/31/the-force-awakens-is-the-worst-thing-ever/.

14 Graeme McMillan, "Boycott 'Star Wars VII' Movement Launched; Movie Called 'Anti-White,'" *Hollywood Reporter*, October 19, 2015, https://www.hollywoodreporter.com/heat-vision/boycott-star-wars-vii-movement-833102.

15 Jessica Valenti, "Sexists Are Scared of Mad Max Because It Is a Call to Dismantle Patriarchies," *Guardian*, May 27, 2015, https://www.theguardian.com/commentisfree/2015/may/27/sexists-are-scared-of-mad-max-because-it-is-a-call-to-dismantle-patriarchies.

16 Kit Daniels, "Mad Max: The Feminist Warrior," Infowars, May 25, 2015, https://www.infowars.com/mad-max-the-feminist-warrior-2/.

17 Mike Sampson, "Why the 'Ghostbusters' Trailer Is the Most 'Disliked' Movie Trailer in YouTube History," Screencrush, April 29, 2016, http://screencrush.com/ghostbusters-trailer-most-disliked-movie-trailer-in-history/.

18 Alexandra Petri, "Donald Trump Is Baffled by Ghostbusters and Change," *Washington Post*, January 28, 2015, https://www.washingtonpost.com/blogs/compost/wp/2015/01/28/donald-trump-is-baffled-by-ghostbusters-and-change/?utm_term=.9d6987d896b4.

19 Aja Romano, "Milo Yiannopoulos's Twitter Ban, Explained," *Vox*, July 20, 2016, https://www.vox.com/2016/7/20/12226070/milo-yiannopoulos-twitter-ban-explained.

20 Rubey, "*Star Wars*: Not So Long Ago, Not So Far Away."

21 Rubey.

22 Rubey.

23 Rinzler, *Making of* Star Wars, 47.

24 Kay Armatage, *The Girl from God's Country: Nell Shipman and the Silent Cinema* (Toronto: University of Toronto Press, 2003), 32–54.

25 Brooker, *Star Wars*, 200.

26 Brooker, 199.

27 Andrew Howe, "Star Wars in Black and White: Race and Racism in a Galaxy Not So Far Away," in *Sex, Politics, and Religion in* Star Wars*: An Anthology*, ed. Douglas Brode and Leah Deyneka (Lanham, Md.: Scarecrow, 2012), 11.

28 Gwynne Watkins, "Carl Sagan Critiqued 'Star Wars' in 1978, and His Complaints Still Will Sound Familiar," *Yahoo Movies*, April 4, 2017, https://www.yahoo.com/entertainment/carl-sagan-critiqued-star-wars -in-1978-and-his-complaints-still-will-sound-familiar-204912662.html.

29 Alex Abad-Santos, "The Fight over Whether Star Wars Is Racist Reveals More about the Media Than Star Wars," *Vox*, December 16, 2016, https://www.vox.com/2015/12/16/10301020/star-wars-racist -harris-perry.

30 Adilifu Nama, "R Is for Race, Not Rocket: Black Representation in American Science Fiction Cinema," *Quarterly Review of Film and Video* 26, no. 2 (2009): 159, https://doi.org/10.1080/10509200600737812.

31 Kevin J. Wetmore, *The Empire Triumphant: Race, Religion, and Rebellion in the* Star Wars *Films* (Jefferson, N.C.: McFarland, 2005), 132–36.

32 Diana Dominguez, "Feminism and the Force: Empowerment and Disillusionment in a Galaxy Far, Far Away," in *Culture, Identities, and Technology in the* Star Wars *Films: Essays on the Two Trilogies*, ed. Carl Silvio and Tony M. Vinci (Jefferson, N.C.: McFarland, 2007), 125.

33 Andrew Gumbel, "Star Wars Accused of Race Stereotypes," *Independent*, June 2, 1999, http://www.independent.co.uk/news/star-wars-accused -of-race-stereotypes-1097783.html.

34 Quoted in Will Brooker, "Readings of Racism: Interpretation, Stereotyping, and The Phantom Menace," *Continuum* 15, no. 1 (2001): 19, https://doi.org/10.1080/713657758.

35 Patricia J. Williams, "Racial Ventriloquism," *Nation*, July 5, 1999, https://www.thenation.com/article/racial-ventriloquism/.

36 Brooker, "Readings of Racism," 17.

37 Brooker, 17.

38 Donald Bogle, *Toms, Coons, Mulattoes, Mammies, and Bucks: An Interpretive History of Blacks in American Films*, 4th ed. (New York: Bloomsbury Academy, 2013), 39–41.

39 BBC Staff, "Star Wars: Lucas Strikes Back," *BBC News*, July 14, 1999, http://news.bbc.co.uk/2/hi/entertainment/394542.stm.

40 Robin DiAngelo, "White Fragility," *International Journal of Critical Pedagogy* 3, no. 3 (2011): 60–61.

41 Brooker, "Readings of Racism," 23.

42 Ron Givens, "Jar Wars: Fame and Blame Ahmed Best's Role as Offbeat Alien Triggers a Hot Debate," *New York Daily News*, June 3, 1999, http://

www.nydailynews.com/archives/nydn-features/jar-wars-fame-blame
-ahmed-best-role-offbeat-alien-triggers-hot-debate-article-1.835585.

43 Jessica Langer, *Postcolonialism and Science Fiction* (New York: Palgrave
Macmillan, 2011), 82.

44 Brooker, "Readings of Racism," 24.

45 Laura Hudson, "Leia Is Not Enough: *Star Wars* and the Woman
Problem in Hollywood," *Wired*, February 15, 2013, https://www.wired
.com/2013/02/opinion-star-wars-females-media/.

46 Ben Child, "Star Wars: Episode VII Casting—Stars React, While the
Press Start to Speculate," *Guardian*, April 30, 2014, https://www.the
guardian.com/film/2014/apr/30/star-wars-episode-vii-casting.

47 Joseph C. Lin, "This Is the Only New Woman to Join the *Star Wars*
Cast So Far," *Time*, April 29, 2014, http://time.com/81427/daisy-ridley
-photo-new-star-wars-cast/.

48 Spencer Kornhaber, "The New *Star Wars* Cast Has Only 1 Woman
Who Isn't Princess Leia," *Atlantic*, April 29, 2014, https://www.the
atlantic.com/entertainment/archive/2014/04/the-one-non-leia-woman
-on-the-new-star-wars-cast/361395/.

49 Rebecca Pahle, "The Mary Sue's Gif-Filled Guide to the Cast of *Star
Wars: Episode VII*," *The Mary Sue*, April 30, 2014, https://www.themary
sue.com/star-wars-episode-vii-cast/2/.

50 Borys Kit, "'Star Wars: Episode VII' Casting: It's Not Over Yet,"
Hollywood Reporter, April 29, 2014, https://www.hollywoodreporter.com
/heat-vision/star-wars-episode-vii-casting-699924.

51 Jeff Labrecque, "'Star Wars': Who Might Lupita Nyong'o and Gwendoline Christie Play?," *Entertainment Weekly*, June 3, 2014, http://
ew.com/article/2014/06/03/star-wars-lupita-nyongo-gwendoline
-christie/.

52 Kyle Buchanan, "This Major Female Villain in *Star Wars: The Force
Awakens* Was Originally a Man," *Vulture*, December 7, 2015, http://
www.vulture.com/2015/12/female-star-wars-villain-originally-man.html.

53 Susana Polo, "Even If The Force Awakens Sucks, It's Made One Big
Diverse Achievement for Hollywood," *Polygon*, December 16, 2015,
https://www.polygon.com/2015/12/16/10236158/force-awakens
-diversity.

54 Jennifer Pearson, "'I Wanted a Movie Mothers Could Take Their
Daughters to': J.J. Abrams on Why He Cast a Strong Female Lead in
Star Wars: The Force Awakens," *Daily Mail*, December 1, 2015, http://
www.dailymail.co.uk/tvshowbiz/article-3339834/J-J-Abrams-cast
-strong-female-lead-Star-Wars-Force-Awakens.html#ixzz56KEhgQQe.

55 Rebecca Sun, "Lucasfilm's Force: Kathleen Kennedy Reveals an
Executive Team More Than 50 Percent Female," *Hollywood Reporter*,
July 12, 2016, https://www.hollywoodreporter.com/news/lucasfilms
-force-kathleen-kennedy-reveals-an-executive-team-more-50-percent
-female-953156.

56 Christopher Palmeri, "Disney Is Making a Killing on Star Wars," *Bloomberg*, December 8, 2017, https://www.bloomberg.com/news /features/2017–12–08/force-is-strong-in-disney-lucasfilm-5-years-after -star-wars-deal.

57 Ben Fritz, "Meet Disney's 'Star Wars' Maestro, Kiri Hart," *Wall Street Journal*, October 2, 2014, https://blogs.wsj.com/speakeasy/2014/10/02 /meet-disneys-star-wars-maestro-kiri-hart/.

58 Nathalia Holt, "The Women Who Run the 'Star Wars' Universe," *New York Times*, December 22, 2017, https://www.nytimes.com/2017/12/22 /movies/star-wars-last-jedi-women-run-universe.html.

59 Megen de Bruin-Molé, "Space Bitches, Witches, and Kick-Ass Princesses: Star Wars and Popular Feminism," in *Star Wars and the History of Transmedia Storytelling*, ed. Sean Guynes and Dan Hassler-Forest (Amsterdam: Amsterdam University Press, 2018), 240.

60 Nick Statt, "Director J.J. Abrams Weighs in on Diversity in the Star Wars Universe," *CNET*, July 11, 2015, https://www.cnet.com/news /director-j-j-abrams-weighs-in-on-diversity-in-the-star-wars-universe /?_escaped_fragment_=.

61 Edward W. Said, *Orientalism* (New Delhi: Penguin Books, 1995), 283.

62 Carol Clover, *Men, Women, and Chain Saws: Gender in the Modern Horror Film* (Princeton, N.J.: Princeton University Press, 1992), 20.

63 Comicbook Staff, "Star Wars: Diego Luna and Kathleen Kennedy Explain Importance of Diversity in Rogue One," *Comicbook*, December 8, 2016, http://comicbook.com/starwars/2016/12/08/star-wars-diego -luna-and-kathleen-kennedy-explain-importance-of-/.

64 Darnell Hunt et al., "2017 Hollywood Diversity Report: Setting the Record Straight" (Los Angeles: Ralph J. Bunche Center for African American Studies at UCLA, 2017), 11–13.

65 Andrew Liptak, "Star Wars Producer Kathleen Kennedy Has 'Every Intention' of Hiring Female Directors," *The Verge*, December 4, 2016, https://www.theverge.com/2016/12/4/13835760/star-wars-kathleen -kennedy-hiring-female-directors-lucasfilm.

66 Marcus Errico, "J.J. Abrams Reveals Shot Suggested by Ava DuVernay in 'The Force Awakens' Climactic Fight (Exclusive)," *Yahoo Entertainment*, October 20, 2016, https://www.yahoo.com/entertainment/j-j-abrams -reveals-shot-suggested-by-ava-duvernay-in-the-force-awakens-climactic -fight-exclusive-130027602.html?soc_src=mail&soc_trk=ma.

67 Martha M. Lauzen, "Where Are the Film Directors (Who Happen to Be Women)?," *Quarterly Review of Film and Video* 29, no. 4 (July 2012): 314, https://doi.org/10.1080/10509201003601167.

68 Jeffrey A. Brown, "#wheresRey: Feminism, Protest, and Merchandising Sexism in *Star Wars: The Force Awakens*," *Feminist Media Studies*, April 24, 2017, 6, https://doi.org/10.1080/14680777.2017.1313291.

69 Janice L. Doane and Devon L. Hodges, *Nostalgia and Sexual Difference: The Resistance to Contemporary Feminism* (New York: Methuen, 1987).

70 Anthony Breznican, "Star Wars: BB-8 Gender Revealed for Force

Awakens Droid," *Entertainment Weekly*, November 13, 2015, http://ew.com/article/2015/11/13/bb-8-gender-star-wars/.

71 Justin Kroll, "'Star Wars: Episode VII' Casts Christina Chong," *Variety*, July 17, 2014, http://variety.com/2014/film/news/star-wars-episode-vii-casts-newcomer-christina-chong-1201264204/.

72 Wilfred Chan, "'Star Wars Episode VII' Actor John Boyega Takes Aim at "Black Stormtrooper" Racism," *CNN Entertainment*, December 1, 2014, http://edition.cnn.com/2014/12/01/showbiz/star-wars-stormtrooper-racism-john-boyega/.

73 Brown, "#wheresRey," 8.

74 Brown, 12.

75 Will Brooker, *Using the Force: Creativity, Community and Star Wars Fans* (New York: Continuum, 2003), 200.

76 Brooker, 15.

77 Brooker, 203.

78 Brooker, 133.

79 Henry Jenkins, *Textual Poachers: Television Fans and Participatory Culture*, updated 20th anniversary ed. (New York: Routledge, 2013), 191.

80 Samantha Schnurr, "*Star Wars: The Force Awakens* Cast Gets Grilled about Their On Screen Romance by Ellen DeGeneres," *E!Online*, December 17, 2015, http://www.eonline.com/news/724844/star-wars-the-force-awakens-cast-gets-grilled-about-their-on-screen-romance-by-ellen-degeneres.

81 Nick Duffy, "Star Wars' Daisy Ridley and Kelly Marie Tran Want Gay Finn/Poe Romance," *Pink News*, December 21, 2017, http://www.pinknews.co.uk/2017/12/21/star-wars-daisy-ridley-and-kelly-marie-tran-want-gay-finnpoe-romance/.

82 Peyton Thomas, "What Will It Take to Get a Gay Character in *Star Wars*?," *Vanity Fair*, December 12, 2017, https://www.vanityfair.com/hollywood/2017/12/star-wars-last-jedi-poe-finn-lgbt-representation.

83 Brooker, *Using the Force*, 205.

84 Hale Goetz, "How 'Star Wars: The Force Awakens' Kylo Ren Is a Gatekeeper," *The Mary Sue*, January 11, 2016, https://www.themarysue.com/the-force-awakens-gatekeepers/.

85 Pablo Hidalgo, "'@Cash_Craig I Will Say Kylo Feels Like the Right Type of Villain for Today,'" Twitter, February 2, 2017, https://twitter.com/pablohidalgo/status/827258169005002754.

86 Anna Menta, "'Star Wars: The Last Jedi' Owes Its Box-Office Success to Women," *Newsweek*, December 19, 2017, http://www.newsweek.com/star-wars-last-jedi-female-fans-747611.

87 Zakarin, "How the Alt-Right and Nostalgic Trolls Hijacked Geek Pop Culture."

88 Scott Mendelson, "As 'Solo: A Star Wars Story' Flops, Are Movies about White Men Box Office Poison?," *Forbes*, May 29, 2018, https://www.forbes.com/sites/scottmendelson/2018/05/29/as-solo-a-star-wars-story-flops-are-movies-about-white-men-box-office-poison/#1a68a1c55d49.

5. JUST LIKE OLD TIMES?

1   Emilio Audissino, *John Williams's Film Music:* Jaws, Star Wars, Raiders of the Lost Ark, *and the Return of the Classical Hollywood Music Style* (Madison: University of Wisconsin Press, 2014), 80.

2   Jon Burlingame, "Mark Hamill Hails 'Star Wars' Composer John Williams: 'He Elevates Every Scene,'" *Variety,* January 11, 2018, http://variety.com/2018/film/news/mark-hamill-on-star-wars-music-compos er-john-williams-1202659494/.

3   Handy, "J.J. Abrams on the Secret Movie References He Snuck into *Star Wars.*"

4   Rinzler, *Making of* Star Wars, 265.

5   Royal S. Brown, *Overtones and Undertones: Reading Film Music* (Los Angeles: University of California Press, 1994), 118; Mervyn Cooke, *A History of Film Music* (New York: Cambridge University Press, 2008), 462.

6   Craig L. Byrd, "The Star Wars Interview: John Williams," *Film Score Monthly* 2, no. 1 (1997): 20.

7   Brown, *Overtones and Undertones,* 118.

8   Audissino, *John Williams's Film Music,* 83.

9   Cooke, *History of Film Music,* 456.

10 Cooke, 463.

11 Cooke, 510.

12 Audissino, *John Williams's Film Music,* 72.

13 Handy, "J.J. Abrams on the Secret Movie References He Snuck into *Star Wars.*"

14 The Star Wars Show, "The Last Jedi Director Talks with the Director of Hamilton, Making BB-8 Sounds, and More!," *Star Wars YouTube Channel,* August 16, 2017, https://www.youtube.com/watch?v=hib2cnhE_fQ.

15 Josephine Reed, "John Williams," *Art Works,* National Endowment for the Arts, 2009, https://www.arts.gov/audio/john-williams.

16 Cooke, *History of Film Music,* 463.

17 Jørn Tillnes, "Soundtrack Review: Star Wars The Force Awakens," *Soundtrack Geek,* December 17, 2015, http://www.soundtrackgeek.com /v2/soundtrack-review-star-wars-the-force-awakens/.

18 Charlie Jane Anders, "Everything That's Wrong with *Star Wars: The Force Awakens,*" *Gizmodo,* January 8, 2016, http://io9.gizmodo.com /everything-thats-wrong-with-star-wars-the-force-awaken-1751756919.

19 Alex Ross, "Listening to 'Star Wars,'" *New Yorker,* January 1, 2016, http://www.newyorker.com/culture/cultural-comment/listening-to -star-wars.

20 Or at least fugue-like: the fugue is from a technical perspective a very strict musical form, and a great many pieces of film music that are commonly labeled as fugues may not actually classify as such under the strictest definitions—even some, such as the one Williams wrote for *Jaws,* which are titled as fugues on the film's soundtrack. To be most accurate, some of these would probably be labeled "counterpoint" instead. However,

given that the setting, the musical tone, and often even the title all evoke the fugue, it makes sense to be slightly more relaxed about technical musicological definitions for our purposes here. For "The March of the Resistance," at least, it is at its most fugal on the official soundtrack cue between 1:11 and 1:46, as the first phrase of the central melody is passed around different sections of the orchestra, in different voicings, keys, and rhythms.

21　Quoted in Cooke, *History of Film Music*, 100.

22　In particular, Jerry Goldsmith is a notable user of the fugue.

23　Jones, *George Lucas*, 185.

24　Jones, 185.

25　Tom Pollard, *Hollywood 9/11: Superheroes, Supervillains, and Super Disasters* (New York: Routledge, 2016), 106.

26　*THX 1138* (dir. George Lucas; Warner Bros., 1971).

27　Robin Gregory, "Dies Irae," *Music & Letters* 34, no. 2 (1953): 133.

28　Philip Keppler, "Some Comments on Musical Quotation," *Musical Quarterly* 42, no. 4 (1956): 485.

29　This section can be heard at 0:14 in the track "Rey's Theme" from the official *Force Awakens* soundtrack.

30　Ndalianis, *Neo-Baroque Aesthetics and Contemporary Entertainment*, 23–24.

31　Ndalianis, 33.

32　Omar Calabrese, *Neo-Baroque: A Sign of the Times* (Princeton, N.J.: Princeton University Press, 1992), 27.

33　Christopher Hooton, "Star Wars Review: The Force Awakens Is the Sequel You're Looking For," *Independent*, December 16, 2015, http://www.independent.co.uk/arts-entertainment/films/reviews/star-wars-the-force-awakens-review-this-is-the-sequel-youre-looking-for-a6774876.html.

34　Calabrese, *Neo-Baroque*, 39.

35　John Powell's *Solo* score from 2018 also includes a fugue. Track 12, "Mine Mission," is entirely a fugue that plays to accompany the wild action-in-disarray sequence on Kessel. It seems that the fugue is to be the sound of the Disney-era of *Star Wars*.

6. YOU HAVE TO START SOMEWHERE

1　Rogers, "Force Will Be with Us."

2　Dan Brooks, "SWCE 2016: 15 Things We Learned from the *Rogue One: A Star Wars Story* Panel," StarWars.com, July 15, 2016, http://www.starwars.com/news/swce-2016-15-things-we-learned-from-the-rogue-one-a-star-wars-story-panel.

3　Anthony Breznican, "Star Wars: Secret Plans for New Movies Discussed after Rogue One," *Entertainment Weekly*, November 22, 2016, http://www.ew.com/article/2016/11/22/rogue-one-lucasfilm-new-star-wars-movies/.

4　Brooks, "SWCE 2016."

5   Adam Rogers, "*Star Wars*' Greatest Screenwriter Wrote All Your Other Favorite Movies Too," *Wired*, November 18, 2015, https://www.wired.com/2015/11/lawrence-kasdan-qa/.

6   Lucasfilm Ltd, "Rogue One: A Star Wars Story—Celebration Reel," *Star Wars YouTube Channel*, July 15, 2016, https://www.youtube.com/watch?time_continue=80&v=HUb_zpdyDpU.

7   Breznican, "Star Wars."

8   Germain Lussier, "Why the *Rogue One* Trailer's Most Iconic Shot Never Appeared in the Movie," *Gizmodo*, January 8, 2017, https://www.gizmodo.com.au/2017/01/why-the-rogue-one-trailers-most-iconic-shot-never-appeared-in-the-movie/.

9   Aynne Kokas, *Hollywood Made in China* (Oakland: University of California Press, 2017), 2.

10   Julia Greenberg, "How *Star Wars* Is Trying to Rule China's Tough Box Office," *Wired*, August 1, 2016, https://www.wired.com/2016/01/star-wars-force-awakens-china/.

11   Ben Child, "Star Wars: The Force Awakens Set to Fall Short of Avatar after Stumbling in China," *Guardian*, January 11, 2016, https://www.theguardian.com/film/2016/jan/11/star-wars-the-force-awakens-avatar-china.

12   Greenberg, "How *Star Wars* Is Trying to Rule China's Tough Box Office."

13   Xi Wei, "Inclusion of Chinese Stars Donnie Yen and Jiang Wen Raises 'Rogue One: A Star Wars Story' Hype in China," *Global Times*, December 21, 2016, http://www.globaltimes.cn/content/1024984.shtml.

14   Fergus Ryan, "Star Wars 'Rogue One' Coming to China on Jan 6," *Beijinger*, December 7, 2016, http://www.thebeijinger.com/blog/2016/12/07/star-wars-rogue-one-coming-china-jan-6.

15   Dan Jolin, "Rogue One: A Star Wars Story—the Complete History, Part II," *Empire*, December 13, 2016, https://www.empireonline.com/movies/features/rogue-one-star-wars-story-complete-history-part-ii/.

16   Patrick Brzeski, "Why Disney's 'Last Jedi' Mind Trick Isn't Working in China," *Hollywood Reporter*, January 16, 2018, https://www.hollywoodreporter.com/heat-vision/star-wars-china-box-office-why-disneys-jedi-mind-trick-isnt-working-china-1075177.

17   Jennifer Drysdale, "EXCLUSIVE: Kathleen Kennedy and Gareth Edwards Tease 'Rogue One' Opening Crawl—See What They Said!," *ET Online*, July 15, 2016, http://www.etonline.com/news/193391_exclusive_kathleen_kennedy_and_gareth_edwards_tease_rogue_one_opening_crawl.

18   Martin Flanagan, Mike McKenny, and Andrew Livingstone, *The Marvel Studios Phenomenon: Inside a Transmedia Universe* (New York: Bloomsbury, 2017), 4.

19   Rogers, "Force Will Be with Us."

20   Jason Mittell, *Complex TV: The Poetics of Contemporary Television Storytelling* (New York: New York University Press, 2015), 18.

21 Calabrese, *Neo-Baroque.*

22 Mittell, *Complex TV*, 27.

23 Breznican, "*Star Wars.*"

24 "'K-2SO': The Droid," special features, *Rogue One* (Disney, 2016), DVD.

25 Brooker, *Star Wars*, 27.

26 "Visions of Hope: The Look of *Rogue One*," special features, *Rogue One* (Disney, 2016), DVD.

27 Kocurek, *Coin-Operated Americans*, 160.

28 "Visions of Hope."

29 Suzanne Scott, "Dawn of the Undead Author: Fanboy Auteurism and Zack Snyder's 'Vision,'" in *A Companion to Media Authorship*, ed. Jonathan Gray and Derek Johnson (Oxford, U.K.: Wiley-Blackwell, 2013), 440, https://doi.org/10.1002/9781118505526.ch23.

30 Tim Robey, "Rogue One: A Star Wars Story's Gareth Edwards: 'The Whole Thing Was One Big Love Letter to Carrie Fisher,'" *Telegraph*, March 31, 2017, http://www.telegraph.co.uk/films/0/rogue-one-star -wars-storys-gareth-edwards-whole-thing-one-big/.

31 Anthony Breznican, "Rogue One Revisions: The TIE Fighter Scene, a Deleted Planet, and Killed Cameos," *Entertainment Weekly*, March 24, 2017, http://ew.com/movies/2017/03/24/rogue-one-revisions-tie-fight er-scene-deleted-planet-killed-cameos/?xid=entertainment-weekly _socialflow_twitter.

32 Breznican.

33 Huw Fullerton, "The Unseen Star Wars Archive Footage Used in Rogue One," *Radio Times*, December 19, 2016, http://www.radiotimes.com /news/2016-12-19/the-unseen-star-wars-archive-footage-used-in-rogue -one/.

34 Dave Itzkoff, "How 'Rogue One' Brought Back Familiar Faces," *New York Times*, December 27, 2016, https://www.nytimes.com/2016 /12/27/movies/how-rogue-one-brought-back-grand-moff-tarkin.html.

35 Itzkoff.

36 Itzkoff.

37 Itzkoff.

38 Kristopher Tapley and Peter Debruge, "'Rogue One': What Peter Cushing's Digital Resurrection Means for the Industry," *Variety*, December 16, 2016, https://variety.com/2016/film/news/rogue-one-peter-cushing -digital-resurrection-cgi-1201943759/.

39 Andrew Pulver, "Rogue One VFX Head: 'We Didn't Do Anything Peter Cushing Would've Objected To,'" *Guardian*, January 17, 2017, https:// www.theguardian.com/film/2017/jan/16/rogue-one-vfx-jon-knoll-peter -cushing-ethics-of-digital-resurrections.

40 Zac Thompson, "Digitally Reviving Peter Cushing for Rogue One Is Disrespectful," *Huffington Post*, December 22, 2016, https://www.huffing tonpost.com/zac-thompson/digitally-reviving-peter-cushing_b_1380 0074.html.

41 Matt Goldberg, "'Rogue One': The Problem with That CGI Charac-
    ter," *Collider,* December 16, 2016, http://collider.com/rogue-one-cgi
    -grand-moff-tarkin/.
42 David Grossman, "How LucasFilm Made Grand Moff Tarkin Look
    Real in 'Rogue One,'" *Popular Mechanics,* January 7, 2017, http://www
    .popularmechanics.com/culture/movies/a24641/grand-moff-tarkin
    -rogue-one/.
43 Itzkoff, "How 'Rogue One' Brought Back Familiar Faces."
44 Erik Davis, "'Rogue One' Director Gareth Edwards Explains Why
    Carrie Fisher Didn't Believe Her Own Cameo," *Fandango,* March 15,
    2017, https://www.fandango.com/movie-news/rogue-one-director
    -gareth-edwards-explains-why-carrie-fisher-didnt-believe-her-own
    -cameo-752037.
45 Itzkoff, "How 'Rogue One' Brought Back Familiar Faces."
46 Ndalianis, "Baroque Facades, Jeff Bridges' Face, and Tron: Legacy," 158.
47 Ndalianis, *Neo-Baroque Aesthetics and Contemporary Entertainment,* chap. 4.
48 Ndalianis, "Baroque Facades, Jeff Bridges' Face, and Tron," 163–64.
49 Svetlana Boym, *The Future of Nostalgia* (New York: Basic Books, 2001), 15.
50 "Visions of Hope: The Look of *Rogue One.*"

7. YOU THINK ANYBODY'S LISTENING

 1 Michelle Ye He Lee, "Donald Trump's False Comments Connecting
    Mexican Immigrants and Crime," *Washington Post,* July 8, 2015, https://
    www.washingtonpost.com/news/fact-checker/wp/2015/07/08/donald
    -trumps-false-comments-connecting-mexican-immigrants-and-crime
    /?utm_term=.18b3e2170276.
 2 Max Fisher and Amanda Taub, "Trump's Threat to Jail Clinton Also
    Targets Democracy's Institutions," *New York Times,* October 11, 2016,
    https://www.nytimes.com/2016/10/12/world/americas/united-states
    -democracy-clinton-trump.html.
 3 Jim Rutenberg, "The Editorialists Have Spoken; Will Voters Lis-
    ten?," *New York Times,* October 5, 2016, https://www.nytimes.
    com/2016/10/06/business/media/the-editorialists-have-spoken-will
    -voters-listen.html.
 4 Patrick Healy and Jeremy W. Peters, "Donald Trump's Victory Is Met
    with Shock across a Wide Political Divide," *New York Times,* November 9,
    2016, https://www.nytimes.com/2016/11/10/us/politics/donald-trump
    -election-reaction.html.
 5 Ed Pilkington and Adam Gabbatt, "How Donald Trump Swept to an
    Unreal, Surreal Presidential Election Win," *Guardian,* November 10,
    2016, https://www.theguardian.com/us-news/2016/nov/09/how
    -trump-won-us-election.
 6 "The Guardian View on the EU Referendum: The Vote Is In, Now
    We Must Face the Consequences," editorial, *Guardian,* June 24, 2016,
    https://www.theguardian.com/commentisfree/2016/jun/24/the

-guardian-view-on-the-eu-referendum-the-vote-is-in-now-we-must
-face-the-consequences.

7 Caroline Mortimer, "Hate Crimes Surge by 42% in England and Wales
since Brexit Result," *Independent,* July 8, 2016, https://www.independent
.co.uk/news/uk/crime/brexit-hate-crime-racism-stats-spike-police
-england-wales-eu-referendum-a7126706.html.

8 Associated Press, "75,000 Far-Right Nationalists March on Poland's
Independence Day," *New York Post,* November 11, 2016, https://nypost
.com/2016/11/11/75000-far-right-nationalists-march-on-polands-inde
pendence-day/.

9 David Crouch and Patrick Kingsley, "Danish Parliament Approves Plan
to Seize Assets from Refugees," *Guardian,* January 27, 2016, https://www
.theguardian.com/world/2016/jan/26/danish-parliament-approves-plan
-to-seize-assets-from-refugees.

10 Adam Harvey, "Controversial Mayor Rodrigo Duterte Wins Philippine
Presidential Election Following Incendiary Campaign," *ABC News,*
May 10, 2016, http://www.abc.net.au/news/2016–05–10/rodrigo
-duterte-wins-philippine-presidential-vote/7399658.

11 Simon Shuster, "European Politics Are Swinging to the Right," *Time,*
September 22, 2016, http://time.com/4504010/europe-politics-swing
-right/.

12 Graeme McMillan, "'Rogue One' Writers Subtly Protest Trump with
Rebellion Safety-Pin Logo," *Hollywood Reporter,* November 11, 2016,
https://www.hollywoodreporter.com/heat-vision/rogue-one-is-a
-political-allegory-tease-writers-946638.

13 Devan Coggan, "Star Wars: Donald Trump Statements Not Included
in Rogue One," *Entertainment Weekly,* December 12, 2016, http://ew.com
/article/2016/12/12/star-wars-rogue-one-anti-trump/.

14 Dan Hassler-Forest, "Politicizing Star Wars: Anti-Fascism vs. Nostalgia in 'Rogue One,'" *Los Angeles Review of Books,* December 26, 2016,
https://lareviewofbooks.org/article/politicizing-star-wars-anti-fascism
-vs-nostalgia-rogue-one/.

15 Michael Wolff, *Fire and Fury: Inside the Trump White House* (New York:
Henry Holt, 2018), 233.

16 Michael Wolff, "Ringside with Steve Bannon at Trump Tower as the
President-Elect's Strategist Plots 'An Entirely New Political Movement'
(Exclusive)," *Hollywood Reporter,* November 18, 2016, https://www.holly
woodreporter.com/news/steve-bannon-trump-tower-interview-trumps
-strategist-plots-new-political-movement-948747.

17 Ben Collins and Gideon Resnick, "Palmer Luckey: The Facebook
Near-Billionaire Secretly Funding Trump's Meme Machine," *Daily
Beast,* September 22, 2016, https://www.thedailybeast.com/palmer
-luckey-the-facebook-near-billionaire-secretly-funding-trumps-meme
-machine.

18 Wolff, *Fire and Fury,* 59.

19 Dan Golding and Leena van Deventer, *Game Changers: From Minecraft*

to Misogyny, the Fight for the Future of Videogames (Melbourne, Aus.: Affirm, 2016), 241–42.

20 Callum Borchers, "White House Press Briefings Could Be Totally Bonkers under Donald Trump," *Washington Post,* November 12, 2016, https://www.washingtonpost.com/news/the-fix/wp/2016/11/12 /white-house-press-briefings-could-be-totally-bonkers-under-donald -trump/?utm_term=.038091a7fef3.

21 Tina Nguyen, "Steve Bannon Half-Heartedly Disowns Mil Yianno- poulos," *Vanity Fair,* October 23, 2017, https://www.vanityfair.com /news/2017/10/steve-bannon-disowns-milo-yiannopoulos.

22 Marlow Stern, "'Alt-Right' Trumpsters Discover True Meaning of 'Star Wars,' Wage #DumpStarWars Campaign," *Daily Beast,* August 12, 2016, https://www.thedailybeast.com/alt-right-trumpsters-discover-true -meaning-of-star-wars-wage-dumpstarwars-campaign.

23 Rinzler, *Making of* Star Wars, 157.

24 Leah Deyneka, "May the Myth Be with You, Always: Archetypes, Mythic Elements, and Aspects of Joseph Campbell's Heroic Monomyth in the Original Star Wars Trilogy," in *Myth, Media, and Culture in Star Wars: An Anthology,* ed. Douglas Brode and Leah Deyneka (Lanham, Md.: Scarecrow, 2012), 34.

25 Hannah Arendt, *Imperialism: Part Two of the Origins of Totalitarianism* (New York: Harcourt, Brace & World, 1968), 17, http://public.eblib .com/choice/publicfullrecord.aspx?p=3302071.

26 *Essential Works of Lenin: "What Is to Be Done?" and Other Writings* (La Vergne, Tenn.: BN Publishing, 2010), 264.

27 Jacob Hall, "Interview: 'Rogue One' Director Gareth Edwards on Why 'Star Wars' Still Matters," *Slashfilm,* December 5, 2016, http://www .slashfilm.com/star-wars-rogue-one-gareth-edwards-interview/2/.

28 Josh Rottenberg, "Making 'Star Wars' Is a Team Sport: 'Rogue One' Director Gareth Edwards on Reshoots, Inspiration, and Trepida- tion," *Los Angeles Times,* December 8, 2016, http://www.latimes.com /entertainment/movies/la-ca-mn-rogue-one-gareth-edwards-20161201 -story.html.

29 N. Virtue, "Poaching within the System: Gillo Pontecorvo's Tactical Aesthetics in *The Battle of Algiers,*" *Screen* 55, no. 3 (2014): 320, https:// doi.org/10.1093/screen/hju022.

30 Michel de Certeau, *The Practice of Everyday Life* (Berkeley: University of California Press, 1984).

31 Eyal Weizman, "Lethal Theory," *Log,* no. 7 (Winter–Spring 2006): 63.

32 James A. Hijiya, "The Gita of Robert Oppenheimer," *Proceedings of the American Philosophical Society* 144, no. 2 (2000): 128.

33 Hall, "Interview: 'Rogue One' Director Gareth Edwards."

34 Jones Vincent, *Manhattan: The Army and the Atomic Bomb* (Washington, D.C.: United States Army Center of Military History, 1985), 12.

35 Hall, "Interview: 'Rogue One' Director Gareth Edwards."

36 Hall.

37 The Star Wars Show, "Lucasfilm President Kathleen Kennedy on All
Things Star Wars, Kylo Ren in Battlefront II, and More!"

38 Stevan Pavlowitch, *Hitler's New Disorder: The Second World War in Yugosla-
via* (n.p.: Oxford University Press, 2008), 61.

39 James Hibbert, "'Star Wars Rebels': New Series Goes to Dark Places,"
Entertainment Weekly, January 23, 2014, http://www.ew.com/article
/2014/01/23/star-wars-rebels-interview/.

40 Rinzler, *Making of* Star Wars, 129.

41 Scott MacLeod, "Global Trouble," *Cairo Review of Global Affairs,* Fall
2016, https://www.thecairoreview.com/q-a/global-trouble/.

42 The Star Wars Show, "Rebels Recon #4.2: Inside "In the Name of the
Rebellion" | Star Wars Rebels," *Star Wars YouTube Channel,* October 23,
2017, https://www.youtube.com/watch?v=XO8tJ4G1mag.

43 The Star Wars Show.

44 Meyer, "Star Wars, *Star Wars,* and American Political Culture," 101.

45 Coggan, "Star Wars: Donald Trump Statements Not Included in
Rogue One."

46 Matt Miller, "Rogue One's Diego Luna Never Thought He'd Be in Star
Wars. Then Hollywood Changed," *Esquire,* December 16, 2016, http://
www.esquire.com/entertainment/movies/a51564/diego-luna-rogue-one
-star-wars-interview/.

47 "Visions of Hope."

48 Jolin, "Rogue One: A Star Wars Story."

49 Owen Gleiberman, "It May Be an Accident, but 'Rogue One' Is the
Most Politically Relevant Movie of the Year," *Variety,* December 24,
2016, http://variety.com/2016/film/columns/rogue-one-donald-trump
-felicity-jones-1201947992/.

50 Brett White, "Rebellions Are Built on Hope: Why Rogue One Matters
Now More Than Ever," CBR.com, November 11, 2016, https://www
.cbr.com/rebellions-are-built-on-hope-why-rogue-one-matters-now
-more-than-ever/.

51 Carolyn Petit and Anita Sarkeesian, "Feminist Frequency on *Rogue
One*: A Diverse Group of People Fighting a Fascist Empire Is Awesome,"
The Mary Sue, December 23, 2016, https://www.themarysue.com/femi
nist-frequency-rogue-one-review/.

52 Darryn King, "The Star Wars Saga's Secret Weapon: A Visual Effects
Nerd with a Big Story to Tell," *Vanity Fair,* December 12, 2016, https://
www.vanityfair.com/hollywood/2016/12/star-wars-rogue-one-john
-knoll-visual-effects.

53 Marlow Stern, "'Rogue One' Director Gareth Edwards Discusses the
Film's Trump 'Fake News' Backlash," *Daily Beast,* March 19, 2017,
https://www.thedailybeast.com/rogue-one-director-gareth-edwards
-discusses-the-films-trump-fake-news-backlash.

54 Sean Hutchinson, "'Rogue One' Shot Amidst a Real-World State of
Emergency," *Inverse,* December 19, 2016, https://www.inverse.com
/article/25224-rogue-one-star-wars-maldives-shoot-corrupt-president.

55 Hutchinson.

56 Hutchinson.

57 Jason Burke, "Maldives President Says He Was Forced to Resign at Gunpoint," *Guardian*, February 9, 2012, https://www.theguardian.com /world/2012/feb/08/maldives-president-resign-gunpoint.

58 Reuters, "Amal Clooney in Maldives Meets Jailed Former President Mohamed Nasheed," *Guardian*, September 9, 2015, https://www.the guardian.com/world/2015/sep/09/amal-clooney-in-maldives-meets -jailed-former-president-mohamed-nasheed.

59 Jason Burke, "Maldives Declares State of Emergency," *Guardian*, November 5, 2015, https://www.theguardian.com/world/2015/nov /04/maldives-declares-state-of-emergency.

60 Oliver Holmes, "Maldives Army Occupies Parliament to Block No-Confidence Vote," *Guardian*, August 22, 2017, https://www.theguardian .com/world/2017/aug/22/maldives-army-occupies-parliament-no -confidence-vote.

61 Roy Greenslade, "News Website in the Maldives under Attack after Abduction of Reporter," *Guardian*, October 1, 2014, https://www .theguardian.com/media/greenslade/2014/oct/01/journalist-safety -maldives.

62 Amnesty International, "Amnesty International Report 2016/17," 2017, 243, https://www.amnesty.org.au/annual-report-2016–17/.

63 Hassler-Forest, "Politicizing Star Wars."

64 Cleve R. Wootson Jr., "Donald Trump Interrupted a Screening of 'Rogue One.' Mark Hamill Had a Forceful Response," *Washington Post*, April 9, 2017, https://www.washingtonpost.com/news/style/wp /2017/04/09/donald-trump-interrupted-a-screening-of-rogue-one-mark -hamill-was-not-amused/?utm_term=.b0817f4845e4.

8. I'VE ALWAYS HATED WATCHING YOU LEAVE

1 Jean Burgess, Peta Mitchell, and Felix Victor Münch, "Social Media Rituals: The Uses of Celebrity Death in Digital Culture," in *A Networked Self and Birth, Life, Death*, ed. Zizi Papacharissi (New York: Routledge, 2018).

2 Melissa Chan, "Did Debbie Reynolds Die of a Broken Heart?," *Time*, December 29, 2016, http://time.com/4619536/debbie-reynolds-dead -carrie-fisher-broken-heart/.

3 Carrie Fisher, *The Princess Diarist* (New York: Blue Rider, 2016).

4 David Kamp, "Cover Story: *Star Wars: The Last Jedi*, the Definitive Preview," *Vanity Fair*, May 24, 2017, https://www.vanityfair.com/holly wood/2017/05/star-wars-the-last-jedi-cover-portfolio.

5 Kamp.

6 Aaron Couch, "Leonard Nimoy's Son on 'Star Trek Beyond's' Spock Tribute and His Dad's 'Incredible Bond' with Zachary Quinto," *Holly-*

wood Reporter, July 25, 2016, https://www.hollywoodreporter.com/heat
-vision/star-trek-beyond-leonard-nimoys-914219.

7   Stacey Menzel Baker and Patricia F. Kennedy, "Death by Nostalgia:
    A Diagnosis of Context-Specific Cases," *Advances in Consumer Research* 21,
    no. 1 (1994): 169–74.

8   Jacob Juhl et al., "Fighting the Future with the Past: Nostalgia Buffers
    Existential Threat," *Journal of Research in Personality* 44, no. 3 (2010): 314,
    https://doi.org/10.1016/j.jrp.2010.02.006.

9   Susan Sontag, *On Photography* (New York: Picador USA, 2001), 71.

10 Bryan S. Turner, "A Note on Nostalgia," *Theory, Culture & Society* 4,
    no. 1 (1987): 150, https://doi.org/10.1177/026327687004001008.

11 Nancy Martha West, *Kodak and the Lens of Nostalgia* (Charlottesville:
    University Press of Virginia, 2000), 202.

12 Katharina Niemeyer and Daniela Wentz, "Nostalgia Is Not What It
    Used to Be: Serial Nostalgia and Nostalgic Television Series," in *Media
    and Nostalgia,* ed. Katharina Niemeyer (London: Palgrave Macmillan
    UK, 2014), 134, https://doi.org/10.1057/9781137375889_10.

13 Boym, *Future of Nostalgia,* 77.

14 Angela Ndalianis, "Television and the Neo-Baroque," in *The Con-
    temporary Television Series,* ed. Michael Hammond and Lucy Mazdon
    (Edinburgh: Edinburgh University Press, 2005), 94.

15 Niemeyer and Wentz, "Nostalgia Is Not What It Used to Be," 135.

16 Niemeyer and Wentz, 134.

17 The Star Wars Show, "Star Wars: The Last Jedi Secrets Explained,"
    Star Wars YouTube Channel, January 10, 2018, https://www.youtube.com
    /watch?v=po9coMXDxto&feature=youtu.be.

18 Jimmy Kimmel Live, "The Cast of *Star Wars: The Last Jedi* Talk Cliff-
    hanger Scene and Luke Skywalker's Beard," *Jimmy Kimmel Live,* January
    10, 2018, https://www.youtube.com/watch?v=bUKhUahlDhA.

19 Empire Staff, "The Making of Indiana Jones and The Kingdom of
    the Crystal Skull," *Empire,* October 8, 2012, https://www.empireonline
    .com/movies/features/indiana-jones-making-crystall-skull/.

20 Michael Rougeau, "How Blade Runner 2049 Resurrected That Charac-
    ter from the Original," *Gamespot,* October 9, 2017, https://www.game
    spot.com/articles/how-blade-runner-2049-resurrected-that-character
    -f/1100–6453912/.

21 Robey, "Rogue One: A Star Wars Story's Gareth Edwards: 'The Whole
    Thing Was One Big Love Letter to Carrie Fisher,'" Telegraph, March
    31, 2017, https://www.telegraph.co.uk/films/0/rogue-one-star-wars
    -storys-gareth-edwards-whole-thing-one-big/.

22 Boym, *Future of Nostalgia,* 543.

23 André Bazin, "The Ontology of the Photographic Image," trans. Hugh
    Gray, *Film Quarterly* 13, no. 4 (1960): 4–9.

24 Robey, "Rogue One: A Star Wars Story's Gareth Edwards.'"

25 Jameson, "Postmodernism and Consumer Society," 197.

26 Boym, *Future of Nostalgia*, 19.

27 Kael, "Whipped."

28 Boym, *Future of Nostalgia*, 534.

29 Göran Bolin, *Media Generations: Experience, Identity, and Mediatised Social Change* (New York: Routledge, 2017), 115.

30 Fisher, *Princess Diarist*, 230.

31 Carrie Fisher, *Wishful Drinking* (New York: Simon & Schuster, 2009), 156.

9. I WILL FINISH WHAT YOU STARTED

1 Whitbrook, "Rian Johnson Is Fully Aware *The Last Jedi* Might Sound Like *Empire Strikes Back,* and He Doesn't Care."

2 Chris Hewitt, "Star Wars: The Last Jedi Spoiler Special," *Empire,* January 16, 2018, https://www.empireonline.com/movies/news/star -wars-last-jedi-empire-podcast-spoiler-special-rian-johnson/.

3 Bill Bradley, "What Really Happened to Luke at the End of 'Star Wars: The Last Jedi,'" *Huffington Post,* January 7, 2018, http://www.huffington post.com.au/entry/star-wars-last-jedi-ending_us_5a4e2de6e4b06d1621 bd7ebc.

4 Taylor, *How Star Wars Conquered the Universe,* 218.

5 Jeff Gomez, "The Self-Disruption of Star Wars," *The Collective Journey (Medium),* January 24, 2018, https://blog.collectivejourney.com/the-self -disruption-of-star-wars-ae3311bedco8.

6 Brian Hiatt, "Jedi Confidential: Inside the Dark New 'Star Wars' Movie," *Rolling Stone,* November 29, 2017, https://www.rollingstone .com/movies/features/the-last-jedi-cover-story-on-the-dark-new-star -wars-movie-w512703.

7 Robbie Collin, "Star Wars: Episode VIII Will Be Classic War Film like The Bridge on the River Kwai, Director Reveals," *Telegraph,* July 17, 2016, http://www.telegraph.co.uk/films/2016/07/17/star-wars-episode -viii-will-be-classic-war-film-like-the-bridge/.

8 David Thomson, "Open and Shut: A Fresh Look at *The Searchers,*" *Film Comment* 33, no. 4 (1997): 31.

9 Brooker, *Using the Force,* 77.

10 Zakarin, "How the Alt-Right and Nostalgic Trolls Hijacked Geek Pop Culture."

11 Caitlin Busch, "The Best Responses to the Crazy Men-Only Cut of The Last Jedi," Syfy Wire, January 16, 2018, http://www.syfy.com/syfy wire/the-best-responses-to-the-crazy-men-only-cut-of-the-last-jedi.

12 BBC Staff, "Star Wars Actress Kelly Marie Tran Deletes Instagram Posts after Abuse," *BBC News,* June 6, 2018, https://www.bbc.com /news/world-asia-44379473.

13 Dan Golding and Leena van Deventer, *Game Changers: From Minecraft to Misogyny, the Fight for the Future of Videogames* (Melbourne: Affirm Press, 2016), 241–42.

14 Jill Pantozzi, "Rian Johnson Responds to Fan Question about 'Polaris-

ing' Last Jedi, But He Shouldn't Have To," *Gizmodo*, December 25, 2017, https://www.gizmodo.com.au/2017/12/rian-johnson-responds-to-fan -question-about-polarizing-last-jedi-but-he-shouldnt-have-to/.

15 Rian Johnson, "'(Want to Make Sure That Didn't Read as Sarcastic—I Honestly Don't Know That It's My Place to Say, the Movie Belongs to You Guys Now),'" Twitter, January 19, 2018, https://twitter.com/rian johnson/status/954174215619452928.

16 Desta, "Disney Is Making More *Star Wars* TV Shows, In Case You Thought There Wasn't Enough *Star Wars*."

INDEX

237

Dan Golding is a lecturer in media and communications at Swinburne University of Technology in Melbourne, Australia.